BOUTIQUE
LODGINGS
New Zealand Ltd

6th **EDITION**

**PERSONALLY REVIEWED AND NARRATED
BOUTIQUE HOTELS, INNS, BED & BREAKFASTS,
RURAL RETREATS, LODGES AND SELF-CONTAINED
COTTAGES THROUGHOUT NEW ZEALAND.**

Boutique Lodgings of New Zealand
6th edition

ISBN 0-476-01661-4

Published by
REL Group Ltd
PO Box 911070
Auckland Mail Centre
Auckland
New Zealand
www.lodgings.co.nz
editor@lodgings.co.nz

Design and typesetting
M3 Integrated, Auckland

Printing
Brebner Print

Disclaimer: All factual information for each property has been provided by the relevant property owner/host. All reasonable efforts have been made to ensure the accuracy of the material printed at the time of printing. The publisher accepts no responsibility or liability for errors, inaccuracies, omissions or changes in respect of this information. Opinions expressed in this book are the personal views of the publisher or its representatives. Readers must make their own inquiries and format their own opinions when selecting accommodation from this book.

Cover Photographs: Front Cover - Essence of New Zealand's Te Kowhai Landing, Taupo. Back Cover - Clockwise left to right: Owen River Lodge, Nelson Lakes; Belvedere Boutique Accommodation, Tauranga; Maison de la Mer, Akaroa; Bellini's of Queenstown, Queenstown; Connells Bay Cottage, Waiheke Island.

Regional photographs supplied by: **North Island, Northland** - Destination Northland. **Auckland** - Tourism Auckland. **West North Island** - Positively Wellington Tourism, Venture Taranaki. **Central North Island** - Destination Lake Taupo/Marcel Tromp, Department of Conservation Turangi, Destination Rotorua Tourism. **East North Island** - Tourism Coromandel, Tourism Bay of Plenty. **South Island, Nelson/Marlborough** - Destination Marlborough, Latitude Nelson. **West Coast** - Tourism West Coast, Doug Johannson. **Canterbury** - Christchurch & Canterbury Marketing. **Otago/Fiordland** - Destination Fiordland, Destination Queenstown, Venture Southland.
Many thanks.

Boutique Lodgings of New Zealand is a collection of unique, intimate places to stay throughout New Zealand. All Boutique Lodging's properties have been selected because of their superior facilities, spectacular locations, warm hospitality, character and ambience or a combination of the above. They are all memorable in some way, and have their own personality.

Emma, Lisa and Rosie Fowler, a family team, are delighted to offer you the 6th edition of Boutique Lodgings of New Zealand. First published in 1997 by Holdsworth Press, the team at Boutique Lodgings of New Zealand continues to source, review and narrate on the diverse selection of quality accommodation that can be found in New Zealand. Boutique Lodgings of New Zealand has evolved into a quality and highly marketable publication appealing to both domestic and international travellers alike.

Our aim is to make a true New Zealand experience available; a holiday away with friends, a romantic getaway, a corporate retreat, a long or short term stay, or a weekend escape. We offer a solution to suit your individual travel needs in a contemporary, user-friendly, conveniently sized guidebook, which stands strongly beside our established and active website.

All of the properties have been personally sought out and experienced by a member of our team. Your experience at a property may differ, so we cannot guarantee your experience will be the same as ours as written in the book. We do however aim to give you the most accurate impression for you to choose if a property is right for you, as we recognise everyone's experience and tastes are different.

We would like to thank everyone who helped make the 6th edition of Boutique Lodgings of New Zealand possible.

Jill Malcolm has now worked on the 4th, 5th and 6th editions of the Boutique Lodgings of New Zealand publication. Her editing skills, expertise and professional, relaxed approach have made her an integral part of the Boutique Lodgings Team.

We would like to thank Katrina for taking care of the office while we were on the road reviewing properties. Her organisational skills and sense of humour have been invaluable to us.

Donna Blaber, who has helped us promote the Boutique Lodgings of New Zealand properties, along with writing and reviewing a number of them listed throughout the publication.

Derek, from our designers, whose commitment and patience has helped ensure the completion of a quality publication.

The Boutique Lodgings hosts, who provide memorable stays for local and international visitors and whose hospitality make our research possible and enjoyable. The standards and selection of accommodation options throughout New Zealand is remarkable and it is only through the lodge host's innovative ideas and commitment to New Zealand tourism that this has happened.

Feedback is crucial to ensuring that future editions of Boutique Lodgings of New Zealand are fulfilling the requirements of you, the user of the publication. Please visit our website or email us to give us an idea of how this publication worked for you, all comments are welcome.

editor@lodgings.co.nz
www.lodgings.co.nz

Table of contents Pages

Colour Coded Regions/Maps

Each of the nine regions has been colour coded as shown on the map opposite. Colour coded maps listing cities and towns with respective property page numbers can be found at the beginning of each section.

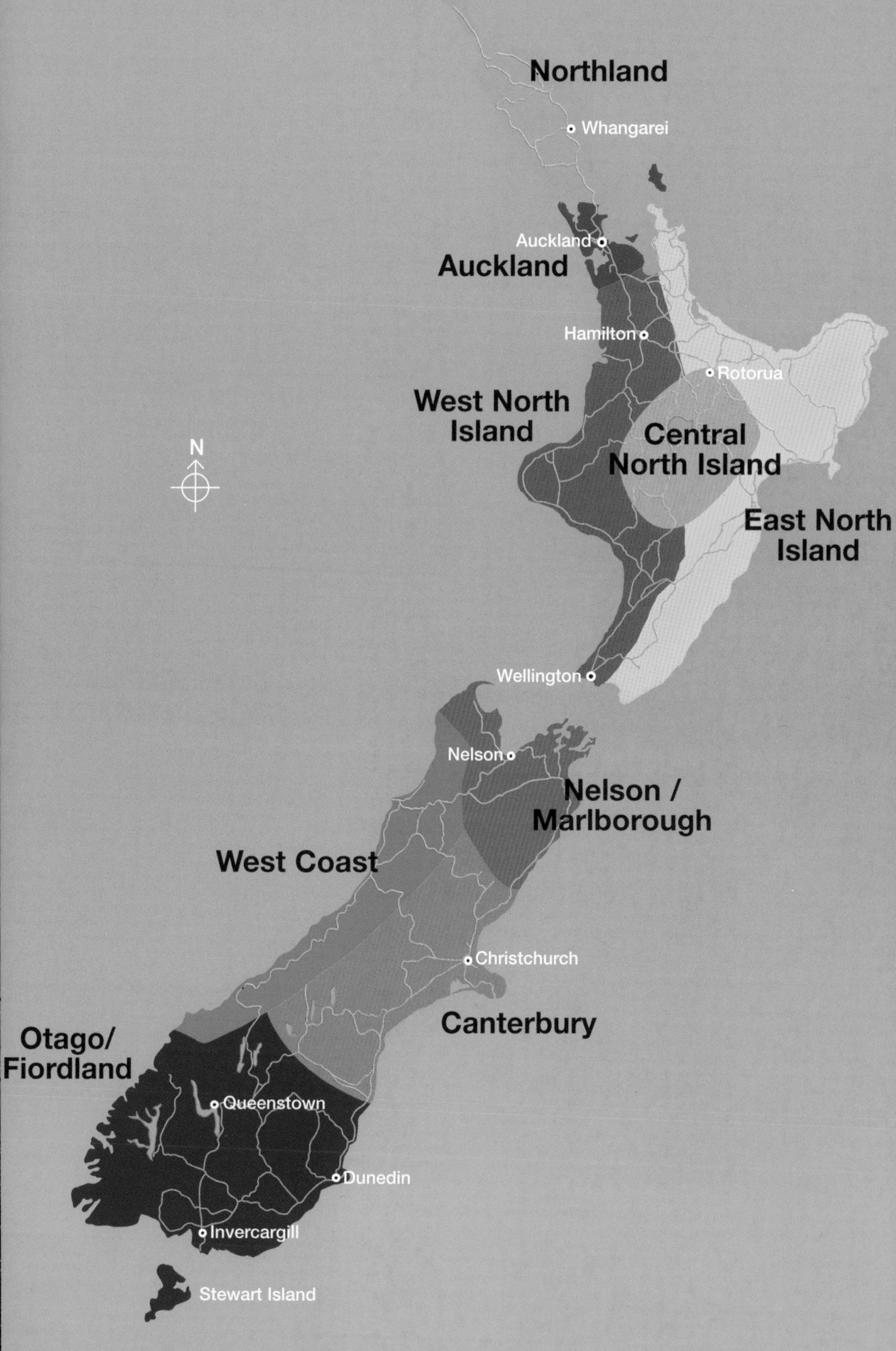

Northland

o Whangarei

Auckland o
Auckland

Hamilton o

o Rotorua

**West North
Island**

**Central
North Island**

N

**East North
Island**

Wellington o

Nelson o

**Nelson /
Marlborough**

West Coast

o Christchurch

Canterbury

**Otago/
Fiordland**

o Queenstown

o Dunedin

o Invercargill

Stewart Island

Cover Flaps

The back and front cover flaps contain important information pertaining to using the book. The flaps also double as bookmarks to help with you travel planning.

Areas / Maps

The properties are divided into 9 regions that generally follow a set travelling route. Properties are listed north to south where possible. On the inside of the front and back covers we have included North and South Island maps and distance charts to help you in your itinerary planning. We suggest a good touring map to be used in conjunction with the book as our maps show only main travelling routes.

Regional Cafes / Restaurants / Events

At the beginning of each region, cafes, restaurants, markets and events are recommended. These are by no means comprehensive lists, but offer readers a choice of diverse, interesting places that we have discovered while travelling or that have been recommended as establishments that are worth a visit.

Check in / Check out Times (approx.)

Check-in: mid - late afternoon
Check-out: between 10am and 11am.
Please check with your host at the time of booking.

Using this Guide

Boutique Lodgings of New Zealand aims to be as user friendly as possible. We welcome any suggestions of improvement for future editions.

Property Pages

Contact a Property

Each property page lists the property's address and phone number. Here, you will also find the property's Boutique Lodgings of New Zealand website address. From this online page you can send an inquiry form straight through to your selected property and/or view further information about them.

Property Features

Activities listed and tea/coffee are generally included in the tariff, please enquire when booking.

Local Features

These include features in the surrounding area specific to the property. The features are personally highlighted by property owners themselves.

Travel Times

All travel times are by motor vehicle unless otherwise stated. This is an indication only and will depend on the driver and road conditions.

Tariff Chart

Tariffs are correct at the time of printing and all prices are in New Zealand dollars and include GST (tax), so please check rates when you book. If applicable please ask about long term and off-season rates.

 1 person occupancy    2 person occupancy

 Extra person if there are facilities to sleep more than 2 people

Property Pages (cont).

Bed Sizes
S.......................... Single bed
D........................... Double bed
Q............................Queen bed
K.......................... King bed
SK..........................Super-king bed
CK..........................Californian-king bed
SK/T...................... Super-king that splits into 2 singles
for twin occupancy

Bathroom Types
EN - Ensuites: exclusive use inside guestroom.
PR - Private: exclusive use outside bedroom
GS - Guest Shared: share with other guests

Helpful Advice:
Using the Telephone:
In emergency.......... **dial 111**
To call from NZ, dial our international access code (00), the country code eg. United States (1), followed by your area code eg. California (619), then the 7-digit telephone number. For example 00 1 619 1234 567.

Conversions

Conversion to imperial	Conversion to metric
1 kph = 0.621 mph	1 mph = 1.61 kph
1 litre = 0.26 US gallons	1 US gallon = 3.79 litres
or 0.22 UK gallons	1 UK gallon = 4.55 litres
1 hectare = 2.471 acres	1 acre = 0.4045 hectares

Public Holidays
New Zealand has 8 national public holidays.
New Year..............................1-2 January
Waitangi Day.........................6 February
Easter (varies)........................March/April
Anzac Day..............................25 April
Queen's Birthday (varies).......June
Labour Day (varies)................October
Christmas Day........................25 December
Boxing Day............................26 December

Regional Holidays
New Zealand also has anniversary days for each of its regions. These are only celebrated within the region and usually fall on the nearest Monday to the dates below:

Southland............................... 17 January
Wellington.............................. 22 January
Auckland................................ 29 January
Northland............................... 29 January
Nelson.................................... 1 February
Otago..................................... 23 March
Taranaki................................. 31 March
South Canterbury.................. 25 September
Hawkes Bay........................... 1 November
Marlborough.......................... 1 November
Westland................................ 1 December
Canterbury............................. 16 December

Kiwi words to learn...
Aubergine............ eggplant
Bach.................... small holiday home (North Island)
Biscuit................. cookie
Bonnet................ car hood
Boot.................... car trunk
Brekkie................ breakfast
Bum-bag.............. fanny pack
BYO..................... Bring Your Own (usually wine or beer)
Capsicum............. bell pepper
Cellotape............. scotch tape
Courgette............. zucchini
Cheers................. goodbye, thank you
Chemist................ pharmacy
Chilli bin............... cooler/eskie
Chips.................... French fries/crisps/potato chips
Crib...................... small holiday home (South Island)
Crook................... be sick, ill
Dairy.................... a convenience store or corner shop
Dunny.................. toilet
Entrée................... appetizer or hors d'oeuvre
Flannel.................. wash cloth
Flat white.............. a short espresso with hot steamed milk
Fortnight.............. fourteen days, two weeks
Holiday................. vacation
Ice block.............. popsicle
Jersey................... sweater
Kia ora................. Maori for hello
Kumara................ sweet potato
Lemonade............ 7up
Licensed............... can legally sell alcoholic beverages
Lift....................... elevator
Lolly..................... candy/sweet
Loo...................... bathroom
Motorway............. freeway
Maori................... indigenous people of NZ
Mossie.................. mosquito
Pakeha................. a non-Maori New Zealander
Spa pool.............. jacuzzi
S/C...................... self-contained – has a kitchen(ette)
Sweet as.............. great, fine
Tiki tour............... roundabout way to get somewhere
Tomato sauce....... catsup/ketchup
Tramping.............. hiking
Torch................... flashlight
Vegemite/Marmite. breakfast spreads (kiwi favourites)

Brown Kiwi - Venture Southland Tourism

Kaitaia

The Beachcomber
222 Commerce St, Kaitaia
Tel: (09) 408-2010. Great
consistent food and service.
Licensed.

Mangonui

Mangonui Fish Shop
Mangonui Village,
Tel: (09) 406-0478. Among the
best fish & chips in NZ.
The Galley Restaurant and Bar
10 Beach Rd, Tel: (09) 406-1233.
Fine dining on the waterfront.
Waterfront Cafe Waterfront Rd,
Tel: (09) 406-0850. Casual. Good
pizza. Open 8am until late.
Licensed.

Kerikeri

Rocket Café Kerikeri Rd,
Tel: (09) 407-3100.
Big reputation. Atomic coffee.
Marsden Estate Winery
Wiroa Road, Kerikeri, Bay of
Islands, Tel: (09) 407-9398.
Great food and wine in a
vineyard setting.
The Landing Restaurant & Bar
Stone Store Basin,
Tel: (09) 407-8479. Enjoy a drink
or dine down by the water and the
Stone Store.
Cafe Jerusalem
Cobblestone Mall, Kerikeri,
Tel: (09) 407-1001.
Middle Eastern cuisine.

Paihia

35 degree South
Paihia Wharf, Paihia.
Tel: (09) 402-6281. Café on the
wharf with an aquarium inside.
Bistro 40 The Strand,
Tel: (09) 403-7771. Sophisticated
dining by the pretty waterfront.
Innovative, fresh seasonal menu.
Sugar Boat Waitangi Bridge,
Tel: (09) 402-7018. A stylish
cocktail bar and elegant
restaurant. Mediterranean food
made with fresh NZ ingredients.
Lips Cafe Selwyn Road, Paihia,
Tel: (09) 402-7185. Café-style
breakfast and lunch. Relaxed
evening dining. Open 7 Days.
The Beachhouse 16 Kings Rd,
Tel: (09) 402-7479
Waikokopu Café Treaty Ground
Waitangi, Tel: (09) 402-6275.
Serious brunches, creative
lunches, dinners in summer.

Boats waiting, Paihia Beach.

Events

Waitangi Day Celebrations
6 February
**Bay of Islands Jazz & Blues
Festival** Early August. National/
international Jazz & Blues, held in
venues around the Bay of Islands.

Opua

Stella Maris Café 3 Beechy St,
Tel: (09) 402-8008. Noted for the
freshest 'ocean to table' fish in the
Bay.

Russell

Duke of Marlborough
35 The Strand, Tel: (09) 403-7829.
Established for over 150 years,
dine in their cosy restaurant with
waterfront views.
Kamakura
The Strand, Tel: (09) 403-7771.
Sophisticated dining by the pretty
waterfront. Innovative, fresh
seasonal menu.

Sunset at Cape Reinga, Northland.

Omata Estate
Off the road between Russell and
the car ferry, Tel: (09) 403-8007.
A boutique vineyard restaurant.
Offers stylish dining using quality
produce.
Sally's Restaurant
25 The Strand, Russell,
Tel: (09) 403-7652. Enjoy coffee
or lunch on the waterfront.
York St Café
1 York St, (09) 403-7360.
Emphasis on fresh ingredients,
friendly service and delicious
desserts.

Events

Russell Tall Ships Race
Early January. Tel: (09) 403-7968
Russell Boating Club's annual tall
& classic ship race.

Dargaville

Funky Fish 34 Seaview Rd,
Baylys Beach, Tel: (09) 439-8883.
Funky, relaxed café. Innovative and
traditional style cuisine with
friendly, happy service.

Whangarei

a Deco 70 Kamo Rd, Kensington,
Tel: (09) 459-4957. Intimate dining
in art deco surroundings. Food &
service of the highest standard.
Fresh 12 James St,
Tel: (09) 438-2921. Vibrant,
extremely tasty fare.
Gybe Quayside, Town Basin
Marina, Tel: (09) 430-0406. Formal
and casual dining options on the
waterfront. Modern menu.
Reva's on the Waterfront
31 Quay Side, Town Basin Marina,
Tel: (09) 438-8969. Overlooking
boat harbour. Popular since 1976.
Vinyl Licensed Cafe Cnr
Riverside and Vale Rd, Town
Basin, Tel: (09) 438-8105. Relaxed
upmarket dining. Legendary
brunches.

Markets

Whangarei Growers' Market
Every Saturday, 6am - 10:30am.
Forum North carpark, Rust Ave.

Mangawhai

Barracuda Café Wood St,
Tel: (09) 431-5587. Lunch/dinner.
A varied, tasty menu. Focus on
seafood, beef and lamb. Licensed.

Naja Garden Café
5 Molesworth Dr, Mangawhai
Heads, Tel: (09) 431-4111. Open
for brunch, lunch and dinner. BYO
with an interesting and evolving
menu.

Quatro Mangawhai Village,
Tel: (09) 431-5226. A buzzy
pizzeria. Eat in or takeaway and
picnic on the beach with a bottle
of wine.

Sail Rock Restaurant and Cafe
Mangawhai Heads,
Tel: (09) 431-4051. Open year
round. Licensed. Eclectic menu.

Smashed Pipi 40 Moir St,
Tel: (09) 431-4849. An adobe-style
café & bar with occasional live
music. Has an excellent gallery of
work by NZ artists.

Roberton Island, Bay of Islands.

Shipwreck Lodge

Roger and Laura
70 Foreshore Road, Ahipara, Northland
Tel: (09) 409 4929
Fax: (09) 409 4928
shipwrecklodge@xtra.co.nz
www.lodgings.co.nz/shipwreck.html

Property features
Luxurious/contemporary home
Unlimited views of 90 mile beach
Brilliant westward sunsets
Private balconies overlooking sea
Local features
90 Mile beach
Golf course
Swimming/surfing/fishing
Adventure activities
Cape Reinga 1.5 hour drive

Ahipara - 3 mins walk
Kaitaia - 14 mins drive

From south of Kaitaia take left turn to Ahipara. From north of Kaitaia turn right to Ahipara. 14 kilometres to Ahipara turn left at school. 600 metres on right.

This purpose built, modern lodge is situated at Shipwreck Bay from which it takes its name. It is only a few metres from the dun-coloured sands of Ninety Mile Beach where the white frilled edges of the sea rolling relentlessly onto the land. I slept upstairs in one of the three guestrooms each opening to private balconies and affording views of the great arc of coastline stretching north to Cape Reinga. The rooms are spacious, uncluttered and fitted with convenient and attractive furnishings and restful décor. There's also a small guest lounge at the top of the stairs, which has a fridge and tea-and-coffee-making facilities. The lower floor has been designed for relaxed living with tiled floors, high studs and wide fold-out doors opening to a small lawn and the beach beyond. To one side of the communal open-plan kitchen/dining room/lounge is a smaller lounge with Sky television for guest's use and this also leads to a small courtyard. The beach is only a short walk away over sand dunes carpeted by natural foliage. In the evening I watched a blazing sunset that often light the sky in this part of the world and by day I enjoyed the fishing, swimming or touring that the area offers.

Accommodation available (NZ$)	👤	👤👤	+👤	🛏	🛁	
1 Room	$200-250	Q	EN			Breakfast: Cooked
1 Room	$250-300	K	EN			Evening meal: $70pp
1 Suite	$300-350	K or 2S	EN			Guest rooms:

Evening meal by prior arrangement.

Ambience:
Setting/location:

LOW   HIGH

Property features
Kayaks/gym
50 channel cable TV
Beachfront location
Host speaks German
Boogie boards
Local features
Quaint fishing village
Golden sandy beaches
Deep sea and fishing charters
Golf course
Cape Reinga day trips

Beach Lodge

Margaret Morrison
121 State Highway 10, Coopers Beach
Tel: (09) 406 0068
Fax: (09) 406 0068
margaret@beachlodge.co.nz
www.lodgings.co.nz/beachlodge.html

Mangonui - 5 minutes
Kaitaia - 30 minutes

Approximately 30 minutes north of Kaeo on SH10 take the Mangonui by-pass. Continue 3km to Coopers Beach. Beach Lodge is on your right (ocean side).

The view from the deck defies description. Because the five self-contained units are elevated just above beautiful Coopers Beach, the outlook from two units is unobstructed across Doubtless Bay. The other units have fabulous sea views through the impressive pohutukawa trees. These two bedroom units are independent and tastefully furnished, each with its own deck leading off the lounge and lower bedroom. The main feature of Beach Lodge is its magnificent location, yet the facilities deserve a special mention. My unit, as all the others, had a full kitchen complete with large fridge/freezer, microwave, under-bench oven, hob and quality crockery and glasses. But I prefered to eat at my favourite fish-and-chip shop, five minutes away in Mangonui. In the units are thoughtful extras such as herbal heatpacks for tired drivers and complimentary packets of fudge. I was there in summer and I lazed on the deck and walked to the beach just thirty seconds away. In winter it would be great to cocoon myself in this self-indulgent luxury in front of the 50-channel cable television. I found Beach Lodge the perfect place to relax. At night, I was lulled to sleep by the sound of lapping water.

Guest pets by arrangement	Accommodation available (NZ$)	♟	♟♟	+♟	🛏	🛁
Breakfast: Not available	4 S/C units	$150-300	$195-400	$30	Q+2S	PR
	1 S/C unit		$250-500		Q	PR

Guest rooms:
Ambience:
Setting/location:

Peak season rates (extra $20) apply 1 Dec - 31 May

Carneval Ocean View

Roly and Martha Fasnacht
360 State Highway 10, Cable Bay, Mangonui
Tel: (09) 406 1012
Fax:(09) 406 1012
fasnacht@xtra.co.nz
www.lodgings.co.nz/carneval.html

Property features
Panoramic seaview
Sauna
Wind surfboard/kayak
Terrace with stunning view
TV/VCR/40 programs
German/French/Swiss spoken
Local features
Safe beaches
Boating/fishing/diving
Historic village Mangonui
Cape Reinga trips etc. organised

Mangonui - 5 mins
KeriKeri - 45 mins/Kaitaia - 30 mins

From the turn off to Mangonui, follow SH 10 to Coopers Beach. Continue to Cable Bay. Cross bridge and opposite the rest area turn left up driveway.

High above Doubtless Bay guests at Carneval Ocean View enjoy the sight of scalloped pink-sand beaches, glittering sea and shadowy headlands. Tables and chairs have been set around the outside of the house to maximise the view whatever the weather. There are two cheerfully furnished guest bedrooms. Mine had a wonderful view through a large picture window; the other has a similar outlook from its adjoining conservatory. Both rooms have large walk-in wardrobes, ensuite bathrooms, televisions, videos and tea and coffee-making facilities, but I was also encouraged to share the other areas of this peaceful and comfortably appointed house. Martha says many people come here as guests and leave as friends. She and Roly came to New Zealand six years ago and speak several languages. Their Swiss name translates as Carneval in English. Roly is a qualified chef and if pre-arranged will cook dinner for his guests. But there are also many excellent restaurants close by which includes the country's best fish and chip shop. Roly's served me his Swiss-style breakfast on the sheltered terrace overlooking Cable Bay. Down the hill I enjoyed the safe swimming beaches using the snorkelling gear and surfboard that are for guests' use.

Accommodation available (NZ$)	👤	👤👤	+👤	🛏	🛁
2 Suites	$180	$30	K	EN	

Breakfast: Special cooked
Evening meal: $45pp
Guest rooms:
Ambience:
Setting/location:

LOW   HIGH

Property features
Stunning sea views
3 safe sandy, swimming beaches
Beach towels supplied
Complimentary port & chocolates
All balcony rooms
CD/Sky TV/tea/coffee
Petanque
Local features
Fishing/diving (Rainbow Warrier)
Kayaking/swimming/walking
Golf course/sailing

Huntaway Lodge

Greg Hunt
1692 Wainui Road, Te Ngaere Bay, Northland
Tel: (09) 405 1611
Fax: (09) 405 1612
greg@huntawaylodge.com
www.lodgings.co.nz/huntaway.html

Kerikeri - 30 mins
Paihia/Waitangi - 45 mins

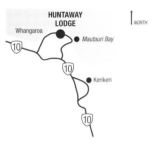

On SH 10 turn right to Matauri Bay, travel 14 km's then turn left in to Wainui Road. Drive through Te Ngaere Bay 600 metres past last house on left turn left up hill.

A road twists steeply up from sea level to access this contemporary lodge perched on a high hill, from which there is a 180-degree panorama over golden sand beaches, rocky promontories and the expansive blue ocean as far as the Cavalli Islands. Up here well away from any disturbance, it was easy to think I was on cloud nine. The three guest rooms of this purpose-built place are romantically named after the beaches that are in closest view from their windows - Te Ngaere, Pia Pia and Wainui. Each is simply designed and furnished with contemporary fittings and decorated with Pacific artworks. Along with bold paintings and tasteful colours throughout, the rooms with full amenities and modern ensuites are restful - and all around are the wonderful views. Adjoining the guest suites is a spacious open-plan sitting room/dining room/bar and a kitchen, which can be blocked off by wooden shutters. Greg has worked in the hospitality industry and the standard of service is excellent but the atmosphere undemanding and relaxing. Guests usually gather for drinks in the lounge before dinner which is cooked by the host. On the menu that night were local delicacies of oysters, pan-fried snapper and char-grilled tenderloin.

Family pets on site

Accommodation available (NZ$)	🧍	🧍🧍	+🧍	🛏	🛁
1 Room	$440	$440		Q	EN
2 Rooms	$375	$375		Q	EN

Breakfast: Special cooked
Evening meal: $80pp
Guest rooms:
Ambience:
Setting/location:

Children by arrangement - house booking only. Min two night stay.

Magic Cottage

Ian and Anna Sizer
Takou Bay Road, SH 10, Kerikeri
Tel: (09) 407 8065   Mob: 027 5457633
Fax:(09) 407 8403
takouriver@xtra.co.nz
www.lodgings.co.nz/magic.html

Property features
Attractive river frontage
Clawfoot bath on deck over river
Completely private and secluded
Extensive gardens/boathouse/jetty
Swimming/kayaking/fishing in river
Access to Takou Bay beach
Local features
Beaches and coastal scenery
Fishing/sailing/diving/surfing
Kerikeri, Waitangi & Russell sites
Golf courses including Kauri Cliffs

Kerikeri - 20 minutes
Paihia - 40 minutes

Travelling north from Kerikeri on
SH10, turn right onto Takou Bay Rd
8km beyond Waipapa. Turn left after
1km. Continue on unsealed road.
Property is at very end.

If you had ever thought of getting away from stress, noise, pollution and anything else that defines a city, Magic Cottage provides the answer. There's not a sound except the occasional bird call and the river lapping against the deck. Modern construction ensured I was comfortable and, tucked away in that secluded enclave, I didn't want for anything. The cottage is intimate studio style and spills onto a deck which holds an antique clawfoot bath, a perfect place to relax and take in your natural surroundings. I could imagine long summer nights, the river running under the deck, the barbecue. The homestead is located a few minutes walk away, and the river is unlikely to have any passers-by to intrude on guests' privacy. The five-acre garden is available for guests to enjoy and Ian and Anna are currently converting the 150 acre property to organics. You are likely to see a variety of birdlife during your visit- tui, fantails, rosellas, heron, shags, geese, paradise ducks or doves. The pontoon and kayaks are available for guests' use, so you can head by boat down the river to the estuary and beautiful surf beach at Takou Bay.

Accommodation available (NZ$)	♦	♦♦	+♦	🛏	🛁	
1 S/C cottage	$170	$170		SK/T	EN	Breakfast: Not available

Guest rooms:
Ambience:
Setting/location:

LOW   HIGH

14   Magic Cottage sleeps two people only.

Property features
River access/secluded gardens
Spacious contemporary design
Tranquil setting/private deck/bbq
Jetty/boathouse/summerhouse
Swimming/Kayaking/fishing in river
Access to Takou Bay beach
Local features
Beaches/coastal scenery
Fishing/sailing/diving/surfing
Kerikeri/Waitangi/Russell sites
Golf courses including Kauri Cliffs

Takou River Lodge Cottages

Ian and Anna Sizer
Takou Bay Road, SH 10, Kerikeri
Tel: (09) 407 8065   Mob: 027 5457633
Fax: (09) 407 8403
takouriver@xtra.co.nz
www.lodgings.co.nz/takouriverlodge.html

Kerikeri - 20 minutes
Paihia - 40 minutes

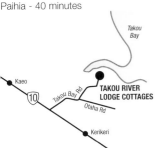

Travelling north from Kerikeri on SH10, turn right onto Takou Bay Rd 8km beyond Waipapa. Turn left after 1km. Continue on unsealed road. Property is at very end.

Takou River Cottages are set in 150 acres of lush green pastures on the banks of the Takou River, just a twenty-minute drive from Kerikeri. The Garden and River Cottages each have two bedrooms, two bathrooms, a lounge with reclaimed wooden floors, and a fully equipped kitchen with a stunning New Zealand timber bench. I admired the collection of art that adorns the walls, most of which comprised artefacts from Ian and Anna's travels- carvings and baskets from Papua New Guinea, clocks and paintings from Russia and kilims from Turkey. These two cottages on the edge of the river and surrounded by gardens and countryside, were so quiet and peaceful I never wanted to leave. Although Kerikeri was near if I'd needed more, I had equipped myself with provisions for a two-day stay. I had plenty of time to enjoy long walks through the stunning sub-tropical gardens, paddled along the Takou River, dreamt and read beside the pond and felt thoroughly relaxed and removed from the rest of the world. Kayaks and canoes are available for guests' use, ideal for heading down the river to the beautiful and deserted beach close by at Takou Bay.

Accommodation available (NZ$)			+		
Breakfast: Not available	2 S/C cottages		$170-220	$40	K or 2S + Q EN

Guest rooms:
Ambience:
Setting/location:

Low season and long stay rates available.

Cavalli View Cottage

Sharon Burges   Rick Harris
27 Te Ra Road, Takou Bay, Kerikeri
Tel: (09) 407 9019   Mob: 021 1185047
Fax: (09) 407 9018
takoubay@acute.co.nz
www.lodgings.co.nz/cavalliview.html

Property features
Ocean/island views
Peaceful private setting
Self contained
Decks and barbecue
Clawfoot bath on deck-hot/cold
Local features
Surf beach
Close to Kauri Cliffs golf course
Whangaroa Harbour/game fishing
Kerikeri
Wineries/art and craft centre

Kerikeri - 20 mins drive
Whangarei - 80 mins drive

Turn right off SH 10 North of Kerikeri onto Takou Bay Rd. Take right fork to Otaha Rd. After 4kms turn left into Te Ra Rd. Go half km veer left, 3rd drive on left go to end.

As I turned off the highway towards the coast of Takou Bay, I realised I was going to arrive at a place with awesome views and a delightful beach. This recently built cottage is completely separate from the hosts' home in a peaceful, spacious garden setting surrounded by fruit orchards and native plantings. The warm interior features an abundance of oiled natural timber and the atmosphere is tranquil. There is a queen-size bedroom that opens on to an expansive deck with a barbecue for private alfresco dining. Before dinner I relaxed in the outdoor claw-foot bath with hot and cold taps and sipped a glass of wine under the stars. You can completely self-cater in the small fully equipped kitchen or eat out at one of the many restaurants of Kerikeri. Bi-fold windows open from the lounge/dining area to a sweeping expanse of lawn which looks to the ocean and beyond to the majestic Cavalli Islands silhouetted against the horizon. The drive down to Takou Bay is only five minutes by car. This spectacular surf beach is popular with local fishermen, but chances are that you could have the beach to yourself. The famous Kauri Cliffs Golf Course is an easy drive away and there are no shortages of idyllic beaches in the vicinity.

Accommodation available (NZ$)	🧍	🧍🧍	+🧍	🛏	🛁	
1 S/C cottage		$150-170		Q	PR	

Family pets on site
Guest pets by arrangement

Breakfast: Not available

Guest rooms:
Ambience:
Setting/location:

LOW   HIGH

Double futon bed also available in cottage.

Property features
Secluded beach
Large garden and bush reserve
Extensive library/open fire
Sea & island views/NZ birdlife
Laundry service
Local features
Historic sites/buildings
Boating/fishing/diving/kauri forest
Several golf courses nearby
Boutique chocolate factory
Art & craft galleries

Fernbrook

Robert and Margaret Cooper
Kurapari Road, Rangitane, RD 1 Kerikeri
Tel: (09) 407 8570
Fax: (09) 407 8572
tfc@igrin.co.nz
www.lodgings.co.nz/fernbrook.html

Kerikeri - 12 minutes
Whangarei - 1 hr 15 mins

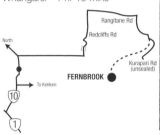

SH 10 past the Kerkeri turnoff, through Waipapa township for 1km and right into Kapiro Rd. Turn left on Redcliffs Rd and follow signs to Rangitane. Turn right into Kurapari Rd for 300 metres. Second driveway on right.

Fernbrook offers the discerning traveller a chance to savour a New Zealand country lifestyle in tranquil, relaxing surroundings. In their attractive, hilltop cedar house Margaret and Robert have two elegant bedrooms, one with its own sitting room. I was invited to share the pleasure of their home's interesting furnishings and the book-crammed library, which has an open fireplace. There is also a self-contained apartment and a waterfront cottage with two bedrooms, both beautifully appointed. One wonderful feature is the expansive, breathtaking view over the Bay of Islands. The house is set on 67 acres, half of which is a flowing country garden with a croquet lawn, petanque court, olive grove and Macadamia nut orchard. Sheep graze the pastures which dip downhill to a secluded beach. The remainder is in native bush with well marked tracks and picnic spots. The hosts told me about the importance of this area as a wildlife habitat where kiwis call at night. Dinner is served by arrangement. Special treats with pre-dinner drinks were pickled olives and Macadamia nuts from the trees on the property.

Breakfast: Cooked
Evening Meal: $55pp
Guest rooms:
Ambience:
Setting/location:

Accommodation available (NZ$)	♦	♦♦	+♦	🛏	🛁
1 S/C unit	$220	$225		Q	EN
1 Room	$185	$200		Q	PR
1 Suite	$200	$225		Q	EN
1 S/C cottage		$300-400		K+Q	EN

S/C cottage has two bedrooms.

17

Paheke

Juen and Frank Duxfield
State Highway 1, Ohaeawai, Northland
Tel: (09) 405 9623   Mob: 027 4485780
Fax: (09) 405 9628
paheke@xtra.co.nz
www.lodgings.co.nz/paheke.html

Kaikohe - 10 mins drive
Kerikeri - 15 mins drive

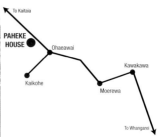

On SH 1 three hours drive north of Auckland Airport pass through the small settlement of Ohaeawai. Paheke is one kilometre further on the left.

Surrounded by a two-and-a-half acre area of enchanting gardens shaded by enormous old trees, The Paheke Homestead brings a slower, more peaceful era, to mind. The house was built in 1862 and, together with the dominating lebanon cedar tree in the front garden, is New Zealand Historic Places trust listed. Frank and Juen welcomed me enthusiastically and after tea I was invited to share the living spaces and verandahs of their comfortable house and wander the charming garden. The well-proportioned rooms of the old house are filled with interesting antique furniture which the couple has collected over many years, but the main accommodation is in the new wing which was seamlessly added in to the house in the old style but with modern convenience and luxuries. The bedrooms are large and airy with views out onto the tranquil gardens. There is additional accommodation in the old house - one double and two small single rooms suitable for children. The couple wholeheartedly encourages families with children to stay, treating them more as friends than paying guests. I joined them for a glass of wine before dinner and the next day enjoyed a picnic in the garden. Like many others I left with warm memories.

Accommodation available (NZ$)	🧍	🧍🧍	+🧍	🛏	🛁	Family dog on site Guest pets by arrangement
1 Room	$150	$150-175	K	EN		Breakfast: Cooked
1 Room	$115	$115-130	Q	EN		Evening meal: $50pp
1 Room	$80	$80-100	Q	PR		Guest rooms:
1 Room	$60	$60-80	S	PR		Ambience:
Family rate (4 persons) $200.						Setting/location:

LOW   HIGH

Property features
Panoramic sea views
Two units with full kitchen facilities
2 acre property/native birds
Indoor heated pool/spa/gym
BBQ/guest laundry
Elevated quiet location
All units have decks/in-room VCR

Local features
Boat trips/fishing/sailing
Swimming beach
Golf course/sightseeing tours

Chalet Romantica

Inge and Edi Amsler
6 Bedggood Close, Paihia
Tel: (09) 402 8270   Mob: 027 2266400
Fax:(09) 402 8278
chalet-romantica@xtra.co.nz
www.lodgings.co.nz/romantica.html

Paihia - Central town
Whangarei - 45 minutes

Find Kings Road and from here turn left into McMurrays Road. Opposite the tennis court, turn right into Bedggood Close and drive to the top.

Located above Paihia Beach on the site of the original Paihia Post Office, this large pleasantly decorated, Swiss-style home has three guest suites. These are roomy and comfortable with facilities, such as televisions, DVDs and CD-players, and private balconies from which guests can enjoy panoramic views over the Bay of Islands. Two suites have king-size beds and kitchen facilities. The third suite has a queen-size bed and is offered as a bed and breakfast. Inge has worked in the hospitality industry most of her life and enjoys spoiling her guests. She also runs the Swiss Cafe & Grill, a waterfront restaurant in town. Edi runs a private yacht charter and assists at the chalet. There is much to do on this two-and-a-half acre property. I enjoyed communing with the farm animals over the fence, swimming in the indoor pool and exercising in the gym, which was set up so that I could take in the view. After all that exercise it was great to be able to soak in the spa pool. Paihia has excellent restaurants, cafes and shops and is only a short walk away from Chalet Romantica. The lodge is convenient for longer stays and an ideal base from which to explore the North.

Accommodation available (NZ$)	🧍	🧍🧍	+🧍	🛏	🛁
1 Room	$80-110	$115-165		Q	PR
2 S/C units	$105-208	$115-225	$25	SK/T	EN

Breakfast: Extra $15pp

Off season discounts available.

Guest rooms:
Ambience:
Setting/location:

LOW   HIGH

19

Vista del Mar in the Heart of Paihia

Marj Browning
25 Sullivans Road, Paihia
Tel: (09) 402 7783   Mob: 027 2105242
Fax: (09) 402 7783
marj@vivid.net.nz
www.lodgings.co.nz/vistadelmar.html

Property features
Self-contained 3 bedroom home
Full kitchen and laundry facilities
Spacious decks and BBQ
Luxurious/spacious interior
Panoramic sea views
Local features
Restaurants/shopping - 10 min walk
Waitangi - Treaty House
Deep sea fishing/golf course/diving
Kayak/canoe/bike hire/tennis
Boat trips/ferry to Russell

Kerikeri - 20 minutes drive
Whangarei - 40 minutes drive

Just south of Paihia township turn off Seaview Rd (as it heads inland) into Sullivans Rd. Vista del Mar (number 25) is on the right - there is an internal access garage for your use.

Before I arrived at Vista del Mar, I could never have imagined how good the views are. I walked out onto the verandah which overlooks the blue water of the Bay of Islands and, as the sun was already setting, I first enjoyed a glass of wine and watched the boats scuttling into harbour, before I unpacked. As Vista del Mar is self-catering I had bought food to prepare and cook on the barbecue. It was easy to feel at home. Vista del Mar has a full kitchen, dining area, lounge and laundry - all that's required for a longer stay. I could easily imagine a small group enjoying this private accommodation and making it their base for several days. In the morning I lingered in bed enjoying the sea view from the bedroom which looks out towards Oronga Bay and an oyster farm. And, after a slow start, I walked down the road to Sullivan's Beach where I spent a large part of the day relaxing and swimming in the warm water. The shops and restaurants of Paihia and the ferry to Russell were only a short drive away.

Accommodation available (NZ$)						
1 S/C cottages	$200	$250	$50	2Q+2S	EN+PR	Breakfast: Not included

Single room has 2 single beds. 2 double rooms have queen beds.

Guest rooms:
Ambience:
Setting/location:

LOW   HIGH

Property features
Extensive sea views
Private decks with all day sun
Nautical theme
Ensuite to each bedroom
Off site host-guests privacy
Local features
Central Bay of Islands location
Boat trips/sailing/fishing
Historic attractions
Golf course/sightseeing

Crows Nest Villas

Marj Browning
20 Sir George Back Street, Opua, Bay of Islands
Tel: (09) 402 7783   Mob: 027 2105242
Fax: (09) 402 7783
marj@vivid.net.nz
www.lodgings.co.nz/crowsnest.html

Paihia - 5 minute drive
Whangarei - 45 minute drive

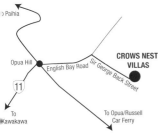

On SH11 from Kawakawa travel 15 mins to Opua hill. Cross into English Bay Rd, take the first right into Sir George Back St. #20 at end of cul-de-sac.

Hidden in the hills overlooking Opua harbour, the Crows Nest Villas are named to reflect a nautical theme. The Bridge Deck and Sails both have breathtaking views and a casual, contemporary feel. The self-contained villas had everything I needed for a weekend escape and were private enough for a romantic getaway or perfect for two families. Each bedroom within the villas has its own ensuite. As there was a barbecue available at Bridge Deck I decided to cook for myself while I enjoyed the afternoon sun. The shops in Paihia were an easy five-minute drive away and I found everything there that I needed for a good New Zealand barbecue. If you are looking for a break from cooking however, Marj, who is the host, is only too happy to organise a chef or restaurant dining for the evening. After dinner I lazed on the indoor swinging chairs, reading books and watching the boats come and go through Opua port. The following day I visited historic Russell, only a short ferry ride away and enjoyed the sights and restaurants.

Breakfast: Provisions provided

Accommodation available (NZ$)	👤	👥	+👤	🛏	🛁
1 S/C House			$280-550	2Q	2EN
1 S/C House			$280-550	Q+2S	2EN

Guest rooms:
Ambience:
Setting/location:

Provisions supplied first morning only.

Harbour House Villa

Robert and Masae Serge
7 English Bay Road, Opua, Bay of Islands
Tel: (09) 402 8087
Fax: (09) 402 8688
stay@harbourhousevilla.com
www.lodgings.co.nz/harbourhouse.html

Property features
Purpose built villa
Best views of Bay of Islands
Guest lounges/viewing deck
Quality furnishings/grand piano
Computer/Internet/hospitality
Local features
Garden, bush & coastal walks
Paihia
Waitangi and cultural heritage
Car ferry to historic Russell
Sailing/fishing/golf/arts/crafts

Opua - 5 min drive
Paihia - 10 min drive

From Auckland, take SH1 past Whangarei to Kawakawa. Take SH11 for 12km towards Opua. At intersection, cross into English Bay Road. Travel 500m to Harbour House Villa on right.

Located on a headland sheltered by two Norfolk pines, Harbour House Villa enjoys panoramic views of the Bay of Islands. A wide viewing deck, with comfortable outdoor furniture, wraps around this delightful home to encompass all aspects of the stunning view. Once I had unpacked, I relaxed and watched the car ferry and the yachts sailing by. Gentle melodies from the digital grand piano floated around me. This charming villa was purpose built providing guests with a lounge, dining area, internet facilities and extensive viewing decks. The bed and breakfast ensuite guestrooms may elect to have their breakfast served in the dining room or on the viewing deck. The one or two bedroom suites also have the option to have breakfast served in their suite and/or have self-catering breakfast provisions supplied promising maximum privacy. Guests may select a continental, full kiwi or Japanese breakfast. Your hosts Robert, from the United States, and Masae, from Japan, are seasoned travellers and experienced in providing hospitality in English and Japanese. It pays to enquire when booking in the winter as Robert and Masae are often known to head away themselves. For yachties needing a break on land, Robert has moorings out in the Bay.

Accommodation available (NZ$)	👤	👥	+👤	🛏	🛁	
2 Rooms	$160-255	$200-295	$40	S+Q/K	EN	Breakfast: Special cooked
1 Suite	$220-310	$260-350	$40	SK+S	EN	Evening meal: $80pp
2 Room Suite		$400-590	$40	S+Q+K	2EN	Guest rooms:

2 room suite tariff is for 4 persons sharing.

Ambience:
Setting/location:

LOW   HIGH

Property features
Separate guest lounge
Historic Kauri Homestead
Guest pick-up available
Adjacent to Matauwhi Bay
Laundry service available
Local features
Sailing/boating/fishing trips
Swimming with dolphins
Waterfront restaurant 10min walk
Museum/Pompallier House
Bush/beach walks

Ounuwhao (Harding House)

Allan and Marilyn Nicklin
Matauwhi Bay, Russell
Tel: (09) 403 7310
Fax: (09) 403 8310
thenicklins@xtra.co.nz
www.lodgings.co.nz/ounuwhao.html

Kerikeri - 35 minutes
Whangarei - 1 hour

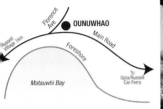

Cross from Opua by car ferry. Proceed on main rd to Russell. Ounuwhao is on the right approx. 100 m past the first 50km/hr sign encountered, about 10 minutes drive from the ferry landing.

Allan and Marilyn have painstakingly restored this beautifully crafted kauri villa which was built in Dargaville in 1894. The spirit of the house has been retained throughout its major relocation and reconstruction which is now settled at Matauwhi Bay as if it has always belonged there. Combined with the happy energy of the hosts, the house has a very inviting atmosphere. The owners have filled their home with whimsical artefacts and period furniture. Marilyn is a well-respected patchwork artist/teacher and walls, beds and furnishings display some of her exquisite work. In the guest's lounge, tea or coffee is set up on a marble dresser. The open fire is surrounded by an art nouveau mantle and next to it is a large screen television. It was summer when I was there, and guests were making good use of the wrap-around verandah. The Nicklins have thought of many details - even a small gift of soap for their guests. I particularly enjoyed the breakfast of lemon, pear and sour cream pancakes with berry sauce served in the old kitchen with its ticking clock and wood burning stove. A detached garden suite on the property offers private, peaceful accommodation suitable for honeymooners.

Family cat on site		Accommodation available (NZ$)	♦	♦♦	+♦	⊑	⊔
Breakfast: Special Cooked		1 Room	$135-170	$185-250	$85	Q+S	PR
		1 Room	$135-170	$185-250	$85	Q	EN
Guest rooms:		2 Rooms	$135-170	$185-250	$85	Q+S	EN
Ambience:		1 Suite	$180	$200-300		SK/T	EN
Setting/location:		1 S/C cottage		$200-290	$45	Q + 2S	PR

Pukematu Lodge

Kay and Colwyn Shortland
Flagstaff Road, Russell
Tel: (09) 403 8500   Mob: 027 2457640
Fax:(09) 403 8501
pukematu.lodge@clear.net.nz
www.lodgings.co.nz/pukematu.html

Property features
360 degree Bay of Islands view
Outdoor spa pool
Surrounded by native bush
Host speaks Maori
Walking distance to historic flagpole
Colwyn is a marriage celebrant
Local features
Bay of Islands dolphin watch
Boating/sailing/fishing
Local oysters and wine
Historic Russell village

Russell - 2 minutes
Whangarei - 1 hour

Find York St in the centre of Russell &
drive north towards Tapeka. This
road becomes Flagstaff Rd as it
climbs hill. At the top there is a sign
to the flagstaff pointing left - the
lodge is on the right down driveway.

Pukematu Lodge is set high on a hill above the historic township of Russell in twelve acres of native forest. This is a haven for bird life including a recently released kiwi that can sometimes be heard calling at night. From the large wooden deck I had commanding views of the town and of the labyrinths of sea winding between the peninsulas and islands of the bay. From another angle there was a view of the famous flagstaff - a local historic icon. The guests rooms are spacious, elegantly appointed and well proportioned with many thoughtful details that help guests feel like special friends. Colwyn, the local policeman, has family roots in the area. He can point across the bay to the place where his grandmother was born and, drawing on a deep knowledge of local customs, is happy to answer any questions about Maori culture. This gregarious fun-loving couple delights in sharing their time and their home and look after their guests with careful and friendly attention. Pukematu Lodge is also a great honeymoon destination and, because Colywn is a marriage celebrant and Kay is a wedding consultant, small weddings are sometimes held at the lodge.

Accommodation available (NZ$)	👤	👤👤	+👤	🛏	🛁
1 Room	$330	$395		Q	EN
1 Room	$330	$395		Q or 2S	EN

Maori hangi evening meals can be arranged - please enquire.
Specialise in small weddings.

Breakfast: Cooked

Guest rooms:
Ambience:
Setting/location:

LOW   HIGH

Property features
Cliff-top location/ocean views
Private terraces
Mediterranean architecture
Separate guest entrances
Local features
Game fishing
Sailing/water sports
Historic areas/museums
Several beaches
Coastal and bush walks
Eco tours and dolphin trips

Russell - 5 minutes
Paihia - 25 minutes

From Russell, drive towards Flagstaff Hill on Tapeka Rd. Continue over hill. Turn right into Du Fresne, Te Pa Helios is up on the left beside the cliff-top.

Te Pa Helios (formerly Villa Helios)
Maggie Duggan
44 Du Fresne Place, Tapeka Point, Russell
Tel: (09) 403 7229
Fax: (09) 403 7229
villa.helios@xtra.co.nz
www.lodgings.co.nz/tepahelios.html

It was 6.30 am, and despite the romance created by the setting and the interior design, I couldn't resist getting up, throwing open all the doors that overlook the sea crashing against the rocks below and having some quiet moments on my own. The sun came up directly in front of me and I was mesmerized by the sound below. All accommodation has its own private outdoor area with panoramic views of the ocean and sea caves. Here, you don't have to see a soul - and yet Maggie, the host, gladly shares a glass of wine or offers suggestions to enhance your visit. Te Pa Helios has more than a little touch of the Greek Islands - lots of terracotta-tiled floors, blues, white and chromes - in the four guest units. The self-contained villa offers several extras: an open fire for warmth and romance in the winter; a video recorder; two bedrooms for extra guests; and an upstairs and downstairs terrace. The newest addition, Paua Cottage, is a self-contained, ocean-front house, designed for longer stays. All units have stereos, televisions, fridges and nicely appointed furnishings, which make a stay at Te Pa Helios comfortable and memorable.

Accommodation available (NZ$)	♦	♦♦	+♦	🛏	🛁
1 Suite	$280	$280		Q	EN
1 Studio	$240	$240		SK/T	EN
1 S/C villa	$350	$350		K+SK/T	1.5PR
1 S/C cottage	$450	$450		K+2Q	2PR

Breakfast: Suite & studio only

Guest rooms:
Ambience:
Setting/location:

Min. night stays: Suite/studio:2, S/C villa:3, S/C cottage:4.

Waipoua Lodge

Nicole and Chris Donahoe
State Highway 12, Waipoua Forest, Northland
Tel: (09) 439 0422   Mob: 027 2572020
Fax:(09) 523 8081
lodgings@waipoualodge.co.nz
www.lodgings.co.nz/waipoualodge.html

Property features
120 year old historic country lodge
Guest lounge/bar/sunroom/library
NZ cuisine enjoyed in dining room
Native bushwalks in gardens
Local features
Waipoua & Tane Mahuta forest walks
Kai Iwi Lakes - fishing and swimming
Night walks to see Kiwi Birds
Golf/horseriding/quad bikes at beach

Dargaville - 40 minute drive
Hokianga Harbour - 40 minute drive

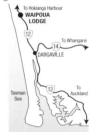

Take Highway 1 north to the Brynderwyns. Follow the "Twin Coast Discovery" signs to Dargaville. Take State Highway 12 north toward the Waipoua Forest. The lodge is 47kms from Dargaville on the main highway on the right hand side.

An absolute calm surrounds this 120-year old kauri villa. Majestic kauri and native trees of Waipoua Forest stretch to the horizon. Waipoua Lodge is an asset to West Coast Northland, perfectly positioned for access to lakes and the beaches of the Pacific Coast nearby. The welcome and charm of Nicole and Chris immediately put me at ease. Nicole guided me to my self-contained apartment, one of four available for guests' use. Housed within the original farm buildings each has been distinctly styled by Nicole with quality new furnishings and attention to detail. My niece was travelling with me and, with children of their own, Nicole and Chris welcomed her. She delighted in the large bath and the sleeping loft in my apartment called the Wool Shed. A memorable dinner served at the time I chose, focused on local organic produce and fresh vegetables from the garden – broccoli and blue-cheese soup was followed by venison steaks, seasonal vegetables and delicious kumara. Dessert was a choice of pickled figs with vanilla bean Kapiti ice cream, or mini sponges with fresh wild strawberries and cream. This understated relaxed accommodation will give luxury and peace to anyone travelling the unspoiled Kauri Coast.

Family dog on site

Accommodation available (NZ$)	👤	👤👤	+👤	🛏	🛁	
1 S/C cottage	$400-550	$420-570		K or 2S	EN	
1 S/C cottage	$400-550	$420-570	$80	2K or 4S	EN	
1 S/C cottage	$400-550	$420-570	$80	K or 2S+2S	EN	
1 S/C cottage	$400-550	$420-570		K or 2S	EN	

Stereo and cds in each cottage. Children welcome, under 6 are free.

Breakfast: Special Cooked
Evening Meal: $70pp
Guest rooms:
Ambience:
Setting/location:

LOW   HIGH

Property features
Spa pool
Kayaks
Mountain bikes available
Water skiing plus tuition
Petanque
Local features
Horse riding
Trout fishing
Golf
Sightseeing

Wai Hou Oma Lodge

Ruby and Noel Martin
357 Kai Iwi Lakes Road, RD3, Dargaville
Tel: (09) 439 7282   Mob: 021 2458368
Fax:(09) 439 7282
info@waihouomalodge.co.nz
www.lodgings.co.nz/waihouoma.html

Dargaville - 30 mins drive
Whangarei - 1 hour drive

From Dargaville, follow state highway 12. Well sign posted to Kai Iwi Lakes approx 35kms we are just 1/2 km on left past main Lake Taharoa.

This lodge overlooks a large private lake as well as white sands and bright-blue waters of Taharoa Lake, which is the largest of the Kai Iwi Lakes. It is a quiet retreat hosted by friendly owners, Ruby and Noel Martin. My accommodation was in one of the two separate, one-bedroom dwellings, both have underfloor heating and are self contained and ultra-modern with internet connections, Sky TVs and CD players. They have, however, kept their New Zealand beach-cottage feel. In each there is a king-size bedroom with ensuite, an open-plan lounge, dining area, and a fully-equipped kitchenette with modern fittings including a dishwasher. I felt pampered by the luxurious bed linen, robes, slippers, plush towels and the range of fine toiletries provided. Ranch sliders opened to my private patio, a pebble garden and barbecue area with comfortable outdoor furniture. By day, pukeko, ducks and black swans swam past on the lake and at night, I heard the call of native frogs. At the lake edge, housed in a boat shed, is a roomy spa. Kayaks are provided for guests' use and there are other activities in the area including water-skiing, fly fishing, hiking across farmland to the ocean beach, kiwi-spotting at night and exploring the Waipoua Kauri Forest.

Family pets on site
Guest pets by arrangement

Accommodation available (NZ$)	👤	👤👤	+👤	🛏	🛁
2 S/C Cottages	$160	$160	$50	D+K	PR

Breakfast: Extra $9-12pp
Evening Meal: Enquire
Guest rooms:
Ambience:
Setting/location:

LOW   HIGH

Parua House

Pat and Peter Heaslip
Parua Bay, Whangarei Heads Road, Whangarei
Tel: (09) 436 5855
paruahomestay@clear.net.nz
www.lodgings.co.nz/paruahouse.html

Property features
Bay and harbour views
Olive grove/house cow
Native bush reserves
Spa pool
Featured on TV
Home grown fruit and produce
Local features
Panoramic ocean views
Golf course nearby/bush walks
Swimming beaches/diving
Fishing/boating/sailing

Whangarei - 20 minutes
Auckland - 2 hrs 30 mins

From Whangarei take road to Whangarei Heads. Continue past the Golf Club and Parua Bay Tavern for 0.7km. Parua House is 100m up the hill on the left.

Elevated high above the road, Parua House enjoys views over Parua Bay and Whangarei Harbour. Although spectacular, the setting is not the dominating factor. People come here just for the superb hospitality. The hosts, Pat and Peter, are passionate about growing food and are involved in Northland's expanding olive industry - a topic that provoked interesting conversation during my visit. The garden around the home is large and colourful. The queen bedroom takes advantage of the view with comfortable chairs in front of double-hung windows that extend to the floor. The twin bedroom in the main house catches the afternoon sun and feels very light. The studio, which is a separate cottage in the garden, is a good option if you want to do your own thing. There are tea and coffee facilities, comfortable seating and modern bathroom facilities. The decor is a blend of modern and traditional, which features some original artwork on the walls. Although it is not much effort to find somewhere to eat, it would be wise to have a meal here at least one night; the location, an antipasto and a glass or two of wine on a balmy Northland evening is something I could get used to.

Accommodation available (NZ$)	👤	👤👤	+👤	🛏	🛁	
1 Room	$90	$150		Q	EN	
1 Studio	$90	$150	$50	Q+S	EN	
1 Room	$90	$150		2S	PR	

Family pets on site
Guest pets by arrangement

Breakfast: Special continental
Evening Meal: $35pp
Guest rooms:
Ambience:
Setting/location:

LOW   HIGH

Property features
Safe swimming and boating
Private beach location/bush walks
Ecologically significant native bush
Moorings for boats up to 10 metres
BBQ and open fire
Historic significance
Local features
Surf beaches nearby
Golf course/bush walks
Diving/fishing trips
Restaurants

Parua Bay Cottage
Greg and Marian Innes
Parua Cemetery Rd, Parua Bay, Whangarei Heads
Tel: (09) 436 5626   Mob: 0274 953382
Free: 0800 116626
paruabaycottage@innes-strategy.com
www.lodgings.co.nz/paruabay.html

Whangarei - 20 minutes
Auckland - 2 hrs 10 mins

From Whangarei, follow signs to Whangarei Heads. Pass Parua Bay tavern and turn second right into Parua Cemetery Rd. Follow to the beach - the cottage is on your right.

   Parua Bay Cottage is located adjacent to a beach shared only with the Innes family. The beach is sandy and is suitable for swimming, fishing, lazing on, and all this not fifty steps from the cottage. The view from the front door is of the beach framed by pohutukawa, while the view from the back door is of the large native tree block behind. The cottage has recently been renovated and has plenty of space for a long summer holiday. There are two bedrooms, a lounge with open fire, dining room and kitchen, bathroom and full laundry. All I needed to bring was plenty of food and wine. Despite being over 120 years old, the cottage had every amenity I needed - the new kitchen comes complete with gas hobs and oven. Marian has, however, gone to a lot of trouble to have everything in keeping with the age of the cottage. There was plenty for this city dweller to do here: bushwalking, birdwatching, feeding the chickens/ducks, beach activities, or relaxing on the verandah reading a good book. Children and/or dogs are most welcome here. This is quite unlike so many seaside experiences - no crowds, no noise - if you can't relax here you need help.

Family pets on site Guest pets by arrangement	Accommodation available (NZ$)	👤	👤👤	+👤	🛏	🛁
Breakfast: Not included	1 S/C cottage	$150	$150	$30	2D+3S	PR

Guest rooms:
Ambience:
Setting/location:

RECOMMENDED
★★★
BOUTIQUE
LODGINGS
LOW   HIGH

Phone available on request.

29

Mangawhai Lodge - a room with a view

Jeannette Forde
4 Heather Street, Mangawhai Heads
Tel: (09) 431 5311
Fax: (09) 431 5312
mlodge@xtra.co.nz
www.lodgings.co.nz/mangawhailodge.html

Property features
Panoramic views
Sep guest lounge & TV room
Conference facilities - sml groups
Large verandahs with sea views
Guest kitchenette/BBQ

Local features
Beaches/walkways
Windsurfing/waterskiing
Bird sanctuary/golf course
Water access - 2 mins
Fishing and kayaking

Mangawhai Heads - 5 mins walk
Auckland - 1 hr 20 mins

From Auckland turn off SH 1 just pas
Te Hana. Follow Twin Coast Route to
Mangawai. Turn right, then left into
Molesworth Dr. Lodge on corner of
Heather St. From north turn off SH1
at Waipu. Follow coastal road.

This large colonial-style property is spread over two levels. The five colourful guestrooms all open onto the expansive verandah that surrounds the building. Most of them face the view over the estuary harbour, surf beach, bird sanctuary and the Hen and Chicken islands. I visited Mangawhai Lodge early one morning and the guests were eating breakfast on the verandah to the background of bird call and soft classical music and the reflection of the sun dancing on the distant water. This is the place I'd come if I wanted some inspiration! Because of the size of the lodge, guests have plenty of space and freedom. With the two guest lounges - one a television lounge, the other featuring a log fire and opening onto the verandahs - there are plenty of places to tuck away and read. There is also a kitchenette for preparing light snacks. A short wander down the road would have taken me to the harbour beach, the 18-hole golf course, or any of the several cafes nearby. A longer walk, or short drive, leads to the Mangawhai Heads surf beach and clifftop walkway. Mangawhai Lodge is popular with golfing groups and city escapees wishing to feel the sand beneath their feet.

Accommodation available (NZ$)	🧍	🧍🧍	+🧍	🛏	🛁	
						Family cat on site Guest pets by arrangement
2 Rooms	$130-145	$150-165		Q	EN	Breakfast: Cooked
2 Rooms	$130-145	$150-165		SK/T	PR	
1 Room	$130-145	$150-165		SK/T	EN	Guest rooms:
						Ambience:
						Setting/location:

LOW   HIGH

Property features
Kayaks/waterfront/sea views
Croquet lawn/feature garden
Swimming pool/petanque court
TV and video in units
Conference facilities;
small groups please enquire
Local features
Surf beach/craft
Golf course and tennis court
Café nearby

Milestone Cottages
Gael McConachy
27 Moir Point Rd, Mangawhai Heads, Northland
Tel: (09) 431 4018
Fax:(09) 431 4018
gael@milestonecottages.co.nz
www.lodgings.co.nz/milestone.html

Mangawhai Heads - 3 minutes
Whangarei - 45 minutes

From Mangawhai turn into
Molesworth Drive (signposted
Mangawhai Heads). Go over
causeway and turn right into Moir
Point Rd, just after Naja Garden
Centre and café. Milestone Cottages
s 200 metres on your left.

Milestone Cottages comprise a mini resort that epitomises 'kiwi style'. All accommodation has been designed around an extensive garden, palm fringed croquet lawn, a swimming pool and views to the estuary and ocean beyond. There are five high-quality self-contained units, each with a unique design, and carefully positioned around the garden to provide maximum privacy. There are three particularly special units here - The Schooner, The Gardners and The Gumdigger's Cottages, each reflecting an element of local history. The Gumdigger's is an earthbrick building and is decorated with reference to the gum digging industry that existed in the area at the beginning of the century. The Gardners which was inspired by English forebears is set on the gardens edge and boasts views over the garden and croquet lawn. The Schooner Cottage (with the best views) is built with reference to the ship-building industry which occurred near this property last century. All accommodation has kitchen facilities. I stayed in The Schooner Cottage, which is also the largest and is suitable for a family, or for a longer stay. There is so much to do on this one-and-a-half acre, estuary-frontage property, and it is also an ideal spot to relax and unwind. Milestone Cottages were NZ Tourism Award winners in 1998.

Breakfast: Café nearby

Guest rooms:
Ambience:
Setting/location:

Accommodation available (NZ$)	♦	♦♦	+♦	⛏	🛁
1 S/C cottage	$170-185	$170-185		K	EN
1 S/C cottage	$170-185	$170-185	$35	Q+S	EN
1 S/C cottage	$195-225	$195-225	$35	K+3S	EN
3 S/C unit	$112.50-175	$112.50-175	$35	Various	EN

Special off-season mid-week rates. Weekend 2 night min.

31

The Ridge Cottages

David and Margaret Barlow
Old Waipu Road, Mangawhai
Tel: (09) 431 4438   Mob: 021 2832990
Fax:(09) 431 4458
theridge@xtra.co.nz
www.lodgings.co.nz/theridge.html

Property features
Superb coastal estuary/bush views
Spa pool with views in Spa cottage
5 acre grounds
Private decks with views and BBQ
Fully self-contained/TV/CD player
Local features
Surf and swimming beaches
Golf course/cafes
Tennis court/coastal walks
Horse riding
Fishing

Mangawhai - 2 mins
Warkworth - 45 minutes

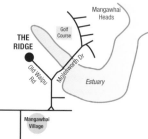

From SH 1 there are 2 roads to Mangawhai - near Te Hana or at Kaiwaka. When you reach Mangawh go past shops & turn left towards Mangawhai Heads. Keep left and continue to end of Old Waipu Rd.

The Ridge has two fully self-contained cottages, the modern Stables cottage and the stylish but more traditional Spa cottage. They are set high on a ridge overlooking the distant ocean and the closer sweep of the tidal estuary which slices through white sand dunes. The view is compelling from both cottages but I didn't feel uncomfortable perched on the side of a cliff because kanuka and ferns threw their fronds around the edge of the decks. The entrance side of the cottages are at ground level but the fronts are in the tree tops shared with grey warblers and silvereyes. I opened the door of the Stables cottage and was greeted by the wonderful aroma of freshly baked bread and comfortable contempory décor. The Spa cottage is a smaller studio cottage and has a private spa pool with a glass ceiling so that I could lie back and contemplate the stars. Perhaps one of the most endearing features of The Ridge is the attention to detail. Both cottages have large private decks with bbq and marvellous views. Inside the cottages, magazines, home-made jams, chocolates, modern entertainment systems, a range of CDs and small kitchens that are thoughtfully equipped with everything you could conceivably require.

Accommodation available (NZ$)	👤	👤👤	+👤	🛏	🛁	
1 S/C cottage	$165-195	$165-195	$40	K+S	EN	Breakfast: Cafés nearby
1 S/C cottage	$165-195	$165-195		K	EN	

Enquire about mid week or long stay rates.

Guest rooms:
Ambience:
Setting/location:

LOW   HIGH

Property features
- Individual BBQs
- Access to lakes/lake views
- Host speaks German
- Mountain bikes/kayaks available
- Petanque

Local features
- Surf beach/trout fishing
- Golf course/tennis court
- Horse riding along beach

Lake View Chalets

Arnim Pierau
662 Ocean View Rd, Mangawhai
Tel: (09) 431 4086   Mob: 021 1487650
info@chalets.co.nz
www.lodgings.co.nz/lakeview.html

Mangawhai - 15 minutes
Wellsford - 30 minutes

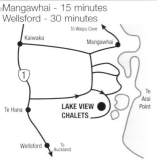

Drive north on SH1. Past Te Hana
take right towards Mangawhai.
Drive 13km. Turn right into Te Arai
Point Rd. Follow signs to Lake
View Chalets.

These six chalets have been designed to maximise the lake view and are separated by gardens and lawn. Each unit is spacious with modern décor and very comfortable furnishings. There are two bedrooms with king-size beds that convert into two singles so that they can be set up to suit different guest groupings. Full kitchen amenities allow people who bring their own food the option of home cooking but the restaurants of Mangawhai Heads are only a 15-minutes drive away. Breakfast can be provided in your chalet if requested. My deck overlooked much of the extensive property which stretches from the hills towards the sand dunes and sea. In the evening, glass of wine in hand, I watched a soft breeze playing with the reeds that fringe Spectacle and Slipper Lakes. By day Arnim showed me where to go kayaking, biking, swimming and fishing or walking through forests. There are horses on the property and experienced guests are welcome to ride them - some guests even bring their horses with them (enquire first). Lake View Chalets are not merely a place to stay; in their lovely setting that offers such a diversity of activity they are a complete destination.

Accommodation available (NZ$)				
Breakfast: Extra $15pp	6 S/C cottages	$150-170	$45	2K or 4S PR

Guest rooms:
Ambience:
Setting/location:

LOW   HIGH

Enquire about mid-week and off-season rates.

Matakana

Ascension Vineyard
480 Matakana Road,
Tel: (09) 422-9601. An hour north
of Auckland, Ascension serves
Mediterranean-style food and its
own wines in a sunny restaurant
just metres from the vineyard.

Herons Flight Vineyard & Cafe
49 Sharps Road,
Tel: (09) 422-7915. A Tuscan style
farm, where vines intermingle with
mulberry & olive trees on the hill
slopes.

Morris & James Café Bar, Pottery & Tileworks
48 Tongue Farm Rd, Tel: (09) 422-7484, Enjoy
lunch and browse their showroom.
Tours available, watch artisans at
work.

The Rusty Pelican Restaurant & Bar
1001 Matakana Rd, Tel: (09) 422-9122.
Relaxed atmosphere, open fire, à
la carte menu, pizzas. Licensed.

Markets
**Matakana Village Farmers
Market** Saturdays from 8am-1pm
(Winter 9am-1pm).

Puhoi

Puhoi Tavern
Off SH 1 between Waiwera and
Warkworth. An old country tavern
in a small Bohemian settlement.

The Art of Cheese Café & Shop
275 Ahuroa Rd, Tel: (09) 422-0670.
Enjoy a cheese platter and a glass
of wine. Watch the cheese makers
at work.

Great Barrier Island

Claris Texas Café
Claris Commercial Centre,
Tel: (09) 429-0852. This relaxed
café is a local favourite. Licensed.

Waiheke Island

Mudbrick Vineyard
Church Bay Rd, Oneroa, Tel: (09) 372-9050.
Superb food and views across
the water back to the city.
Book ahead in summer.

Stonyridge Vineyard
80 Onetangi Rd, Tel: (09) 372-8822.
Fabulous al fresco dining amongst
the vines and olive trees.

The Shed
76 Onetangi Rd,
Tel: (09) 372-6884. While away a
day in this unique setting on the
Te Motu Vineyard. Enjoy the wine
and share one of their fabulous
platters.

Maraetai Beach

Vino Vino Café & Winebar
3/153 Ocean View Rd, Oneroa,
Tel: (09) 372-9888. Great for long
lunches looking out over idyllic
Oneroa Bay.

Waimauku

The Hunting Lodge
Waikoukou Valley Rd, Tel: (09) 411-8259.
Great after many years. Vineyard
setting, open fire in winter, quality
cuisine.

Beesonline Honey Centre & Café
791 SH 16, Tel: (09) 411-5216.
An urbane café at the centre of a
high-tech beehive, the focus is on
native Kiwi ingredients.

Devonport

Esplanade Hotel Dining Room
1 Victoria Rd, Tel: (09) 445-1291.
One of the most pleasant and
professional dining experiences.
Pick and mix several dishes to
create a multi-course culinary
extravaganza.

Ponsonby

Bambina
268 Ponsonby Rd,
Tel: (09) 360-4000. Popular with
the locals, simple but clever food
combinations keep the blackboard
menu interesting.

Chandelier
152 Ponsonby Rd,
Tel: (09) 360-9315. Opulent décor,
splendid food. Dress to impress in
this chic Ponsonby establishment.

Prego
266 Ponsonby Rd,
Tel: (09) 376-3095. Consistently
great food, setting and service.

Rocco
23 Ponsonby Rd,
Tel: (09) 360-6407. The influence is
rustic Spanish, but there's more
than tapas at this great restaurant
along with an admirably eclectic
wine list.

SPQR
150 Ponsonby Rd,
Tel: (09) 360-1710. This place is
hip and happening and at the
heart of the Ponsonby scene.

Kingsland

Bouchon
479 New North Rd,
Tel: (09) 845-1680. A lovely little
creperie. Eat inside where it's cosy or
catch the afternoon sun on the deck.

Kalaloo Café
480 New North Rd,
Tel: (09) 815-1025. Tiny, chaotic,
atmospheric and fantastic Italian
food. Ruby Bar a few doors along is
good if you have to wait for a table.

Auckland City

Cin Cin on Quay
99 Quay St,
Tel: (09) 307-6966. A waterfront
institution that serves up dishes
with flair. Great for a late-night bite
(the kitchen closes at 11pm).

Soul Bar & Bistro
Viaduct Basin,
Tel: (09) 356-7249. A highly-
regarded restaurant in Auckland's
Viaduct Basin.

Superette
18 Drake St,
Tel: (09) 373-3664. Where the
city's fashionista hang. Browse the
clothes racks then enjoy a coffee
at this unique café.

The French Cafe
210 Symonds
St, Tel: (09) 377-1911. This elegant
restaurant is famous for its inspired
menu and fantastic reputation.

Vivace
Level 1, 50 High St,
Tel: (09) 302-2303. Nibble tapas
beside the fire in the back bar or
savour an Italian-style repast in the
restaurant.

White Hilton Hotel
Prince's
Wharf, Tel: (09) 978-2000. Fine
dining using the best of local
ingredients with great views of the
harbour. Also lovely for a lazy
Sunday brunch on the terrace.

Markets
Aotea Market All day
Fridays/Saturdays.
Interesting food, fashion.
Takapuna Market Sunday
early - 12pm. Local produce,
various products for sale.

Events
Pacifika March: Western Springs
The Food Show Auckland
August: Auckland Showgrounds,
Greenlane

Great Barrier Island page 43

Warkworth page 36

Puhoi page 42

Mahurangi page 40

Orewa page 49

Waimauku page 50

Waiheke Island page 45

Auckland page 51

Bombay Hills page 63

Newmarket & Mt Eden

Zarbo 24 Morrow St, Newmarket, Tel: (09) 520-2721. Foodie heaven, this café and deli offers a blackboard menu or tasty lunches from the chiller.

Rikka 73 Davis Cres, Newmarket, Tel: (09) 522-5277. Order the tenshin set menu at this modern Japanese restaurant and watch a parade of edible artworks appear on your table.

Gina's Pizza and Pasta Bar 209 Symonds St, Eden Terrace, Tel: (09) 302-2061. Authentically tiny, crowded and loud. Popular with the locals so book in advance.

Benediction Site 3, St Benedicts St, Newton, Tel: (09) 309-5001. Enjoy a morning latté or lunchtime ravioli in industrial surroundings opening to an internal courtyard in the revamped Symond St stables.

Parnell

Antoines 333 Parnell Rd, Tel: (09) 379-8756. This is high cuisine at its best.

The Java Room 317 Parnell Rd, Tel: (09) 366-1606. Licensed and BYO restaurant serving delectable dishes from all corners of Asia - from Japan to Java.

Metropole 223 Parnell Rd, Tel: (09) 379-9300. Sleek and stylish, the menu is fresh New Zealand cuisine with Asian and Mediterranean influences.

St Heliers

Halo 425 Tamaki Dr, Tel: (09) 575-9969. Take a drive along the waterfront to this upmarket yet understated restaurant. The menu is Pacific Rim with an oceanside flavour.

Westhaven Marina.

Karaka

Truffle Café & Deli
257 Linwood Rd,
Tel: (09) 292-7017. Great coffee, all day breakfasts.

Alegria Beautyfarm

Claudia and Alex Schenz
180 Monarch Downs Way, Matakana, RD 2, Warkworth
Tel: (09) 422 7211
Fax:(09) 422 7833
alegriabeautyfarm@xtra.co.nz
www.lodgings.co.nz/alegria.html

Property features
Beautyfarm
Pampering holiday
Peaceful rural setting
Stunning panoramic views
Overlooking vineyards
Delicious European breakfasts
Local features
Close to wineries/2 golf courses
Beaches/Kawau Island Ferry
Pottery/Matakana market
Diving/snorkeling at Goat Island

Matakana - 5 mins drive
Auckland - 60 mins drive

From Auckland take SH 1 to Warkworth. At 2nd lights follow the road to Matakana, after 5 km turn right into Sharp Road, go 1.2 km. Turn right into Monarch Downs Way. Drive to end 2km.

Here's an opportunity for a pampered night or two at this modern house with a Mediterranean ambience, which stands high on a hill overlooking vineyards, olive groves, a deer farm and Kawau Bay. You will possibly wish you had booked in for a week. I arrived early on a bright clear morning to be greeted by Claudia who had prepared a magnificent breakfast, including excellent German coffee, home-baked, wheat free bread and delicacies from all around Europe - decorated with herbs from her garden. Another special aspect of Alegria is the beauty studio in a delightful separate group of rooms. Claudia is a German qualified beauty therapist, offering her guests sensational face and body treatments. Her specialty starts with a back massage, followed by an application of self-heating mud on the spine, using French Phytomer products. According to Claudia, these products are the best in marine cosmetology. The favourite of the guestrooms is the adjoining, pleasantly serene Spanish Room with its elegant theme of olives, and an enormous bed covered in crisp white linen. It opens to a terrace overlooking the green countryside and has a roomy ensuite bathroom.

Accommodation available (NZ$)	🧍	🧍🧍	+🧍	🛏	🛁
1 Studio	$145-180		SK or 2S	EN	
1 Room	$145-180		SK	PR	

Breakfast: Special cooked
Evening Meal: Enquire
Guest rooms:
Ambience:
Setting/location:

LOW   HIG

Property features
Swimming pool
Separate guest area
Rural and vineyard outlook
Restaurants close by
Large rose garden & orchard

Local features
Goat Island Marine Reserve
Kauri Museum
Golf Courses
Vineyards
Cafes/art galleries

Rosemount Homestead Bed & Breakfast

Libby Dykes
25 Rosemount Road, RD 5, Warkworth
Tel: (09) 422 2580   Mob: 027 4966654
enquiries@rosemount.co.nz
www.lodgings.co.nz/rosemount.html

Warkworth - 5 mins drive
Auckland - 60 mins drive

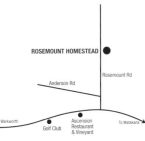

Take SH 1 to Warkworth. Turn right into Matakana Road towards Leigh. Past Ascension Vineyard turn left into Rosemount Road. Drive 500 metres following signs.

The wooden picket gate brushed with lichen sets the atmosphere for this rustic two-storeyed homestead set amongst the rolling hills of the Matakana Valley. Libby's love of old houses culminated in the acquisition of the 105 year-old, kauri-built Rosemount and its recreation into a vision of how it could have been in the Victorian era. Inside are high coved ceilings, polished kauri floors and simple folk-antique furniture. The serene interiors open up to the outside light through sash windows and French doors. Upstairs are the three spacious guest ensuite bedrooms, all of which have doors leading to a wrap-around verandah and views over lush pastures and verdant lawn which stretches to a spreading plum tree. All the bedrooms are airy, sunny and comfortable and Libby says guests like to spend time in them as much as they do in the downstairs guest lounge with its tiled fireplace and antique Italian tool bench. One special touch at Rosemount is the lavish breakfast accompanied by candlelight and jazz music, which I was served on a bench table in a separate dining room. I enjoyed a selection of seasonal fruits and traditional eggs, bacon and spiced mushrooms.

Family dog on site	Accommodation available (NZ$)	👤	👤👤	+👤	🛏	🛁
Breakfast: Cooked	1 Room	$175	$200		Q	EN
	1 Room	$175	$200		Q	EN
Guest rooms:	1 Room	$175	$200		2S	EN
Ambience:						
Setting/location:	Winter rates apply. Not suitable for children.					

LOW   HIGH

The Castle Matakana

Val and Ross Sutherland
378 Whitmore Rd, Matakana, Warkworth
Tel: (09) 422 9288
Fax:(09) 422 9289
mail@the-castle.co.nz
www.lodgings.co.nz/thecastle.html

Property features
Panoramic sea and rural views
Unique architectual design
Large outdoor chess set
Small vineyard on site
Local features
Vineyards/wineries
Kawau Island & Mansion House
Surf and swimming beaches
Marine reserve - Goat Island
Cafes/restaurants

Warkworth - 15 minutes
Auckland - 1 hour

From Warkworth follow signs east towards Matakana/Omaha. Continue through Matakana and turn right and right again onto Takatu Rd. Take the first turn right (Whitmore Rd). The lodge is on the left.

This is what boutique lodgings are about - interesting architecture, stunning location and outstanding hosts. Due to time constraints, I was unable to stay the night here but will not make that mistake next time. The architecture is reminiscent of Moroccan and Greek villas with additional features such as the floor to ceiling windows that take in the views over the rolling countryside and the islands of Kawau Bay. The home is set on fifteen acres of land planted with pasture, bush, and vineyards. Inside this home, the guest wing is off to one side with the grandest guestroom situated upstairs. All three have spectacular views with french doors opening directly onto the verandah or terrace. Rooms have been tastefully decorated and there is original art, beautiful linen, and plenty of fresh flowers. Facilities are as you would expect in top quality accommodation. Val's innovative meals can cater to any dietary requirements and feature local organic produce. Breakfast focuses on fresh produce from the region such as melon, cape gooseberry jam or plums. To follow the fresh fruit, muesli and homemade bread, Val also cooks wonderful dishes, such as a specialty organic blueberry dish.

Accommodation available (NZ$)					
1 Room	From $270	SK	EN	Breakfast: Special cooked
1 Room	From $300	SK/T	EN	Evening Meal: $75pp
1 Room	From $375	SK	EN	Guest rooms:

Our own vintages are available, only to in-house guests.
Phone, fax, fast internet available.

Ambience:
Setting/location:

LOW   HIGH

Property features
Secluded, tranquil position
Views of estuary and vineyard
Refreshments upon arrival
Separate guest lounge
Local features
Pottery and craft galleries
Vineyards/wineries/restaurants
Seashore/café - short walk
Harbour Cruises - Kawau Island
Golf course/beaches
Marine reserve diving/sailing

The Saltings Estate

Terry and Maureen Baines
1210 Sandspit Road, Sandspit, Warkworth
Tel: (09) 425 9670   Mob: 021 625948
Fax:(09) 425 9674
relax@saltings.co.nz
www.lodgings.co.nz/saltings.html

Warkworth - 5 minutes
Auckland - 55 minutes

From Auckland take SH 1 north.
From Warkworth at the second turn
off take right hand road to Sandspit.
Travel 5 mins. Take signs to
Sandspit. The Saltings is on your
right.

I found The Saltings Estate up a meandering tree-lined driveway, where there is a choice of gourmet bed & breakfast at The Saltings or self catering luxury accommodation at The Vintner's Haven. The locality, the light uncluttered interiors and creative paint effects have resulted in unique accommodation of excellent quality. The Saltings and The Vintner's Haven have a Mediterranean ambience and a feeling of romance which is emphasised by the fresh white linens, tiles and soft lighting. Generously proportioned rooms open to their own private courtyard or deck. The décor is delightful with plaster walls, inlaid ceramics and impeccable character furnishings. Several of the rooms open to stunning views of the vineyard and estuary and as I entered my room drifts of lavender perfumed the air. Others open to the sloping garden of mature trees under-planted with aloes, cacti, native flax and grasses. Terry is developing a vineyard and olive grove on the property with the first vintage in 2006 and ready to drink in 2007. Everything here is presented with consummate good taste and I can particularly recommend Maureen's breakfast of Potato Rosti with Eggs Benedict. There is plenty to do in this area: wine trails, ferry trips to Kawau Island, walks and good restaurants.

Accommodation available (NZ$)	👤	👥	+👤	🛏	🛁
Breakfast: Special cooked	1 Room		$225-$255		K	EN
Breakast not on offer for S/C Apt	1 Suite		$265-$280		SK	EN
Guest rooms:	1 Room		$225-$255		SK	EN
Ambience:	1 S/C Apt		$265-$495	$50	2SK	2EN
Setting/location:	1 S/C Apt		$200-$260		Q	EN

LOW   HIGH

Waipiata

Natalie and Ross Aitken
657 Pukapuka Rd, Mahurangi West
Tel: (09) 422 0156   Mob: 027 4408312
Fax:(09) 422 0157
info@waipiata.co.nz
www.lodgings.co.nz/waipiata.html

Property features
20m swimming pool/hot tub
Spectacular coastal/bush views
Private cove for swimming/kayaking
Contemporary NZ architecture
Local features
Beaches/walks
3 regional parks/marine reserves
Golf course - incl Gulf Harbour
Vineyards/cafes/art galleries
Waiwera thermal hot pools
Puhoi historic village

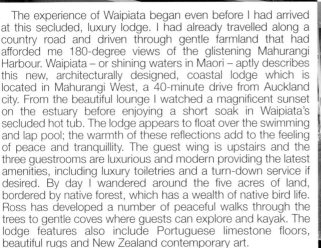

Orewa/Warkworth - 20 min drive
Auckland - 40 min drive

From SH1 take turnoff to Mahurangi Regional Park. After 1 km turn left (Pukapuka Road). Drive through entrance to Uhuru Farm, taking left fork. Waipiata is at end of road, turning left at each fork.

The experience of Waipiata began even before I had arrived at this secluded, luxury lodge. I had already travelled along a country road and driven through gentle farmland that had afforded me 180-degree views of the glistening Mahurangi Harbour. Waipiata – or shining waters in Maori – aptly describes this new, architecturally designed, coastal lodge which is located in Mahurangi West, a 40-minute drive from Auckland city. From the beautiful lounge I watched a magnificent sunset on the estuary before enjoying a short soak in Waipiata's secluded hot tub. The lodge appears to float over the swimming and lap pool; the warmth of these reflections add to the feeling of peace and tranquillity. The guest wing is upstairs and the three guestrooms are luxurious and modern providing the latest amenities, including luxury toiletries and a turn-down service if desired. By day I wandered around the five acres of land, bordered by native forest, which has a wealth of native bird life. Ross has developed a number of peaceful walks through the trees to gentle coves where guests can explore and kayak. The lodge features also include Portuguese limestone floors, beautiful rugs and New Zealand contemporary art.

Accommodation available (NZ$)	![person]	![two people]	+![person]	![bed]	![bath]	Family dog on site
1 Room	$360	$390		K	EN	Breakfast: Cooked
1 Room	$390	$420		SK/T	EN	Evening Meal: $80pp
1 Room	$420	$450		SK	EN	Guest rooms:

Evening meals include: Pre dinner drink with antipasti, 3 course NZ specialty produce, with complimentary bottle of quality NZ wine (per couple).

Ambience:
Setting/location:

LOW   HIGH

Property features
Games room/library/tennis court
Heated swimming pool/spa pool
400 acre farm with native bush
Panoramic views
Sea swimming in private bay
Canoes and dinghy available
Horse riding/fishing
Local features
Restaurants/cafes 20 min drive
Vineyards/wineries/bush walks
Regional parks

Uhuru
Bob and Sue Stevenson
390 Pukapuka Road, RD 3, Mahurangi West
Tel: (09) 422 0585   Mob: 021 739294
Fax:(09) 422 0545
suestevenson@xtra.co.nz
www.lodgings.co.nz/uhuru.html

Orewa - 20 minute drive
Auckland - 40 minute drive

Take SH1 14km north of Orewa or just south of Warkworth to Mahurangi Regional Park turnoff. Travel .5km, turn left into Pukapuka Rd. Follow for 3.5km, and take left fork, Uhuru at end on right.

Arriving at Uhuru, which is set in rolling farmland on a peninsula, that juts into the Mahurangi Harbour, I had the wonderful sensation of coming home. Strong, healthy cattle stared at me curiously, while I in turn gazed at the outstanding aspect from this 400-acre property. In the Swahili language 'Uhuru' means 'freedom'. It certainly felt like freedom to stand and absorb the view that sweeps toward the heads and the islands of the Hauraki Gulf. Two luxurious, self-contained, guest apartments open to a pool and spa. Steps from the deck lead down to a small cove where there are canoes for guests' use. I walked down a track in another direction and came across the tennis court which is surrounded by a grove of native trees. From every angle there were wonderful views. Bob and Sue are great hosts and, understanding my need for peace, took care not to intrude. I had, by prior arrangement, organised to have a family-style meal at the property that night. A barbecue is also provided for guests' use. But there are restaurants in the region if you prefer to go out. Uhuru is a well-designed homestead with a relaxed and casual ambience, and a great spot for anyone who loves land and sea.

	Accommodation available (NZ$)					
Family dog on site Guest pets by arrangement						
Breakfast: Provisions on first day	1 S/C unit	$300			K	EN
Evening Meal: $45pp	1 S/C unit	$450	$50		K+Q+S	PR

Guest rooms:
Ambience:
Setting/location:

Surcharge of $50 for 1 night stays. Long term rates avail.

The Ridge Luxury Country Lodge

Maralyn and Ian Bateman
147 Greenhollows Road, Puhoi 1243, North Auckland
Tel: (09) 426 3699   Mob: 021 999095
Fax: (09) 426 3695   Free: 0508 843743
relax@theridge.co.nz
www.lodgings.co.nz/theridgepuhoi.html

Property features
Modern design using local materials
Bush country setting
Rural and sea views
Seclusion/superb food/local wine
Local features
Matakana coast/vineyards
Beaches and regional parks
Historic Puhoi village and pub
(Early Bohemian settlement)
Kayaking/fishing/sailing/golf
Bush walks/mountain biking

Orewa - 15 minute drive
Warkworth - 15 minute drive

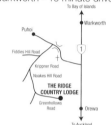

Turn off SH 1 to Puhoi (approx. 10 km north of Orewa). Take first left after church into Krippner Rd. At the top of the hill (2km) turn left into Noakes Hill Rd and left again into Greenhollows Rd. Follow for 1.5 km (left at fork). The Ridge is down the drive to the left.

This Luxury Country lodge is built high on a ridge above the historical village of Puhoi and affords a marvelous view over a hundred acres of native bush, the river estuary and out to the distant sea. I certainly found peace here along with a friendly welcome from owners Maralyn and Ian and their dog Charlie. The modern, purpose-built lodge, with three sunny private guest suites that take in the view is designed with innovation; combining the benefits of an environmentally friendly home with contemporary interiors and a high level of comfort. I loved the uncluttered spaces, the glowing, oiled, red eucalyptus floor and the corrugated metal and brushed chrome details. After I'd spent the day exploring the vineyards of Matakana, Maralyn prepared me a delicious three-course dinner - beetroot mousse with spinach, bacon and walnut salad, stuffed chicken breast followed by fresh strawberries topped with a sweet green and black pepper sauce and accompanied by an excellent local wine. I then rested comfortably on leather settees around a large, central, log fire to watch my favourite television programme and listen to music. This is a healthy and deeply restful environment in the countryside, which is perfect for a weekend break or a stay en route to Northland.

Accommodation available (NZ$)	🧍	🧍🧍	+🧍	🛏	🛁	Family dog on site Guest pets by arrangement
3 Suites	$175-195	$250-295		K or 2S	EN	Breakfast: Special cooked Evening Meal: $65pp Guest rooms: Ambience: Setting/location:

Evening meal price includes pre-dinner drink. Exclusive party bookings for 6 available - please enquire.

Property features
Set in 20 acres of isolated bush
Spectacular ocean/beach views
Private track to sandy beaches
Windsurfers/dinghy/boogie boards
No TV/phone/enquire for internet
Potbelly fire

Local features
Natural hot pools/surfing/swimming
Vineyard and wine tasting
Walking tracks/fishing/diving/kayaking
Local restaurant nearby

Bay Lodge

Neil and Carole Wright
Okupu, Great Barrier Island
Tel: (09) 429 0916
rightway@xtra.co.nz
www.lodgings.co.nz/baylodge.html

Auck - 30 mins by air to Claris
Claris - 10 min drive

Hosts can arrange travel. Flight time to Claris airport 30 mins then 10 mins by 4WD to Bay Lodge. Hosts will transfer.

The breathtaking 30-minute scenic flight from Auckland seemed a distant memory as I concentrated on Neil skillfully manoeuvring the Range Rover along the private access road towards Bay Lodge. My attention was immediately drawn to the front of the cottage and the spectacular view before me; twenty acres of native bush and the deep blue of Okupu Bay below. The music from within welcomed me into the tastefully modernised little cottage. This cottage was indeed perfect for my weekend away from the city; chilled wine in the fridge; flowers and fruit; home-made bread baked daily, and all of my favourite mod cons, minus a television and mobile coverage! I couldn't help but relax. Carole and Neil were there if I needed them, living 100m through the bush, otherwise I was left alone to relax and listen to the waves and tui calling. Guests' access to the beach is by a private track. Neil takes guests out to fish for snapper in the bay, and they can also wander over to the only vineyard on Great Barrier Island, Mellars Boutique Vineyard, for wine tasting. Bay Lodge is perfect for a romantic weekend or as a place to just relax and get back to nature.

Accommodation available (NZ$)			+👤	🛏	🛁
1 S/C cottage	$165-240	$165-240		Q	PR

Breakfast: Continental

Guest rooms:
Ambience:
Setting/location:

LOW   HIGH

Supplies stocked by prior arrangement. Enquire for internet & phone access.
Rate incl. comp dive/fish in Bay, weather permitting.

Mount St Paul Lodge

Trish Andrews   Ivan McMannaway
29 Kaitoke Lane, Claris, Great Barrier Island
Tel: (09) 429 0861
Fax: (09) 429 0863
trish@mountstpaullodge.com
www.lodgings.co.nz/mountstpaul.html

Property features
108 acres native bush/bush walks
Panoramic ocean views
15 min to white sandy beaches
3 metre deep verandah around house
Four Wheel Drives for hire
Local features
Museum 15 min walk
Fishing/horse riding
Hot springs
Bush walks
Kayaking

Auck - 30 mins by air to Claris

Flight time to Claris airport from Auckland 30 mins.

Travelling to Great Barrier Island, only a thirty-minute flight from Auckland, is always something I do with happy anticipation because I know the sort of peace and beauty I will find when I arrive. Despite it only being a short flight away, the island feels well out of the mainstream. The island boasts rugged mountains, miles of white sandy beaches, rainforests and hot pools. Mount St Paul Lodge is a luxury retreat in the style of a 19th century manor house. For the utmost in space and comfort six guests can relax in luxuriously appointed suites, whilst taking in the sweeping ocean views from their private balconies. Although the lodge itself impressed me, it was hosts Ivan and Trish that made my experience special. Ivan, who has lived on the island for most of his life, has so much history and information at his fingertips. I accompanied Ivan on a fishing trip and we managed to catch dinner which Trish, a world travelled chef, turned into a feast. I was delighted by the way the meal was presented as much as by the sensational tastes. The experience of both the lodge and the island is one I'll find hard to forget.

Accommodation available (NZ$)	👤	👤👤	+👤	🛏	🛁	Family pets on site
1 Room	$400	$720	$185	K or 2S	EN	Breakfast: Cooked
1 Room	$400	$720		K	EN	Evening meal: Included
1 Room	$400	$720		K	EN	Guest rooms:
1 Room	$280	$560		2S	PR	Ambience:
						Setting/location:

LOW   HIGH

Property features
North facing/quiet location
Seaviews - Oneroa Bay/Hauraki Gulf
Private terraces/kitchenette
TV/DVD/CD player
BBQ/laundry on request
Local features
350 mtrs to beach and store
300 mtrs to bus stop
Short drive to wineries
10 min stroll to village/cafes/shops

Watermark

Jo Underwood   Charles Hrasky
17 Tawa Street, Little Oneroa, Waiheke Island
Tel: (09) 372 2862   Mob: 021 1845410
Fax:(09) 372 2862
info@watermarkwaiheke.com
www.lodgings.co.nz/watermark.html

Oneroa - 10 minute walk
Auckland - 35 minute ferry

From Matiatia ferry, straight up hill
through Oneroa village. After church
turn right into Moa Ave then left into
Tawa St. Lodge on right #17.

Purpose built in late 2003, Watermark's three stylish, self-contained studio apartments contain everything I needed to make my visit to Waiheke Island comfortable and enjoyable. Elevated on the hill overlooking Little Oneroa beach, two of the studios have superb views, while the third has a small outlook to Great Barrier, Little Barrier and The Noisey Islands. Every time I turned around, there was an aspect of the view to enjoy. Jo has thought of everything her guests might need – televisions, DVD's, movies, CD players, electric barbecues, comfortable king or twin beds and quality linens with modern furnishings. Large sliding windows open out to each terrace and I plugged in the barbecue to cook and eat my breakfast of bacon and eggs outside in the sun. Breakfast provisions are provided by prior arrangement. Throughout each studio the flooring is rimu timber and the bathrooms have heated floors of Italian porcelain tiles and heated towel rails. For lunch or dinner guests can easily walk down to nearby restaurants and shops or drive the short distance to the local supermarket and vineyards. Jo and Charles live upstairs and are on hand but separate. You don't need to see them unless you want to as all studios have private entrances and terraces.

Accommodation available (NZ$)					
3 S/C units	$175-250	$175-250		K or 2S	EN

Breakfast: Extra charge

Guest rooms:
Ambience:
Setting/location:

LOW   HIGH

45

Te Whau Lodge

Liz Eglinton   Gene O'Neill
36 Vintage Lane, Te Whau Point, Waiheke Island
Tel: (09) 372 2288   Mob: 0274 308222
Fax: (09) 372 2218
lizandgene@tewhaulodge.co.nz
www.lodgings.co.nz/tewhau.html

Property features
Spectacular sea & bush views
Contemporary NZ architecture
Separate guest lounge & dining
Superb cuisine
Hot tub with a view
Fully licensed
Local features
Vineyards and wineries
Bush and coastal walks
Artists studios
Watersports and beaches

Oneroa, Waiheke - 10 mins drive
Auckland CBD - 35 mins Ferry ride

Take Fullers ferry from Auckland
downtown, or Subritzky vehicular
passenger service from Halfmoon
Bay. Hosts will pick up from arrival
point

   Te Whau Lodge perches high on Waiheke Island on the crest of a peninsula of the same name. From this purpose-built building the views are unparalleled – over a plunging hillside of grapevines and olive trees, the convoluted coastline, the deep inlets of the bay dotted with watercraft and the distant vista of Auckland City across the Waitemata Harbour. As I sat on the wide verandah sipping a local wine I was treated to a lingering neon-bright sunset. Te Whau is a long, low, quintessentially New Zealand building made of timber, corrugated iron and concrete. Inside, wandering around the spacious lounge and separate dining room with their timber walls, leather couches, ceramic artifacts and intriguing Pacific art, you couldn't really be anywhere but New Zealand. Each of the four well-appointed guestrooms is subtly themed according to its view. Liz and Gene fled a corporate life in Auckland to live on Waiheke and their enthusiasm for their new lifestyle is evidenced by their warm welcome and their attention to the comfort and enjoyment of their guests which culminates each evening with Gene's superbly presented canapes and dinner. Seated around the large dining table, it was easy to pick up the atmosphere and new acquaintances began to feel like old friends.

Accommodation available (NZ$)						Family cat on site
4 Rooms	$350	$410		SK	EN	Breakfast: Special Cooked

Evening meal and 4 courses $100pp on Saturday night.
Evening meal and 2 courses $50pp other nights.

Breakfast: Special Cooked
Evening Meal: Enquire
Guest rooms:
Ambience:
Setting/location:

LOW   HIGH

Property features
3 minutes walk to sandy beach
Extensive sea view
Large combined bedrooms/lounges
Own kitchen
Self catering breakfast
Spacious private decks/gas BBQ
Local features
All-tide, safe swimming beach
Coastal walkways
Cafes and vineyards
Golf/sea kayaking

Palm Beach Lodge

Marion and Peter Robertson
23 Tiri View Road, Palm Beach, Waiheke Island
Tel: (09) 372 7763
Fax: (09) 372 7763
palmbeachlodge@xtra.co.nz
www.lodgings.co.nz/palmbeach.html

Oneroa, Waiheke - 5 mins drive
Auckland - 35 mins ferry

Take Fullers ferry from Auckland
downtown terminal or Subritzky
vehicular/passenger service from
Half Moon Bay. Arrange with hosts
for pick-up or taxi

Large separate apartments step down a steep hillside dotted with holiday baches overlooking the sandy curve of Palm Beach and a vista of sparkling water to Little Barrier Island. On the extensive patios outside each unit the rhythm of waves against the shore gave me an urge to sink onto a lounger and succumb to the peace. Each unit has two spacious lounge/bedrooms with two televisions, videos, and stereo. These open to the view of the bay and are comfortably furnished in Wedgwood blue and white and decorated with dramatic artwork from the Pacific. A romantic touch is provided by nets which are draped softly above the beds. Between the bedrooms is a well-equipped kitchenette complete with self-catering breakfast provisions, and a spacious bathroom. All rooms lead to the very extensive outdoor patios which are set up with barbecues and plenty of seating. Hosts Marion and Peter Robertson told me how, during their years of living there, Waiheke Island had gone straight to their hearts. Sipping coffee in the clear bright air, with the beach only three minutes walk away, it was easy for me to see why.

Accommodation available (NZ$)					
Breakfast: Provisions provided	1 S/C unit	$190	$280	$80	2K	PR
	1 S/C unit	$190	$280	$80	2K	PR
Guest rooms:	1 S/C unit	$190	$280	$80	2Q	PR
Ambience:						
Setting/location:	Seasonal discounts apply.					

Connells Bay Cottage

John and Jo Gow
Cowes Bay Road, Waiheke Island
Tel: (09) 372 8957   Mob: 021 363613
info@connellsbay.co.nz
www.lodgings.co.nz/connellsbay.html

Property features
10 metres from beach/private bay
2 hr sculpture park tours
Swimming/kayaks/bbq/laundry
4WD vehicle available for hire
Fishing dinghy provided
Bird watching/bush walks
Local features
Vineyards/wineries/restaurants
art galleries/golf course
all within 20 mins drive
Stony Batter nearby

Auckland - 35 minute ferry + drive

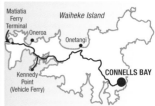

Take Waiheke Ferry to Matiatia. Drive to Onetangi, turn right into Waiheke Rd towards Orapiu. Continue past Passage Rock Vineyard & at 'T' junction turn left into Cowes Bay Rd. Property is 1.2kms on right. Yellow letterbox.

This turn-of-the-century, stylishly refurbished, guest cottage is set in privately owned Connells Bay. I sat on the porch only metres from the beach, and looked out on the expanse of turquoise water between Rotoroa and Ponui Islands, and distant Castle Rock, which forms part of the Coromandel Range. It felt as if I'd found a slice of heaven. The cottage has two double guestrooms and two bathrooms, a small lounge and fireplace, a full kitchen, a sunny dining area and a deck. If guests catch a snapper, or some other fish, from the three-metre dinghy that's provided, they can cook it for themselves on the barbecue. Jo and John's vision was to unite art and nature. They planted native trees and commissioned, site-specific, New Zealand sculpture. Now their 60-acre property is one of New Zealand's most celebrated, private sculpture parks. I thoroughly enjoyed walking around it for two hours with Jo guiding. There is much to see on Waiheke Island, but I was pleased I'd taken provisions so that I didn't have to leave Connells Bay until it was time to catch the ferry home. It's recommended that you pre-book a four-wheel-drive vehicle from a hire company or from your hosts.

Accommodation available (NZ$)	👤	👥	+👤	🛏	🛁	Family cat on site
1 S/C house		$350		2 D	EN+PR	Breakfast: Provisions provided

Sleeps 2 couples - Minimum 2 nights stay.

Guest rooms:
Ambience:
Setting/location:

LOW   HIGH

Property features
Panoramic sea views
Beach access
Private balcony in two rooms
Small conference venue
Local features
Bush walks/beaches
Native reserve
Hot pools
Horse riding
Golf course
Kayak tours

Moontide Lodge

Andy and Rony
19 Ocean View Road, Hatfields Beach, Auckland
Tel: (09) 426 2374   Mob: 021 2386010
Fax: (09) 426 2398
moontidelodge@hotmail.com
www.lodgings.co.nz/moontide.html

Orewa - 5 minutes
Auckland - 30 minutes

From Auckland, take SH1 north to Orewa. Continue through town to Hatfields beach (3km). Turn right into Ocean View Road. Lodge on left.

I was struck by the hosts willingness to make my stay as perfect as it could be. The night I stayed I had meant to be back in Auckland, but Andy and Roney were so generous that within minutes a room was ready for me, my luggage delivered to my room and I was enjoying the unobstructed view out over Orewa Bay. Guest bedrooms and living areas have been furnished to a high standard and all rooms offer breathtaking sea views. I recommend leaving all the curtains open so the sunrise can wake you in the morning. The guest bedrooms have been named after particular aspects of the view. All have stunning but different sea views. There is also beach access from the property. Probably the most beautiful of the large guestrooms is the Whangaparaoa Suite that has its own private balcony. There is a choice for breakfast. I opted for the traditional bacon, eggs, tomatoes, mushrooms and hashbrowns. Breakfast can be served in the dining room or alfresco on the deck. Personalised tours of the country or day trips for small groups can be arranged.

Family dog on site	Accommodation available (NZ$)	�standing	�	+♂	🛏	🛁
Breakfast: Cooked	1 Suite	$190	$200		Q	EN
Evening meal: $45pp	1 Room	$140	$150		Q	PR
Guest rooms:	1 Room	$150	$160		Q	EN
Ambience:	1 Room	$170	$180		Q	EN
Setting/location:						

LOW   HIGH

Vineyard Cottages

Kristine and David Simpson
1011 Old North Road, Waimauku, RD 2, Auckland
Tel: (09) 411 8248   Mob: 027 2963452
Fax: (09) 411 9626   Free: 0800 846800
info@vineyardcottages.co.nz
www.lodgings.co.nz/vineyardcottages.html

Property features
Surrounded by vineyard
Private patio and BBQ area
Rural memorabilia
Local features
Wineries/restaurants
Four golf courses
Horse riding/hot mineral pools
Gannet colony/surf beach
Coastal and forest walks
Quad biking

Kumeu - 10 minutes
Auckland - 30 minutes

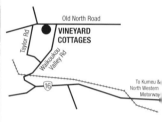

Just south of Waimauku turn off SH 16. Follow signs to Matua Valley Wines & Hunting Lodge. Continue past Matua. Turn left at T junction onto Old North Rd. Take first drive on left. Check in at reception.

In the thick of Auckland's vine-growing region, these seven rustic cottages make reference to both the current wine industry and the earlier timber-milling industry for which the area was known. The wooden cottages are set along the slopes of a small valley with a central stream and are separated for privacy. Grapevines hang from the verandah roofs and the private, backyard patios have their own barbecues. Collected memorabilia is used artfully to underline the rural/pioneer theme. Old machinery makes interesting garden sculptures. My cottage had a pit-saw, a horse collar and a pole-jack hung on the verandah wall and inside were other old items, among them an anvil, scales and a bed warmer. I enjoyed the comfort that the golden glow of oiled timber brings and the way the décor is coloured to reflect wine styles. Mine - Sauvignon Blanc Cottage - was, for instance, sage green; the Champagne Cottage is cream and gold and the Pinot Noir shades of mulberry. In each cottage there is a wood-burning stove, a full kitchen, stocked pantry, breakfast supplies and a torch to guide you through the vines to the adjacent Hunting Lodge Restaurant.

Accommodation available (NZ$)	♦	♦♦	+♦	🛏	🛁	Family pets on site
7 S/C cottages	$245	$245	$50	K	PR	Breakfast: Provisions provided

Guest rooms:
Ambience:
Setting/location:

LOW   HIGH

Prior bookings are essential.

Bethells Beach Cottages

Trude and John Bethell-Paice
267 Bethells Rd, Waitakere, Auckland
Tel: (09) 810 9581
Fax: (09) 810 8677
info@bethellsbeach.com
www.lodgings.co.nz/bethells.html

Property features
Scandinavian hot tub
Sunset views over the Tasman Sea
South End cave
Games pavillion/gardens
Table tennis/pentanque/volleyball
Local features
Swimming at Lake Wainamu
Te Henga walkway to Murawai
Walk to O'Neills beach/surfing spot
Private walk to Bethells Beach
Glow worms/phosphoresence

Waitakere - 15 minute drive
Auckland - 40 minute drive

Take the Lincoln Rd turnoff on
Northwestern motorway turn right
on Universal Dr, follow straight
through to Swanson Rd then
Scenic Dr, turn off at Te Henga Rd
to Bethells Beach.

Set among giant pohutukawa with panoramic views of Auckland's stunning west coast, Bethells Beach Cottages is a relaxing retreat where it is easy to unwind and enjoy the natural surroundings. The cottages – Te Koinga and Turehu, have private outlooks, barbecues and are fully self-contained. Te Koinga has two bedrooms and is the larger of the two. It's suitable for two couples travelling together but also comfortably accommodates a large family. A large private deck set beneath sprawling pohutukawas looks out over the surf crashing on the beach below. It's totally private and outdoor furniture is provided for alfresco dining. Alternatively, a beautiful handcrafted wooden table inside can seat up to 16 people! A shower and a bath are provided and the open plan kitchen is well equipped with a microwave, stove, large fridge/freezer, dishwasher and coffeemaker. Turehu Cottage offers spectacular views of the beach through its cosy conservatory windows. Bi-folding doors open out to a patio area and onto extensive lawns. Creativity is encouraged here – both cottages have easels and paints at the ready and the lush forest and dramatic coastline has provided inspiration to many artists, poets, writers, singers, musicians and film makers who come to recharge and nourish their creative spirit.

Family cats on site

	Accommodation available (NZ$)					
	1 S/C studio	$281.25	$22.50	Q+Divan	2PR	
	1 S/C cottage	$393.75	$33.75	Q+3S+Divan	2PR	

Breakfast: Extra $28pp
Evening meal: $35-45pp
Guest rooms:
Ambience:
Setting/location:

LOW   HIGH

Studio: internet & phone avail. 2 or 3-course dinner options avail by prior arrangement, min. 6 people. 2 night min stay.

Titirangi Coastal Cottages

Fiona Jeaffreson   Mike Reynolds
12 Opou Road, Titirangi, Auckland
Tel: (09) 817 8323   Mob: 021 897731
Fax: (09) 817 6896
info@coastal-cottages.co.nz
www.lodgings.co.nz/titirangicoastal.html

Property features
Sauna/spa/bush walks/native birds
Bush and sea views
Plasma screen/full A/V system
Peaceful setting
Local features
Arts and crafts
Cafes and restaurants
Beaches
Monthly Titirangi markets
Art Gallery/theatre
Arataki visitor centre

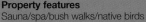

Titirangi - 3 mins drive
Auckland - 25 mins drive

From city take SH16 west to Great North Road exit, travel to New Lynn. Continue into Titirangi Rd. Turn left into Park Rd. Left into Otitori Bay. Left into Opou Rd. Park on platform – take left stairs to cottage.

The beaches and forest-clad hills of Titirangi comprise a small but growing community only thirty minutes from downtown Auckland. The Coastal Cottage is a hidden gem that is surrounded by native forest yet still has a peep of the sea. It is absolutely private. The only noises I heard for the few days I stayed were from the birds in the trees around. The cottage has two bedrooms, a full kitchen, a huge, open living-area, a sauna and two large decks, one of which has a spa pool. The kitchen, which is bright and cheerful, was equipped with all that I needed, and hosts, Fiona and Mike, had stocked the fridge with a full variety of breakfast foods. This luxurious home away from home has been decorated with modern art and craft, much of it produced by local people. I felt rather spoilt and decided that I could easily have lived at The Coastal Cottage for quite some time. It is only a two-minute drive from the village of Titirangi and I visited the cafes, restaurants and art and craft shops. I was also lucky enough to be there on the last Sunday of the month when the very colourful local market is held.

Accommodation available (NZ$)	🧍	🧍🧍	+🧍	🛏	🛁	Guest pets by arrangement
1 S/C house	$450	$450	$30	SK/2S + 1K	PR	Breakfast: Special continental

Evening meal: Enquire
Guest rooms:
Ambience:
Setting/location:

LOW   HIGH

Property features
Waterfront location
10 minute ferry to Auckland CBD
Located in quaint maritime village
Antiques/art/library/sub-tropical gdn
Separate guest lounge
Local features
Ferries to central AK & islands
Beaches/coastal walks/views
Antique shops/galleries/boutiques
Restaurants/cafes/cinema
Golf course/gym/tennis

The Peace & Plenty Inn
Peter and Judy Machin
6 Flagstaff Tce, Devonport, Auckland
Tel: (09) 445 2925   Mob: 021 665661
Fax:(09) 445 2901
peaceandplenty@xtra.co.nz
www.lodgings.co.nz/peaceandplenty.html

Downtown - 10 mins (ferry)
Downtown - 20 mins (off peak)

Take Esmonde Rd exit from
motorway (SH1). Follow signs to
Devonport. When you reach the
village, proceed to the last of the
shops on the left. Turn left into
Flagstaff Tce, first house on the left.

From the moment the front door opened and I was welcomed to The Peace and Plenty Inn, I felt at home. Judy's perfectionist nature is reflected in the wonderful attention to detail. The Peace and Plenty, a gorgeous and graciously restored 1880's Victorian villa, overlooks a park, the waterfront and the quaint maritime village of Devonport and is just a short stroll to the ferry which leaves for central Auckland and the surrounding islands of the Hauraki Gulf. The spacious guestrooms have been decorated so that each has its own special style. Furnishings are a mix of New Zealand and English antiques. I liked the additional touches which included complimentary specialty teas, coffees, handmade chocolates, port, sherry and lavender bags in all guestrooms. Breakfast was served in a spacious, open and sunny room overlooking the secluded tropical garden. In summer, guests can breakfast alfresco on the verandah. Even the menu is beautifully presented and sets the scene for a superb breakfast, starting with fresh Kerikeri orange juice, home-made muesli and tropical fruits. I ordered eggs Devonport – scrambled with herbs and smoked salmon and served on a toasted English muffin.

Family dog on site
Guest pets by arrangement

Breakfast: Special cooked

Guest rooms:
Ambience:
Setting/location:

Accommodation available (NZ$)	👤	👥	+👤	🛏	🛁
2 Rooms	$265	$295-325	$100 K		EN
4 Rooms	$265	$295-325	$100 Q		EN
1 Room	$265	$295-325	$100 2 SK		EN

Additional child $50pp. Direct dial telephones.
Wireless high speed internet (wi-fi). Selective organic produce.

Braemar on Parliament Street

John and Sue Sweetman
7 Parliament Street, Auckland Central
Tel: (09) 377 5463   Mob: 021 640688
Fax: (09) 377 3056   Free: 0800 155463
braemar@aucklandbedandbreakfast.com
www.lodgings.co.nz/braemar.html

Property features
Central location
Historic home in Auckland CBD
Local features
High court - 1 min walk
Old government house - 3 min walk
University of Auckland - 3 min walk
Queen street - 6 min walk
Sky tower - 10 min walk
Parnell shops/cafes - 10 min walk
Museum - 15 min walk
Viaduct Basin bars/restaurants

CBD - 5 mins walk
Parnell - 10 mins walk

Take 'Port' exit from motorway. At traffic lights take the free left turn up Alten Rd. Turn right at lights into Anzac Ave. Parliament St is the first street on the left, it is opposite the High Court.

A 1901 Edwardian townhouse in the heart of Auckland City, Braemar on Parliament Street has been elegantly refurbished with modern comforts but still retains a suggestion of yesteryear. When I arrived, my hosts, John and Susan, welcomed me with tea, coffee and fresh muffins. I had booked the spacious Batten Suite for my stay. A private lounge with Sky television and an open fireplace and the adjoining bedroom with an ensuite was a great place to unwind in privacy. I soaked in the large clawfoot bath and cosied into a bathrobe and pair of slippers. The two other suites, similarly appointed, shared the large original bathroom. That evening I sipped a complimentary glass of port in the downstairs guest lounge and looked at the historic photographs and drawings on the walls of early days in Auckland. Then I strolled downtown to inspect Auckland's selection of cafes and restaurants. In the morning I enjoyed a sumptuous breakfast in the Rose dining room. Braemar on Parliament Street is centrally located, yet very peaceful. It is a haven in the city, ideal for both corporate and pleasure travellers.

Accommodation available (NZ$)	🧍	🧍🧍	+🧍	🛏	🛁	Family pets on site Guest pets by arrangement
2 Rooms	$180	$225		Q+D	GS	Breakfast: Special cooked
1 Suite	$295	$295	$25	Q	EN	Evening meal: On request
1 Room	$150	$150		D	PR	Guest rooms:
						Ambience:

Evening meal available by prior arrangement.

Setting/location:

LOW   HIGH

Property features
Wrap around sea and city vistas
Exclusive use/fully self-contained
Private spa and sun loungers
BBQ and alfresco dining
Home theatre/multi-room audio
Full office/security/garaging

Local features
Luxury health and beauty spas
Restaurants/cafes/fashion
Sailing/fishing/cruises/ferries
Art galleries/museums/CBD

Viaduct Landing
Essence of New Zealand
Apartment 32, Shed 24, Prince's Wharf
147 Quay St, Auckland
Tel: 027 5424202
Fax:(07) 574 8096   Free: 0800 ESSENCE (3773623)
stay@essencenz.com
www.lodgings.co.nz/viaductlanding.html

Auckland central
Hamilton - 1 hour drive

VIADUCT
LANDING

Auckland
Viaduct

Prince's Wharf
Queens Wharf
Cpt Cook Wharf
Quay St
Hobson St
Customs St East
Fanshawe St
Albert St
Queen St
Nelson St

Prince's Wharf access from Hobson
St or Quay St. From Nth, use
Fanshawe St exit, From South exit
Nelson St - link into Sturdee St, then
Hobson St. Approach via Quay St
from the East.

Nearby the vibrant cafes and restaurants of the Viaduct Basin in the heart of Auckland, Viaduct landing is an oasis that captures the essence of New Zealand. This elegant, three-bedroom apartment offers guests a luxurious place to stay in one of Auckland's most sort-after locations. The apartment is fully self-contained - furnished with every convenience. An extensive collection of the works of New Zealand artists adorn the walls, and a compendium of the work gives information about the artists and the images. Viaduct Landing is surrounded by 200 square metres of deck and I was captivated by the extensive vistas of city and sea. The simple, clean lines of this architecturally designed building were contrived so that little distracted from the view. The building mimics a cruise ship on the water and I felt as if I could have been on board a boat in the harbour. I spent the evening wandering around the Viaduct Basin, admiring the yachts and deciding on which of the enticing restaurants I would dine at. It was a very pleasant experience to return to the apartment and sip a wine on the large, all-weather, outdoor area, and then taking a dip in the spa pool which is positioned on the deck to provide sweeping views of the lighted Sky Tower.

Accommodation available (NZ$)			+		

Breakfast: Provisions provided	1 S/C Suite	2SK/T+Q EN+PR
Evening meal: Enquire	High season	$1,114
Guest rooms:	Low season	$889
Ambience:		
Setting/location:		

Chef available by prior arrangement. Charges apply. Tariff is for up to 4 people.

Moana Vista

Tim Kennedy   Mathew Moran
60 Hamilton Road, Herne Bay, Auckland
Tel: (09) 376 5028   Mob: 021 376150
Fax:(09) 376 5025   Free: 0800 213761
info@moanavista.co.nz
www.lodgings.co.nz/moanavista.html

Property features
Highspeed wireless internet in rooms
Central to city/quiet city street
Friendly flexible hosts
Stylishly renovated villa/sea views
Piano and open fire
Local features
Nearby cafes/restaurants/beaches
Nearby Ponsonby shops
City - 20 mins walk
Beaches short walk
Urban and park walks

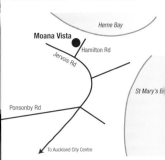

Auckland CBD - 20 mins walk

From Auckland head towards Ponsonby up College Hill into Jervois Road. Travel through the Curran Street lights and turn right into Hamilton Road.

The hosts, Tim and Mathew, have renovated and furnished this pretty, two-storeyed villa close to the sea in an inner-city suburb of Auckland. The house was built as a private home in 1896. Now the kitchen, dining room and casual lounge are open plan and adjoining these areas is a larger lounge with an open fireplace, comfortable sofas, a grand piano and state of the art television. My room was downstairs and there are also two upstairs guestrooms opening to a verandah, which overlooks the quiet suburban street and views of the Waitemata Harbour. All are furnished with elegant simplicity in keeping with the style of the house. Breakfast is served in the dining area - a platter of fresh fruit and cereal, baking, coffee and tea. The hosts like the atmosphere to be relaxed and unstructured, so that people can enjoy the friendliness of the place, or keep to themselves if they are seeking solitude. In the evenings many guests like to join Mathew and Tim for a glass of wine on the balcony, or by the fire, before walking to one of the many local cafes for dinner.

Accommodation available (NZ$)	🧍	🧍🧍	+🧍	🛏	🛁	
1 Room	$140-180	$180-240	$40	Q	EN	Breakfast: Continental
1 Room	$140-180	$180-240		Q	EN	
1 Room	$140-180	$180-240		Q	PR	Guest rooms:

Enquire about low season and long term rates (3+ nights).
Extra bed available on request.

Ambience:
Setting/location:

LOW   HIGH

Property features
- Free wireless internet
- Quiet location no traffic noise
- Bicycles/beach towels avail
- Outdoor courtyards
- Close to city
- City circuit bus every 10 mins

Local features
- Cafes/restaurants - 5 mins walk
- Boutique shopping/galleries
- Harbour - 20 mins walk
- Victoria Park Market

Downtown - 10 minutes
Airport - 30 minutes

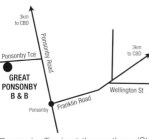

Ponsonby Tce is at the northern (St Marys Bay) end of Ponsonby Rd. From downtown take Victoria St West, continue past Victoria Market. At top of Hill turn left into Ponsonby Rd. Ponsonby Tce is third on right.

The Great Ponsonby B&B

Sally James   Gerry Hill
30 Ponsonby Terrace, Ponsonby, Auckland
Tel: (09) 376 5989
Fax:(09) 376 5527   Free: 0800 766792
info@greatpons.co.nz
www.lodgings.co.nz/ponsonby.html

Situated in a quiet street in the middle of a very colourful suburb of Auckland City, this historic ten-room small hotel accommodation displays a very strong sense of place. Its décor reflects its location with a happy blend of Pacific and New Zealand elements - Polynesian masks, tapa cloth, sculptures and ceramics and paintings - and a sunny mix of blue aqua and earth-yellow colours on the walls. Many of these artefacts were bought from the boutique shops of Ponsonby. Within walking distance is, probably, the widest selection of restaurants and cafes in New Zealand. The rooms and suites are spacious, comfortable and bright and a lot of thought has gone into equipping them with almost anything you might need for a stay. I particularly like the sitting room with its comfortable loungers, tea and coffee making facility and loads of books, magazines and CDs, and the adjacent breakfast room which spills out onto a wide verandah. Here the Great Ponsonby's breakfast was served. It was a congenial affair with lots of good-hearted banter between guests and hosts. All the classical dishes are available but I chose one that further enhanced the local flavour – kumera cakes, and grilled fish.

Family pets on site	Accommodation available (NZ$)	♟	♟♟	+♟	🛏	🛁
Breakfast: Special cooked	4 Rooms		$180-220	Q	PR	
	1 Room		$215	K/T	PR	
Guest rooms:	1 S/C unit		$215-225	Q	PR	
Ambience:	4 S/C units		$225-350	K/T	PR	
Setting/location:	Seasonal rates apply.					

Amitees on Ponsonby

Ian Stewart   Jill Slee
237 Ponsonby Road, Ponsonby, Auckland
Tel: (09) 378 6325
Fax:(09) 378 6329
bookings@amitees.co.nz
www.lodgings.co.nz/amitees.html

Property features
Guest lounge with fireplace
High speed wireless internet
Guest computer
Laundry facilities/Sky TV/DVD
Local features
Auckland's finest restaurants
Café's/boutique shopping
Harbour/city centre/Sky tower
Gym - 10 mins walk
Parks/galleries/Victoria Park market
Bungy jumping/harbour tours

Ponsonby - central
Auckland City - 5 mins drive

From south take motorway to Nelso
St exit. Turn left into Union St &
Wellington St, & left into Franklin Rd
Turn right into Ponsonby Rd to
Amitees on right. From north take
Shelly Beach Rd exit.

This boutique hotel, located in the heart of Auckland's trendy suburb of Ponsonby, has contemporary furnishings and a relaxed casual ambience. The hosts, Jill and Ian, live in their own wing and bestow a friendly welcome to everyone who visits. Guests frequently comment about Jill and Ian's hospitable attention and willingness to share their local knowledge. Ponsonby Road is lined with boutique shops, award-winning cafes and restaurants and is near the city centre and the stunning 'City of Sails' harbour. The luxurious Penthouse suite is located on the upper floor and has a private lounge with spectacular views out to the Sky Tower and the city. The other six guestrooms and the guest lounge are on the ground floor. All have luxury beds, quality cotton linens and robes, Sky TV, DVD players and direct dial phones – making it ideal for both corporate and leisure travellers. The guest lounge has a cosy fireplace, internet service, and a range of magazines and books. A continental breakfast is laid out here for guests to help themselves. From the ground floor I wandered out to a small garden of native grasses and flax bushes - a lovely taste of nature to balance the bustle of the city.

Accommodation available (NZ$)	👤	👥	+👤	🛏	🛁	Family cat on site
1 Room	$180			D	EN	Breakfast: Continental
1 Room	$195			2KS	EN	
3 Rooms	$235		$35	Q	EN	Guest rooms:
1 Room	$275		$35	K	EN	Ambience:
1 Room	$400		$35	SK	EN	Setting/location:

LOW   HIGH

Property features
1878 colonial mansion
Swimming pool/spa pool
Tropical landscaped grounds
Library/home theatre
Early NZ period furniture
Local features
Western Springs Park-5 mins
MOTAT (Museum)-5 mins
Auckland Zoo-15 mins walk
Aviation Museum/golf course
Kingsland cafes/rests. 5mins

Downtown - 10 minute drive
Airport - 25 minute drive

Take Northwestern Motorway from city. Veer off motorway at Western Springs off-ramp then turn left and left again onto Western Springs Road. Hastings Hall is on your left opposite Fowlds Park.

Hastings Hall
Malcolm Martel
99 Western Springs Road, Western Springs
Tel: (09) 845 8550   Mob: 021 300006
Fax:(09) 845 8554
unique@hastingshall.co.nz
www.lodgings.co.nz/hastingshall.html

As in a secret enclave Hastings Hall sits in a large rambling garden hidden from the houses that have joined it on the once open hillside. There is so much within walking distance including parks, museums, shops and, if you are fit, a great range of cafes and restaurants in nearby Kingsland village. The property itself retains much of the charm of yesteryear with the added intrigue of themed guestrooms. A few are Isabella's Suite, William's Grand Suite, Casablanca Studio and Moulin Rouge Studio. If money is no barrier, my recommendation would be Williams Grand Suite with its own lounge and sound system in addition to features found in other rooms such as Sky television and direct dial phones. Several rooms have baths and private verandahs with tables and chairs. I enjoyed a gourmet breakfast in the dining room but it is also served in the conservatory or in the privacy of your own room or suite. Offerings could include blueberry and guava buttermilk pancakes with Canadian maple syrup or Gruyere cheese-and-basil omelette with peppered grilled tomatoes. Both the property and the location are out of the ordinary - a pleasant surprise.

Family dog on site Guest pets by arrangement	Accommodation available (NZ$)	♦	♦♦	+♦	⇥	🛁
Breakfast: Special cooked Evening meal: from $50pp	7 Rooms	$135-295	$175-350	$35	Q	EN

Guest rooms:
Ambience:
Setting/location:

LOW   HIGH

Rooms with GS bathrooms share with only one other room.

Aachen House Boutique Hotel

Joan and Greg McKirdy
39 Market Road, Remuera, Auckland
Tel: (09) 520 2329   Mob: 021 670044
Fax: (09) 524 2898   Free: 0800 222436
info@aachenhouse.co.nz
www.lodgings.co.nz/aachen.html

Property features
Large luxurious rooms and suites
Secure complimentary parking
Comp tea/coffee/port/pre-dinner drks
Gourmet breakfast
NZ owners and operators
Conference/meeting/function room
Local features
Antique shops - 300 metres
Golf courses/beaches/park nearby
Restaurants - 5 min walk
Museum/city centre - 10 mins

Downtown - 10 minutes
Airport - 20 minutes

Exit SH 1 (motorway) at Market Rd
and travel east towards Remuera.
Aachen House is on the left
(approximately 100 metres).

This five-star luxury boutique hotel is situated in the exclusive central Auckland suburb of Remuera close to the city. Safe, tree-lined streets and gardens lead to local cafes, shops and art galleries. Inside an extraordinary collection of antique furniture and porcelain pieces is displayed adding to the sense of elegance and style. Rated five star by Qualmark, the nine large luxury guestrooms are decorated in period style each with a spacious ensuite bathroom. Modern facilities have been introduced with the business traveller in mind. I started the day with a gourmet breakfast in the beautiful conservatory and adjoining garden. These serene areas are also often used for conferences, weddings and other special occasions. Aachen House is perfect for discerning International travellers and corporate clients and with nine rooms the hotel lends itself to "exclusive use" for families and clients. The property is private and secure, provides complimentary parking and is only 20 minutes from the airport and ten minutes from the city. The guest book is full of praise for the attention and hospitality guests have received during their stay. You may not be royalty but here, it seems, you will be treated as if you are.

Accommodation available (NZ$)	👤	👤👤	+👤	🛏	🛁
2 Rooms	$332	$332		K	EN
4 Rooms	$398	$398		2K+2KT	EN
2 suites	$493	$493		CK	EN
1 Suite	$574	$574		CK	EN

Lunch, cocktails or evening meals can be arranged for special occasions.

Breakfast: Special cooked

Guest rooms:
Ambience:
Setting/location:

LOW   HIGH

Property features
Solar heated swimming pool
Spa/sauna/BBQ/antiques
Guest entertainment lounge
Views to One Tree Hill/Mt Hobson
Spacious residential setting
Privacy
Central heating
Local features
Auckland city/harbour-10 mins drive
Walk to city/parks/shops
Parnell - 7 minutes drive

Omahu Lodge

Robyn and Ken Booth
33 Omahu Road, Remuera, Auckland
Tel: (09) 524 5648   Mob: 021 954333
Fax:(09) 524 5108
omahulodge@xtra.co.nz
www.lodgings.co.nz/omahulodge.html

Auckland - 10 mins drive
Auckland Airport - 20 mins drive

OMAHU LODGE

Travelling north or south on Southern Motorway, take Market Road exit. Travel east and continue to Remuera Rd. Turn right, then right again into Omahu Rd. Omahu Lodge on the right.

A short drive to downtown Auckland and the suburbs of Remuera, Newmarket and Parnell and only a 20 minute drive from Auckland Airport, Omahu Lodge is ideal for both corporate and leisure travellers. As I entered the large airy reception area, I was drawn to the textured walls, colourful artworks, comfortable furnishings and striking antiques. A mottled kauri antique dining table, chiffonier and a radio gram are the envy of the National Museum. The three upper-level guest rooms have lovely outlooks over the suburbs, in particular One Tree Hill/Cornwall Park and Mt Hobson which two of the rooms have taken themes from. Two of the guestrooms also face the pool and spa and all are ensuite. On the lower level there is a separate lounge and an entertainment room with a large plasma screen television, DVD and CD player. One guestroom beside the pool has its own spacious ensuite, guest lounge, private entrance and an outlook to a native garden and the pool. All guests' breakfast in the conservatory looking over the pool. The house is tastefully appointed with stunning floral arrangements displayed throughout. Omahu Lodge is a small haven for visitors to Auckland.

Accommodation available (NZ$)	👤	👥	+👤	🛏	🛁
Breakfast: Special cooked	2 Rooms	$160-200	$175-225	D	EN
Evening meal: On request	1 Suite	$160-200	$175-225	Q	EN
Guest rooms:	1 Suite	$160-200	$175-225	Q	EN
Ambience:					
Setting/location:					

LOW   HIGH

Seahaven

Terry and Carmel Connolly
605 Riddell Rd, Glendowie, Auckland
Tel: (09) 575 8169
Fax:(09) 575 4072
tandc.connolly@xtra.co.nz
www.lodgings.co.nz/seahaven.html

Property features
Panoramic coastal and gulf views
Quiet seaside location
Swimming beach below property
Full laundry and kitchen facilities
Separate phone line
Bus stop at bottom of drive
Local features
Kelly Tarltons - 10 mins
Seaside village/cafes etc - 5 mins
Tennis courts
Golf courses

Auckland - 30 minutes
Airport - 40 minutes

From city drive along waterfront to S
Heliers. Turn right into Vale Rd. Veer
left into Bay Rd then turn left into
Riddell Road Proceed onto the ram
on left hand side to "605" (right of
way).

Walk into this private, self-contained apartment in the Auckland suburb of St. Heliers and you will immediately appreciate the peace of its unique position and uninterrupted view. I was mesmerised by the large window in front of me, exposing the deep blue of the Hauraki Gulf with Browns Island at centre stage. French doors from the lounge open to a small private deck, where guests can sit and watch the yachts sail gracefully past the end of the garden. If the timing is right, you might also catch the full moon on the water. Back inside, the apartment is of generous proportions with a separate bedroom and kitchen. Homely touches include fresh fruit, flowers and homemade biscuits. A private telephone is also provided and the kitchen and laundry have everything guests need. Carmel and Terry are happy to assist with travel plans or leave you in peace to enjoy your stay. Close to Auckland and yet quiet enough to have you almost believe you are on an island, Seahaven is particularly suited to those who like comfort and space. This spot would be great for a longer stay. Many good restaurants are to be found at St.Heliers by the sea.

Accommodation available (NZ$)	👤	👥	+👤	🛏	🛁	
1 S/C unit	$130	$150		Q	EN	Breakfast: Provisions first morning

Enquire about low season and long stay discounts.

Guest rooms:
Ambience:
Setting/location:

LOW   HIGH

Property features
Swimming pool
Projector TV in lounge
Gym facilities
Rural setting/doves/sheep/cattle
Local features
Information centre - 5 mins drive
Eftpos facilites - 5 mins drive
Walks

Flinders Landing

Carol and Ian Hobbs
RD 1963 Great South Rd, Bombay
Tel: (09) 236 0550   Mob: 027 4947272
Fax:(09) 236 0550
flinders@xtra.co.nz
www.lodgings.co.nz/flinders.html

Pukekohe - 10 mins drive
Auckland - 35 mins drive

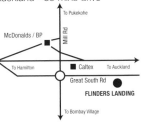

From SH1 take Bombay exit, drive towards the Caltex service station and turn left at roundabout into Great South Rd. Stone entrance with black gates is 300 metres on right hand side.

Approximately forty minutes from Auckland and an easy drive from Auckland airport is Flinders Landing. This architecturally designed, modern house, which has already won accolades for its design, is sure to impress. The building is large and private. The electric gates, set in a stone entranceway, opened as I approached and I passed sheep and cattle as I drove to the house. There are two guestrooms at Flinders Landing. The bathroom is guest-shared and it has a large bath and a walk-in shower. Both rooms back onto the courtyard where I settled in by relaxing and reading a book. Later I cooled off with a pleasant dip in the swimming pool. Dinner that evening was the typical New Zealand fare of roast lamb and vegetables, and afterwards I tucked up on a comfortable sofa in front of the fire and drank a port with the Whitney's family dog snuggled on my lap. The projector television is bound to be a hit with sport's fans. In the summer months, Carol often prepares a barbecue for her guests and I thought how enjoyable that would be in this rural setting. There are many activities in the area, but I only had time for a walk around the fifteen acres of land, where the farm animals are an added interest.

Family pets on site Guest pets by arrangement	Accommodation available (NZ$)	![person]	![two people]	+ ![person]	![bed]	![bath]
Breakfast: Special cooked	2 Rooms	$175-200	$250-300		K	GS
Evening meal: Enquire						
Guest rooms:						
Ambience:						
Setting/location:		Please enquire about children.				

Wellington Cable Car.

Hamilton

Hydro Majestic Café and Restaurant 33 Jellicoe Dve, Tel: (07) 859-0020. Eclectic retro décor with river views.

Rocket Espresso Lounge 109 Victoria St, Tel: (07) 839-6422. Great coffee.

Scott's Epicurean 181 Victoria St, Tel: (07) 839-6680. Contemporary style, latest mags, good music. Licensed.

Tables on the River 12 Alma St, Tel: (07) 839-6555. Overlooking the Waikato River.

Events

Balloons Over Waikato April - 5 days. Hamilton Lake. NZ's premier ballooning festival.

Field Days - June (held annually)

Cambridge

The Boatshed Café 21 Amber Ln, Tel: (07) 827-8286. Entire menu is gluten-free with dairy-free options.

Matamata

Workmans Café & Bar 52 Broadway, Tel: (07) 888-5498. Popular with locals and visitors.

Otorohanga

Copper Tree Restaurant 80 Maniapoto St, Tel: (07) 873-7777.

Te Kuiti

Bosco Café 57 Te Kumi Rd, Tel: (07) 878-3633. Good place to stop for coffee and snack.

New Plymouth

Andre's L'Escargot Restaurant 37 Brougham St. Tel: (06) 754-8544. Dine in casual elegance. French cuisine with a Mediterranean influence.

Nice Hotel & Bistro 71 Brougham Street, Tel: (06) 758-6423. Light, airy dining room with sheltered deck and subtropical gardens. Great seasonal menu.

Pankawalla 85 Devon St, Tel: (06) 758-4444. A contemporary upmarket Indian restaurant.

Ultra Lounge Manchester Unity Arcade 75 Devon St East, Tel: (06) 758-8444. An innovation in dining and relaxation in the world of cafes.

Events

Oakura Carnival New Years Day

Pukeiti Rhododendren & Garden Festival October

Taranaki Arts Festival July 2007 - held bi-annually

World Of Music Art & Dance (WOMAD) March 2007 - held bi-annually

Hawera

The Fuse Factory 47 High St, Tel: (06) 278-4444. Enjoy upmarket dining. New Zealand cuisine.

Stratford

Collage Cnr Miranda St & Prospero Pl, Tel: (06) 765-7003. Part of the Art Gallery, enjoy relaxed café-style dining.

Palmerston North

Barrista 77 George St, Tel: (06) 357-2614. "The" café in Palmerston North, serving brunch, café and evening meals.

Bella's Café 2 The Square, Tel: (06) 357-8616. Italian, Thai, Pacific Rim menu. Popular with the locals.

Déjeuner 159 Broadway Ave, Tel: (06) 952-5581. Operating for almost 20 years, fine-dining.

Vavasseur 201 Broadway Ave, Tel: (06) 359-3167. Boutique restaurant with great food & service.

Events

Palmerston North Market Every Saturday 6am-10am. Corner of Albert and Main Sts.

Waikanae

Rumours SH1, Tel: (04) 293-4564. Intimate with consistently good food and service.

The Easter Egret 4A Ngaio Rd, Tel: (04) 293-4772. 'Best takeaway on the Kapiti Coast'.

Vella on the Coast Café & Restaurant SH1, Tel: (04) 902-6200. Café style, large portions and good service.

Wellington

Amba Bar 21 Blair St, Tel: (04) 801-5212. Young and old frequent this laid back style spot for their weekend live jazz.

Caffe L'Affare 27 College St, Tel: (04) 385-9748. Great coffee & tasty Italian-inspired cuisine.

Chocolate Fish 497a Karaka Bay Rd, Scorching Bay Tel: (04) 388-2808. All day breakfasts and some of the best views in Wellington.

Chow 45 Tory St, Tel: (04) 382-8585 A hip noodle bar serving fine cocktails.

Dojo 11 Woodward St, Tel: (04) 437-4474. Asian fusion cuisine. Vibrant contemporary atmosphere.

Hummingbird 22 Courtenay Pl, Tel: (04) 801-6336. Serving NZ style tapas in a fun vibrant environment.

Logan Brown 192 Cuba St, Tel: (04) 801-5114. Award winning restaurant. Creative cuisine, stylish surroundings, serious about food.

Maria Pia 55-57 Mulgrave St, Thorndon, Tel: (04) 499-5590. A popular Italian trattoria serving fresh homemade pasta.

Parade Café 148 Oriental Parade, Tel: (04) 939-3935. Overlooks harbour and city, excellent coffee & decadent sweets.

Pravda 107 Customhouse Quay, Tel: (04) 801-8858. Located in one of Wellington's elegant older buildings. Serving bistro food & great coffee.

Smith the Grocer 19/233 Lambton Quay, Tel: (04) 473-8591. Café & deli in the refurbished Old Bank Arcade. Serves great coffee & food.

Solstice 27 Dundas St, Seatoun, Tel: (04) 388-8299.

Tinakori Bistro 328 Tinakori Rd, Thorndon, Tel: (04) 499-0567. Good food, licensed – in the heart of Tinakori Village.

Toast Bistro 120 The Terrace, Tel: (04) 499-1656. Cocktails, mixed drinks and nourishing food.

Events

The Food Show June. Westpac Stadium.

WOW – World Of Wearable Arts Festival September.

Mt Taranaki.

Brooklands Country Estate

General Manager: Marion Jarman
RD 1, Ngaruawahia
Tel: (07) 825 4756
Fax:(07) 825 4873
relax@brooklands.net.nz
www.lodgings.co.nz/brooklands.html

Property features
5 course meal included in tariff
Tennis court/swimming pool/croquet
Broadband access
Purpose built conference room
Native bush with beautiful bird life
Forest park - 10km of walking tracks
Local features
Glow worm caves/golf courses
Waingaro hot springs
Caving/abseiling/flying fox
Raglan village & beaches

Hamilton - 40 minutes
Auckland - 80 minutes

Turn off SH 1 at Huntly or
Ngaruawahia and follow signs to
Waingaro Springs (20 mins).
Brooklands is 4km north of
Waingaro Springs.

Four kilometres west of Waingaro Hot Springs, I arrived at one of the original homesteads of this attractive rural area. Brooklands Country Estate has been transformed into a luxury retreat with ten ensuite double bedrooms, which are stylish and contemporary but have kept their homely ambience. Aperitifs and canapés were served on the expansive return verandah overlooking the croquet lawn and the pool. Sometimes they are also served in the outside pavilion, with the stars as company, and on chilly nights, they are enjoyed inside the house around one of the open fireplaces. In the evening, I ate a delightful five-course meal. This was produced by the lodge's renowned chef and served at the large oak table where I sat enjoying the company of other guests. Guests can also choose to dine privately in the library/lounge among candles, chandeliers and crystal. A well-equipped, modern conference room is also available. Groups gather on the wide verandah that overlooks a flood-lit tennis court. This is also an ideal property for small intimate wedding receptions. Often couples have married in the charming, historic St Albans Church, which is 500 metres away from the lodge, and then return to Brooklands to celebrate in the elegant surroundings of this delightful property.

Accommodation available (NZ$)	♦	♦♦	+♦	🛏	🛁		
1 Room	$499	$799		K+S	EN	Breakfast: Special cooked
8 Rooms	$499	$799		K/T	EN	Evening meal: Included
1 Studio	$499	$799		K+Q	EN	Guest rooms:
						Ambience:
						Setting/location:

Enquire about conference rates and weekend specials.

LOW   HIGH

Property features
Garden ramble/rose garden
Croquet and petanque
10 acre drystock farm/beef cattle
Extensive rural views
Local features
Airport/Mystery Creek 5 mins
Horse stud tours
Waipa Delta paddle steamer
Fly fishing - guide available
Waitomo Caves/Rotorua 60 mins
Jet boating/bush walking

Glengariff 1877

Virginia and John Mathieson
235 Kaipaki Road, Ohaupo, Hamilton
Tel: (07) 823 6131   Mob: 025 948484
Fax: (07) 823 6178
glengariff@clear.net.nz
www.lodgings.co.nz/glengariff.html

Cambridge - 10 minutes
Hamilton - 15 minutes

From Hamilton take SH 3 south
towards Ohaupo / Te Awamutu. At
Cambridge sign turn left into Kaipaki
Rd. Continue 2.35km to Glengariff
on left.

Set among the lush pastoral plains of the Waikato, Glengariff has an impressive presence at the end of a long driveway. The two-storeyed building's most distinctive feature is a bell tower which is said to have been a watchtower during the land wars and later was used to call farm hands to lunch. The bell is no longer there but the tower affords good views of the countryside and is a quiet place for guests to get away from the household for a quiet read. Built in 1877, the house is one of the earliest pioneer homesteads in the Waikato. Of course there have been alterations over the years. The latest is a large air-conditioned conservatory where small conferences and weddings are sometimes held. Above this is the honeymoon suite and the original kauri staircase leads up to the other suite and bedroom. The suites open onto the balcony, which extends the length of the house with views over the grand sweep of lawn and garden. I enjoyed joining in with the household in front of the lounge fire, in the dining room and in the conservatory. The house has a comfortable, lived-in feel that encourages easy communication. Glengariff is well situated to visit the Waitomo Caves or Rotorua.

Family cat on site	Accommodation available (NZ$)					
Breakfast: Continental	1 Suite	$145	$170-195	SK/T	EN
	1 Room	$130	$155-170	Q	PR
Guest rooms:	1 Room	$110	$145	2S	PR
Ambience:					
Setting/location:					

LOW   HIGH

Alternative mobile phone: 025-297 1322.

The Woolshed

John and Sandra Cottle
625 Scotsman Valley Road, RD 1, Morrinsville
Tel: (07) 824 0992   Mob: 027 5240992
Fax:(07) 824 0982
thewoolshed@paradise.net.nz
www.lodgings.co.nz/woolshed.html

Property features
400 acre hill country dairy farm
Converted woolshed accommodation
Farm trips to top of farm
Sky TV/laundry/garden setting
Local features
Karangahake walkway - 45 mins
Lake Karapiro - 15 mins
Te Aroha hot pools - 30 mins
Raglan beach - 1 hr
Mystery Creek (Field Days) - 20 mins
Rotorua - 1 hour

Cambridge - 10 mins drive
Hamilton - 20 mins drive

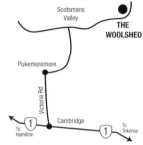

Take SH1 south. Take left at Taupiri.
Follow signs to Cambridge. Follow to
end of Church Rd turn left at sign to
Morrinsville. Take third turn-Hiwi Rd.
Follow to T intersection, turn right.
Woolshed 4kms on left.

As I drove the country roads in Central Waikato, I noticed how brilliantly green the rolling pastures were. It was easy to find this converted woolshed, which is located on a 400-acre, working dairy farm. I was impressed by its character and sophistication; it must be one of the most luxurious woolsheds around. The building has a corrugated-iron roof and its plastered exterior walls are covered by pretty Virginia vines. Decorative white shutters surround the interior windows, which are covered with fly screens and allow the country breezes to flow through the house. Inside, the walls are exposed concrete-block and the flooring is made of rimu timber. Macrocarpa, stable-style doors separate the guest quarters from the lodge's main living areas. Sandra is wonderful in the kitchen because she previously worked with a top New Zealand celebrity chef. On the menu the night I stayed, was fillet of beef on rocket lettuce, with baby potatoes and fresh vegetables, followed by dessert, cheeses and fudge. Guests can bring their own wine to dinner, although a selection is also available for purchase. The Woolshed's central location is ideal for exploring the Central North Island, The Coromandel and the Bay of Plenty.

Accommodation available (NZ$)	🧍	🧍🧍	+🧍	🛏	🛁
1 Room	$190	$190-250		SK or 2S	EN
1 Studio	$190	$190-250		SK or 2S	EN

Breakfast: Special cooked
Evening meal: $45pp
Guest rooms:
Ambience:
Setting/location:

LOW   HIGH

Evening meal by prior arrangement. Studio has kitchenette & laundry.

Property features
Themed garden/tranquil setting
Mt Karioi/rural views
All comforts/modern kiwi design
Quality bed linen/robes
Unique cosy central fire
Complimentary NZ wine/chocs

Local features
Surf beaches (lessons available)
Cafes/shops/galleries - 5 mins
Golf/bushwalks/horse riding
Fishing/kayaks/windsurfing

Raglan - 5 mins drive
Hamilton - 45 mins drive

From Auckland head south on SH1,
turn right at BP Ngaruawahia onto
SH39. 17km to SH23 T junction,
turn right, travel 35km. Turn right into
Greenslade Rd, Hideaway first on
left.

Hideaway Cottages

Rob Gillard   Margot Bowen
91 Greenslade Road, RD 1, Raglan
Tel: (07) 825 8868   Mob: 027 52607520
Fax: (07) 825 8868
info@hideawaycottages.co.nz
www.lodgings.co.nz/hideaway.html

  12

Rob and Margot have built these three cottages in a peaceful, landscaped valley near Moonlight Bay, in the West Coast town of Raglan. Extensive landscaping, using native trees and local sculptures, connects guests to the environment. A stony track, which borders a large pond, is linked by a bridge and boardwalk. The cottages encourage rest and romance. Each has a good-sized deck area, which takes advantage of the sun during the day and the stars at night. Once inside my cottage, I found no good reason to leave: I had a surround-sound stereo and speaker system; a two-way fireplace warming the open-plan lounge and kitchen; and a bedroom with a super-king-size bed and blackout curtains if I needed to catch up on sleep. The spacious ensuite bathroom had a double massage shower, heated mirrors and a large bath. Was I in heaven? Rob and Margot support their community by having as much made locally as possible. The ceiling beams, doors, floors and furniture are made of macrocarpa timber; the artworks are original; bathroom products are made by a local herbalist. Across the road there is access to the beach of Moonlight Bay, and the beaches of Raglan only a short drive away.

Accommodation available (NZ$)	♦	♦♦	+♦	🛏	🛁
3 S/C cottages	$245	$295	$50	SK+D	EN

Breakfast: Provision provided
Evening meal: Enquire
Guest rooms:
Ambience:
Setting/location:

Breakfast provisions are for continental and cooked.
Local chef for evening meals by prior arrangement.

Kamahi Cottage

Elisabeth and Evan Cowan
229 Barber Road, RD 5, Otorohanga
Tel: (07) 873 0849   Mob: 021 0551818
Fax: (07) 873 0849
enquiries@kamahi.co.nz
www.lodgings.co.nz/kamahi.html

Property features
1120 acre sheep & beef farm
Guided farm tours in 4WD vehicle
Landscaped country garden
BBQ/hammock chairs
Walks/views
Local features
Garden tours can be arranged
Guided trout fishing by arrangement
Golf course - 25 min drive
Waitomo glow worm cave - 30 min
Horse trekking/4WD bikes/rafting

Otorohanga - 15 min drive
Hamilton - 60 min drive

South of Otorohanga township (on State Hwy 3) turn onto Otewa Rd follow for approx. 12 kms. Turn right onto Barber Rd go to 229 Barber Rc Kamahi Cottage is on the left.

This stylish country cottage offers peace and privacy to guests. I was warmly welcomed by Liz, my host, who has created a delightful environment with the use of fresh, modern colours and fittings. The panoramic outlook from Kamahi Cottage is over sweeping landscapes of lush rolling farmland and volcanic mountain ranges. The cottage itself has high-pitched ceilings, a loft-style bedroom with a queen-size bed and pure cotton linen. Downstairs is a comfortable lounge area and a large bathroom and, hidden behind crafted wooden doors, a kitchenette. I found numerous books and magazines and a small stereo to occupy me. Best of all, the cottage is located in a region where there is plenty of action and adventure. By day I explored the nearby Waitomo Caves area, and in the evening I relaxed in the swinging hammock chairs on the porch of the cottage to watch the sunset, while I reflected on the day's events. Liz serves specialty breakfasts in the cottage, or at the homestead just a short walk away through the country garden. She loves creating culinary delights and, because so many guests asked for it, has created a web page of her recipes. Situated on a 1,120-acre sheep and cattle farm Kamahi Cottage is a delightful home away from home.

Accommodation available (NZ$)   Family cat on site

	♂	♂♂	+♂	🛏	🛁
1 S/C cottage	$200	$225	$55	Q+Sofa	PR

Farm tours $25 up to 4 people. Dinners by prior arrangement.
Cottage can take 4 guests.

Breakfast: Special cooked
Evening meal: Enquire
Guest rooms:
Ambience:
Setting/location:

Property features
360 degree elevated north views
Magical country retreat
Gourmet meals/fine wines
Spa pool/helipad
Local features
Golf course - 7 mins drive
Helicopter tour packages
Whitebaiting - 5 mins drive
Swimming and fisihing - 7 mins drive
Vineyard Café - 7 mins drive
Beach

Urenui - 7 min drive
New Plymouth - 30 min drive

From north at BP in Urenui Village, turn left into Ngakoti St. Follow road for approx 7 mins. Mataro Lodge is number 676 on right hand side. With signage.

Mataro Lodge

Kevin and Lynda Ingram
676 Mataro Road, RD 45, Urenui
Tel: (06) 752 3926
Fax: (06) 752 3926
info@mataro.co.nz
www.lodgings.co.nz/matarolodge.html

New owners, Lynda and Kevin sold their farm in South Taranaki to move north to the 12-acre hillside Mataro Lodge. The three stylish ensuite bedrooms have unobstructed views to Mokau, Raglan and the Pacific Ocean to the north and the awe inspiring Mt Taranaki to the south, with rolling hills and pastures in-between. The open-plan modern living areas take full advantage of the location and views and has huge sliding windows that open out to native flax and grasses blowing gently in the wind and a small lime tree orchard. I sat on the large Macrocarpa seat enjoying the warmth of the sun on my face. Polished concrete floors and underfloor heating throughout the lodge ensure warmth in the cooler seasons. This casual hilltop hideaway encourages guests to relax. The tariff includes breakfast and dinner, which Lynda prepares. I dined on smoked salmon vol-au-vent to start, followed by beef fillet with pesto and beetroot Cumberland sauce on a parsnip and kumera mash, with wilted spinach and green beans. Of course I couldn't say no to the homemade Tay berry cheesecake served with ice cream and a shot of Baileys Irish Cream. Food, fine wine and great coffee are integral parts of this contemporary country retreat.

Family cat on site
Guest pets by arrangement

	Accommodation available (NZ$)			+image		
Breakfast: Special cooked	3 Rooms	$330	$400		K	EN
Evening meal: Included						
Guest rooms:						
Ambience:						
Setting/location:						

LOW   HIGH

Cottage Retreats

Selwyn and Lorraine Phillips
564 Mangorei Road, New Plymouth
Tel: (06) 758 3633
sel.lorraine@xtra.co.nz
www.lodgings.co.nz/cottageretreats.html

Property features
Historic Places Trust Building
Semi-rural setting and view
Full kitchen facilities
Pet donkey and Kune Kune pig
Swimming pool/country garden
Local features
Golf course/cafes/restaurants
Tupare gardens/Burgess House
Pukeiti rhododendron gardens
Mt Egmont/walks/skiing
Beach/surf/coastal walkway

New Plymouth - 5 minutes
Inglewood - 10 minutes

Entering city from north turn left at third set of lights into Mangorei Rd & continue 5.2km to cottage. From south (SH 3) pass Burgess Park Restaurant, turn left into Mangorei Rd. Cottage is on right.

Set at the rural edge of New Plymouth but not too far from town, Lorraine and Selwyn (who live close by) provide superb hospitality with many detailed touches. The heritage-rated, 1840's kauri cottage was brought to this country site from the centre of town, authentically restored and then modernised. Lorraine and Selwyn are passionate about the history of the place and the journey of the cottage to its present location makes an interesting story. The two bedrooms, lounge, kitchen/dining and bathroom facilities ensure that there is plenty of room for four guests, or a treat for couples to really spread out, as I did – if only I had more time to enjoy it! There are many elements that bring the early 19th century to mind; the pretty country garden, the views of rolling countryside, wood burning stove in the kitchen, polished kauri floors, the hip bath, wrought iron bed heads, rag mats and, wandering the section, a donkey called Harry and a Kune Kune piglet called Henrietta. These elements combine with 20th century requirements such as CD player, television, shower, bathrobes, microwave, stove, dishwasher and washing machine. A great array of breakfast ingredients including a loaf of home-made bread were left for me in the kitchen.

Accommodation available (NZ$)	👤	👥	+👤	🛏	🛁	Family pets on site Guest pets by arrangement
1 S/C cottage	$160	$160	$20	K+2S	PR	Breakfast: Cooked Evening meal: $25pp Guest rooms: Ambience: Setting/location:

Breakfast prepared for you or self-prepared. Evening meal BYOW.

LOW   HIGH

Property features
Inner city tranquility
Unique architecture & contemp décor
Separate guest lounge & S/C kitchen
Designer ensuites - 2 spa baths
Guest deck & BBQ with bush outlook
Local features
Pukeariki & costal walkway - 5 mins
Pukekura Park - 2 mins
Surf beach/golf courses
Cafes/restaurants - walking distance
Art gallery - 5 mins

Issey Manor

Jan and Brian Mason
32 Carrington Street, New Plymouth
Tel: (06) 758 2375   Mob: 027 2486686
Fax: (06) 758 2375
issey.manor@actrix.co.nz
www.lodgings.co.nz/isseymanor.html

Wanganui - 2 hours
Hamilton - 2.5 hours

Arriving from North turn left into
Liardet St at traffic lights, first right
into Pendarves St and you will see
Issey Manor to your left.

Issey Manor is a combination of historical architecture and modern living and suits both corporate and leisure travellers visiting New Plymouth. Painted orange and brown on the outside, this stylish urban bed and breakfast began life as a coach-house in 1857. The guestrooms are all spacious, styled in bright colours and contemporary furnishings with outlooks to the surrounding rooftops and trees of the residential neighbourhood. Contemporary New Zealand artwork is displayed throughout and a private guest lounge has a well-stocked library, with Sky television, a DVD player and stereo. Jan and Brian serve breakfast and guests are welcome to use the fully equipped, modern guest kitchen throughout the day and evening. Although Jan and Brian live on-site, I was amazed at how much privacy I had; the main portico entrance and private locations of the four guestrooms allow guests to come and go undisturbed. That afternoon after exploring the numerous sights of New Plymouth I discovered a large deck area hidden at the rear of the property that looked out to a small valley lined with native trees – a nice little place to unwind. I thought the table and chairs and barbecue would be perfect for alfresco dining on a summer evening.

Family pets on site	Accommodation available (NZ$)	👤	👥	+👤	🛏	🛁
Breakfast: Special cooked	1 Room	$120	$170	$45	SK or 2S	EN
	1 Room	$110	$150		Q	EN
Guest rooms:	1 Room	$100	$140		Q	EN
Ambience:	1 Room	$100	$120		Q	EN
Setting/location:						

LOW   HIGH

73

Nice Hotel and Bistro

Terry Parkes
71 Brougham Street, New Plymouth
Tel: (06) 758 6423   Mob: 027 4576633
Fax:(06) 758 6433
info@nicehotel.co.nz
www.lodgings.co.nz/nicehotel.html

Property features
Award winning bistro
Deck/tropical garden
Contemporary NZ art/bikes
Jetstream/business centre
Meeting room/weddings/functions
Local features
Pukekura Park/Pukeariki museum
Walk to contemporary art museum
Historic St Mary's Church
Len Lye Wind Wand
Coastal walkway

New Plymouth - 1 min walk
Hamilton - 2 hour drive

Entering into New Plymouth stay on the main Northgate Rd follow to the lights by the fire station. Nice Hotel is across the viaduct on the right diagonally across from St Mary's.

Located in New Plymouth's city centre, Nice Hotel & Bistro is the only luxury boutique hotel in town. The hotel boasts chandeliers and rich-coloured halls lined with contemporary New Zealand artworks. It has seven large, bright, airy guestrooms which have ensuites with double spa baths or massage showers. All guestrooms have their individual charm, each named and decorated after an element of New Plymouth's history – the Redcoats room, the Pukeariki room or the Windwand room. Within walking distance of numerous tourist sites, the hotel's location also caters for business travellers. Each room has a large desk and broadband internet connection. Terry has developed the nooks and crannies of this 140 year-old New Plymouth residence. I relaxed, for instance, in an alcove found on the second floor where there was a small library, plush armchairs and the sound of classical music. The on-site award winning Bistro has an a-la-carte menu catering for in-house guests during the day, and open to the public for dinner. Outside, a large deck, surrounded by a tropical garden, is an oasis in this central city location. By day the Nice Hotel & Bistro is run with slick and professional service but when the sun goes down the ambience is more romantic in style.

Accommodation available (NZ$)	👤	👤👤	+👤	🛏	🛁	Family dog on site Guest pets by arrangement
5 rooms	$225	$225		Q	EN	Breakfast: Extra $15pp
2 Rooms	$225	$225		SK	EN	Evening meal: Menu
1 Suite	$333	$333		SK	EN	Guest rooms: Ambience:

Ensuites have massage showers or spa baths.

Setting/location:

LOW   HIGH

Property features
Award winning architecture
180 degree Tasman Sea views
Kayaks and mountain bikes to hire
Outdoor hot showers
Fire pit
Local features
Beaches/swimming/surfing/fishing
Mt Taranaki/hiking
Cafes/restaurants/shops - 5 min drive
Outstanding ancient Pa site
Surf Coast highway

Ahu Ahu Beach Villas

David and Nuala Marshall
321 Ahu Ahu Road, Oakura, RD 4, New Plymouth
Tel: (06) 752 7370   Mob: 027 4781206
holiday@ahu.co.nz
www.lodgings.co.nz/ahuahu.html

Oakura - 5 min drive
New Plymouth - 15 min drive

Take Surf Highway 45 from New Plymouth, travel approx. 3km past Oakura. Ahu Ahu Road is the first road on your right, the Villas are on your left 3km down.

The spell of Mt Taranaki is forever present in this special region of New Zealand, as is the sound of the surf, the stillness of the wind and the peace. These two award-winning, studio-style villas have two units in each of them and their interiors reflect the tones of the land and sea around. All the units are loft-style, sleep up to four and have private bathrooms, kitchenettes, outside terraces with tables and chairs and views that are hard to beat. Finished in undulating plaster, the villas were built using Australian hardwood timber taken from the old ports of Taranaki and Nelson. Large recycled hospital windows have been used to frame extensive north-facing views over the Tasman Sea. Before I arrived, I'd bought provisions from the nearby village of Oakura. I swam in the sea in the late afternoon sun and then walked along the beautiful, black sand of Oakura beach. The sand is typical of that found on New Zealand's west coast. Hosts, David and Nuala, hire mountain bikes and kayaks to any of their guests with adventurous desires and the couple are happy to background the history and attractions in the Taranaki region.

Guest pets by arrangement	Accommodation available (NZ$)			+		
Breakfast: Extra charge	4 S/C units	$150-195	$150-195	$35	Q+2S	PR

Guest rooms:
Ambience:
Setting/location:

LOW   HIGH

75

Tairoa Lodge

Linda and Steve Morrison
3 Puawai Street, Hawera
Tel: (06) 278 8603   Mob: 027 2435782
Fax: (06) 278 8603
tairoa.lodge@xtra.co.nz
www.lodgings.co.nz/tairoa.html

Property features
Victorian kauri villa
Established gardens
Separate guest dining & sitting rms
Swimming pool
Romantic getaways/small functions
Local features
Mt Egmont/Taranaki/hiking/skiing
Tawhiti Museum/antique shops
Surf to mountain - 20 min drive
Restaurants/cafes 2mins
Fishing/waterskiing

Hawera - 10 minute walk
New Plymouth - 50 minute drive

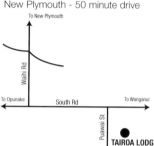

From North travel from Hawera towards Wanganui. Turn right into Puawai St before overhead subway. From South turn left into Puawai St as you enter Hawera, after the overhead subway.

The word Tairoa in Maori means "to linger" and that is exactly what you will want to do at this elegant bed and breakfast lodge and self-contained cottage. Secluded behind a stand of mature kauri trees in a large established garden on the fringes of Hawera township, the house is one of Hawera's oldest residences still standing. Linda and Steve have restored its original structure and renovated the interior to make the most of the high stud, the elegant proportions and the golden timber floors and joinery. There are two spacious ensuite guestrooms upstairs which are faithful to the gracious era that the house was built in, but also provides a high degree of modern comfort. Downstairs I found privacy in the separate guests' sitting room with open fire, television and deep leather armchairs. Across the passage is the dining room where Linda, who is a very fine cook, served me dinner (which I'd pre-arranged) and full cooked breakfast. A specialty is a romantic candlelight dinner for celebrating couples. Venture through the gardens and The Cottage can be found, providing privacy and tranquillity. Recently restored, The Cottage offers space and comfort with modern touches. The ambience at Tairoa is friendly and relaxed. I thoroughly enjoyed my stay.

Accommodation available (NZ$)	🧍	🧍🧍	+🧍	🛏	🛁	Guest pets by arrangement
1 Room	$120	$150-175		Q	EN	Breakfast: Special cooked
1 Room	$120	$150-175		Q+S	EN	Evening meal: $50pp
1 S/C cottage		$195-250	$30	Q+2S	PR	Guest rooms:
						Ambience:
						Setting/location:

LOW   HIGH

Enquire about packages. Breakfast provisions provided in cottage.

Property features
1100 acre working farm
Sweeping lawns/mature gardens
Romney & Poll Dorset sheep stud
Spa in secret garden/wine cellar
Entertaing hall/beauty therapist
Local features
Private jet boat/Manawatu gorge
Guided fly fishing/5 golf courses
Adidas rugby institute home
Massey Uni/Manfield autocourse
Historic Fielding saleyards

Hiwinui Country Estate

Dave and Jan Stewart
465 Ashurst - Bunnythorpe Road, Palmerston North
Tel: (06) 329 2838   Mob: 025 2680173
Fax: (06) 329 2828
jan@hiwinui.co.nz
www.lodgings.co.nz/hiwinui.html

Palmerston North - 15 mins
Wellington - 2 hrs

From the centre of Palmerston North drive along Tremaine Avenue which becomes Kelvin Grove Road. At the T junction with the Ashhurst Bunnythorpe Road, turn left. The entrance is on the right.

On the grassy plains of the Manawatu, this sprawling modern house surrounded by broad areas of lawn and bordered by trees, ponds and gardens has all the characteristics of a traditional farm homestead. The Stewart family have farmed here since 1887 and Hiwinui is now one of New Zealand's best known sheep studs. Staying here is a multi-faceted experience. In the house three handsomely decorated bedrooms with well-appointed ensuites, and a choice of spa bath or double shower, provide every comfort and open through glass doors to the garden. The living areas are large and lofty with leather lounge chairs and locally crafted furniture and art. In one of the two lounge areas divided by a splendid double fireplace made of schist stone, I enjoyed a drink before Jan and Dave served my finely presented dinner. I had already selected a New Zealand wine from the underground cellar. At Hiwinui you can be private or sociable. You can go on a farm tour with Dave, fly-fish with a local guide and walk over the farm. You can also indulge in a massage or treatment in the beauty salon or in a romantic part of the garden, luxuriate in the private alfresco spa bath next to a roaring stone fire. Hiwinui is a favoured place for honeymooners.

Accommodation available (NZ$)	🧍	🧍🧍	+🧍	🛏	🛁
1 Room	$250	$330		SK	EN
1 Room	$250	$330		K	EN
1 Room	$160	$250		Q	PR

Breakfast: Special cooked
Evening meal: $60-75pp
Guest rooms:
Ambience:
Setting/location:

LOW   HIGH

Te Horo Lodge

Craig Garner
109 Arcus Road, Te Horo, Kapiti Coast
Tel: (06) 364 3393   Mob: 027 4306009
Fax: (06) 364 3323   Free: 0800 483467
enquiries@tehorolodge.co.nz
www.lodgings.co.nz/tehoro.html

Property features
Swimming pool/spa pool
Petanque court/5 acre bush
Small conference room
Tranquil setting/open fire
Rural/garden views
Local features
Southward Car Museum - 20 mins
5 golf courses within 30 mins
Ruth Pretty Cooking School
Kapiti Island excursions - 25 mins
Kapiti 4x4 quad bike - 30 mins

Wellington - 50 minutes
Levin - 20 minutes

Approx. 8km south of Otaki, turn off SH 1 opposite the Red House Cafe onto School Rd. Turn left onto Arcus Rd. Lodge is number 109.

The drive into Te Horo Lodge winds through a stand of native kohekohe trees before opening out into a courtyard and the entrance to this impressive purpose-built accommodation. In this fertile pocket of land close to the Otaki River, Craig has built an elegant cedar building against a backdrop of native bush and a sheltered, two-and-a-half acre lawn brightened with flower gardens and an orchard of citrus, kiwi fruit and stone fruit beyond. The result is a place that has two great luxuries: the peace and the view. I imagined myself breakfasting in the gazebo by the outdoor pool or relaxing in the jacuzzi under the stars. In the lodge's interior Craig has combined timber shutters and frames with fruity-coloured walls bright curtaining and a tiled floor. The result is chic and sophisticated without being the least bit pretentious. The ensuite bedrooms are understated and cheerfully coloured, with glass doors that lead to the garden. My upstairs suite featured a large round window looking right into the treetops and the serenity of the forest. There is a small conference room, but the most charming room in the house is the lounge with its dominant stone chimney which is a work of art that has been crafted by a local stone mason.

Accommodation available (NZ$)	👤	👤👤	+👤	🛏	🛁		
3 Rooms	$150	$210-305		K	EN	Breakfast: Cooked	
1 Room	$165	$265-345	$55-85	K+S	EN	Evening meal: $50-60pp	

Guest rooms:
Ambience:
Setting/location:

Evening meals by prior arrangement.

Country Patch

Sue and Brian Wilson
18 Kea Street, Waikanae
Tel: (04) 293 5165   Mob: 027 4578421
Fax: (04) 293 5164
stay@countrypatch.co.nz
www.lodgings.co.nz/countrypatch.html

Property features
Views of Kapiti Coast
Quiet location - semi rural
French tub overlooking view
Character cottages/privacy
Local features
Beaches nearby
Restaurants - 5 mins
Golf courses
Southward car museum
Kapiti Island
Bush walks

Waikanae - 3 minutes
Paraparaumu - 10 minutes

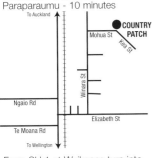

From SH 1 at Waikanae turn into
Elizabeth St and cross railway line.
Take the third road left (Winara St)
and then the fourth road on the right
(Mohua St) which becomes Kea St.
Country Patch is on your left.

There are two self-contained lodging options at Country Patch and I would be happy to stay in either of them. A split barn door leads to The Apartment, which has a sloped ceiling, a small mezzanine for two single beds and the main ensuite bedroom tucked behind the kitchen for privacy. The kitchen/lounge has all the inviting charm of a cosy loft. A large glazed alcove with a snugly fitting daybed takes in the tree-speckled view over Waikanae and beyond are steep, bush-clad hills. The most overwhelming feature of the new Cottage is the stunning, ever-changing view over the Waikanae Coast, Kapiti Island. The day I was there was fine and I could see as far as the Marlborough Sounds. Sue has kept elements of a country cottage in the décor, such as the hearth of sleepers in front of the open fire, but there are also some well-thought-out, modern features, such as a double French tub (with a view), a bathroom with disabled facilities, a second ensuite bedroom with a private courtyard and a laptop table. Both the apartment and cottage have telephone connections. The couple are generous, involved and cheerful hosts and it would be hard to not enjoy a stay here.

Family dog on site
Guest pets by arrangement

Accommodation available (NZ$)	👤	👥	+👤	🛏	🛁
1 S/C unit	$135-150	$135-150	$30	Q+2S	EN
1 S/C house	$190-210	$190-210	$40	2Q or 4S	2EN

Breakfast: Provisions provided

Guest rooms:
Ambience:
Setting/location:

LOW   HIGH

Disabled facilities available in large cottage only.

Hurunui Boutique Lodge

Erica and Geoff Lineham
15 Hurunui Street, Waikanae, Kapiti Coast
Tel: (04) 902 8571
Fax: (04) 902 8572
relax@hurunuihomestead.co.nz
www.lodgings.co.nz/hurunui.html

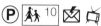

Property features
Private setting/romantic rooms
Cotton linen/bathrobes/slippers
Exquisite French toiletries
Port/sherry/chocs/tea/coffee
French doors to large sunny patio
Heated pool/private spa room
Tennis court/petanque piste
Local features
Sandy beaches/safe swimming
Restaurants/cafes/golf courses
Nga Manu Nature Reserve (kiwis)

Waikanae shops - 15 mins walk
Wellington CBD - 50 mins drive

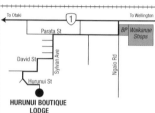

Take SH1 to Waikanae. Turn at BP Petrol Station into Ngaio Rd. Take first right - Parata St, left into Sylvan Ave, right into David St, left into Hurunui St. Hurunui Boutique Lodge is signposted at the end of the cul-de-sac.

Every aspect of this lodge is presented with artistic flair. Erica's consummate creativity is evidenced in the fresh flowers, fine china collections, luxury furnishings and the design of the park-like grounds. Here I could wander through the water gardens, a grove of native trees, play petanque and tennis, or relax in the shade of the gazebo. Spoiled for choice, guests can enjoy the swimming pool, private spa and an extensive tiled courtyard with outdoor furniture that leads to sweeping lawns. Two guest lounges are beautifully furnished and include every comfort including guest computer with free broadband internet and WiFi. Downstairs, the spacious Water Garden Suite's floor-length windows offer dreamy garden and pond views. The South Pacific Room is adjacent and can only be booked by guests using the suite, assuring privacy. Upstairs are two queen-size ensuite bedrooms and a gallery sitting room. My romantic Country Garden Room (pictured) was decorated in French-country style with a hand-painted armoire. The Romantiques Room has mahogany antiques and views to the Tararua Ranges. Erica thoroughly spoils her guests with a generous gourmet breakfast, and a different table setting daily. Hurunui Boutique Lodge is an enchanting place to stay for several days. Leaving was difficult.

Accommodation available (NZ$)	🧍	🧍🧍	+🧍	🛏	🛁	Family cat on site
1 Suite	$285	$310		SK/T	EN	Breakfast: Special cooked
1 Room	$255	$280		Q	EN	
1 Room	$225	$250		Q	EN	Guest rooms:
1 Room	$145	$195		D	PR	Ambience:
Laundry service and packages available.						Setting/location:

LOW   HIGH

Broadeaves Bed & Breakfast

Liz and Andrew Kirkland
24 Ngarara Road, Waikanae
Tel: (04) 293 1483   Mob: 027 5545175
Fax: (04) 293 1583
stay@broadeaves.co.nz
www.lodgings.co.nz/broadeaves.html

Property features
Petanque
Large garden/BBQ area
Hot tub in master suite
Kids playground and playroom
Local features
Nga Manu nature reserve - 5 min
Ferndale horse riding - 5 min
Southwards car museum - 10 min
Kapiti Island charter boat tour - 15 min
Bush and river walks
Beach
Waikanae - 10 min walk
Wellington - 50 min drive

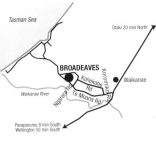

Turn off SH 1 into Te Moana Rd,
take 2nd R Koromiko Rd, follow to
end (now Kohekohe Rd) at T
junction Broadeaves is the driveway
in front of you.

Situated on a large, private section in a residential area of Waikanae on the Kapiti Coast and only a short 50 minute drive to Wellington, makes Broadeaves Bed and Breakfast a great option for corporate and leisure travellers, honeymooners and families alike. As they have school aged children themselves, Liz and Andrew will happily mind children while parents dine out at one of the several local restaurants nearby. Outside, gardens wrap around the house creating vistas from all rooms. Inside, the large comfortable lounge has an entertainment area for adult guests and a well-equipped playroom for children. Two of the three guestrooms have French doors opening out to the central garden. The third guestroom captures the morning sun. With the large Magnolia suite is a private, outdoor, hot tub, which is a warm place from which to watch the stars. All of the bathrooms are spacious with dual basins, heated towel rails and quality bath linen. Liz offers two- and three-course dinner options by prior arrangement. The warmth and love in this energetic household is infectious and I felt included in the family. Liz and Andrew also offer accommodation at The Boathouse, a self-contained house with a nautical theme, only a short walk from Raumati Beach a little further down the coast.

Family pets on site Guest pets by arrangement	Accommodation available (NZ$)	👤	👥	+👤	🛏	🛁
Breakfast: Special continental	1 Room	$120	$165-225		Q	EN
Evening meal: $25-45pp	1 Room	$100	$120		K or 2S	PR
Guest rooms:	1 Room	$100	$120		Q	PR
Ambience:						
Setting/location:	TV available on request.					

The Boathouse

Liz and Andrew Kirkland
39 Matatua Road, Raumati
Tel: (04) 293 1483   Mob: 027 5545175
Fax:(04) 293 1583
stay@theboathouse.co.nz
www.lodgings.co.nz/theboathouse.html

Property features
Nautical theme/BBQ
28" whale chaser boat
Outdoor bath
Marine artifacts
Large decks/views over Raumati
Local features
Beach - 3 minutes walk
7 x restaurants - 4 minutes walk
Swimming pool - 3 minutes walk
Park - 4 minutes walk

Raumati - 4 minutes walk
Wellington - 40 minutes drive

Turn at the Nyco chocolate on State Highway No 1 (Raumati Road). Follow to end. Turn right into Matatua Road. Pass the bowling club and its approximately 150 m on the left.

Treat your friends or family for a weekend at this self-contained, romantic, holiday cottage, which is set up for one-party occupation. It is located a four-minute walk away from Raumati Beach and within harpooning distance of a variety of restaurants and cafes. Built from recycled native and exotic timbers and decorated with a range of quirky nautical pieces, The Boathouse is a sight to behold. A large deck, complete with fish sculpture and fishing nets hanging from overhead beams, overlooks the eastern hills and provides guests with two large areas for entertaining. Inside, The Master Cabin has a queen-size bed made up with quality linens, and French doors open to a courtyard. Upstairs on a mezzanine floor there are two single beds. There's a stylish kitchen with all mod cons, a bathroom with an "aquarium" toilet, and fully equipped laundry. The rear garden has a garden path leading to a double hammock slung between the trees, an outdoor bath (with hot and cold running water) and a 28-foot whale-chaser boat which provides extra accommodation if its needed. There is ample outdoor furniture to lounge on, tables to set for meals, and a gas barbecue for cooking. Refreshments and breakfast provisions are provided.

Accommodation available (NZ$)	![]	![]	+![]	![]	![]	Guest pets by arrangement
1 S/C house			$200-225	$30	Q+2S	EN	Breakfast: Provisions provided

Guest rooms:
Ambience:
Setting/location:

LOW   HIGH

The house is a 2 bedroom with boat sleepout.

The Cottage Ohariu Farm

Jude Best
184 Takarau Gorge, Ohariu Valley, Johnsonville
Tel: (04) 477 3374   Mob: 027 4773064
Fax:(04) 499 9781
info@ohariufarm.co.nz
www.lodgings.co.nz/cottage.html

Property features
Total privacy
Rural setting
Outdoor fire-heated bath
Comfortable and cosy
Close to city
Local features
Horse riding
Country walks
Nine-hole golf course
Wellington highlights
Restaurants and cafes 10 mins

Wellington - 20 mins drive
Johnsonville - 10 mins drive

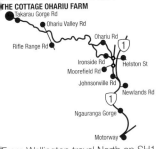

From Wellington travel North on SH1.
Exit left into Johnsonville. At second
roundabout turn left onto Ironside
Road. Travel 6 km to cross roads.
Continue straight onto Takarau
George Road for 1.84k.

If you really want to get away from it all, this rustic little cottage is only twenty minutes from Wellington's CBD but, surrounded by the steep hills of a peaceful 1200-acre farm, a world away from the city. An old army barracks building was moved to the property for shearers' quarters in the 1960's and has now been renovated into a cosy self-contained place furnished with leather couches. The bedroom of the cottage merges with the dining area and kitchen and the spaces are freshly painted and decorated in a simple and comfortable style. Jude feels that privacy is important for her guests, and apart from being greeted on arrival, I was left alone, but invited to call on the farmhouse if there was anything I needed. In the garden is the piece de resistance of the property - a romantic outdoor bath heated by a wood fire underneath it. Relaxed under the stars in the warm water and soaking in the stunning quiet of the countryside, I couldn't think of a better way to refresh a weary body. Breakfast ingredients are in the cottage. I didn't feel like cooking my own dinner but there were good restaurants in Johnsonville around ten minute's drive away.

Family pets on site	Accommodation available (NZ$)					
Breakfast: Continental	1 S/C cottage		$150		PR	

Guest rooms:
Ambience:
Setting/location:

7 day stay - $120/night.
4 day stay - $130/night.

Woodhaven Country House & Cottage

Anne and James Conder
20 Rifle Range Road, Ohariu Valley, Wellington
Tel: (04) 477 4047
Fax: (04) 477 4047
anne@woodhaven.co.nz
www.lodgings.co.nz/woodhaven.html

Property features
Rural setting/4 acre garden
Pond and bird life
Sheep/alpacas and chickens
Private decks/BBQ/petanque
Character cottage/quality furnishings

Local features
Horse riding
9 hole golf course
Kapiti Coast - 30 min drive
Country walks/gardens to visit
Fishing/scenic walks

Johnsonville - 5 minute drive
Wellington - 15 minute drive

From Wellington, turn left at the second roundabout into Ironside Rd Follow for 4.5 kms until the Ohariu Valley intersection turning left into Rifle Range Rd - #20.

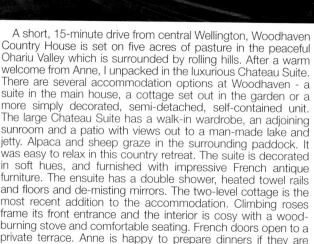

A short, 15-minute drive from central Wellington, Woodhaven Country House is set on five acres of pasture in the peaceful Ohariu Valley which is surrounded by rolling hills. After a warm welcome from Anne, I unpacked in the luxurious Chateau Suite. There are several accommodation options at Woodhaven - a suite in the main house, a cottage set out in the garden or a more simply decorated, semi-detached, self-contained unit. The large Chateau Suite has a walk-in wardrobe, an adjoining sunroom and a patio with views out to a man-made lake and jetty. Alpaca and sheep graze in the surrounding paddock. It was easy to relax in this country retreat. The suite is decorated in soft hues, and furnished with impressive French antique furniture. The ensuite has a double shower, heated towel rails and floors and de-misting mirrors. The two-level cottage is the most recent addition to the accommodation. Climbing roses frame its front entrance and the interior is cosy with a wood-burning stove and comfortable seating. French doors open to a private terrace. Anne is happy to prepare dinners if they are ordered in advance. Alternatively it's a short taxi ride to the plethora of restaurants in Wellington city or Johnsonville.

Accommodation available (NZ$)	👤	👥	+👤	🛏	🛁	Family cat on site Guest pets by arrangement
1 Suite	$275	$275		Q	EN	Breakfast: Special cooked
1 S/C unit	$200	$200		Q + SB	PR	Evening meal: Enquire
1 Cottage	$230	$230		K + Q	PR	Guest rooms:

Continental breakfast provisions provided for cottage and unit.
Dinners by prior arrangement. Also sofa bed in cottage.

Ambience:
Setting/location:

LOW   HIGH

Property features
Central city - suburb location
Contemporary home
Spacious private guest wing
Café style breakfast
Local features
Parliament - 10 mins walk
Botanic gardens - 10 mins walk
Stadium - 20 mins walk
Ferry - 5 mins drive
Te Papa Museum - 45 mins walk
Shopping/cafes/restaurants

@ The Stables

Gill and John Olifent
3 Poplar Grove, Thorndon, Wellington
Tel: (04) 972 4796   Mob: 021 433712
atthestables@paradise.net.nz
www.lodgings.co.nz/thestables.html

Wellington CBD - 10 minute walk
Airport - 20 minute drive

From city - up Bowen Street, right into Tinakori Road. Little lane on left 0.55ks. From North - take Hawkestone St off ramp, turn right. At Tinakori Road, left and immediate right.

Simple clean lines and uncluttered spaces are the hallmark of this contemporary bed and breakfast in the Wellington city suburb of Thorndon. The accommodation is ideal for corporate travellers, parties of up to four, international travellers wanting extra comforts, and domestic travellers on short escapes. Wellington's culture is at the doorstep. Te Papa Museum, Parliament buildings, Lambton Quay, the Botanical Gardens and the cable car are all only short walks away. There are two guestrooms with walk-in wardrobes and desks. The bathroom is shared, but Gill only takes single-party bookings, so guests have the whole downstairs wing to relax in. Blonded-maple flooring and white-painted brick walls create a slightly industrial feel to this converted stable building, but Gill's attention to design detail also creates a warm and inviting ambience. Cooked breakfast is served upstairs where the kitchen, dining room and lounge flow out to a large patio area with rooftop views over Wellington. I welcomed the warmth of the sun beaming through the windows on the morning I visited. Near to the motorway, in a quiet lane, with easy access to the ferry terminals and airport, @The Stables is a good choice of accommodation for anyone visiting Wellington.

Accommodation available (NZ$)	![person]	![couple]	+![person]	![bed]	![bath]
1 Room	$180-200	$195-250		Q	PR
1 Room	$180-200	$195-250		2SK	PR

Breakfast: Special cooked
Evening meal: On request
Guest rooms:
Ambience:
Setting/location:

LOW   HIGH

Single party bookings for up to 4 persons only.

Edgewater and Villa Karaka Bay

Stella Lovering
459 Karaka Bay Road, Seatoun, Wellington
Tel: (04) 388 4446   Mob: 021 613357
Fax: (04) 388 4446
edgewaterwellington@xtra.co.nz
www.lodgings.co.nz/edgewater.html

Property features
Located opp Karaka Bay beach
Award winning architecture
Laundry facilities available
Creative cuisine/quality produce
Central heating/guest balcony
Local features
Cable car/botanic gardens
Parliament/National Museum
Café close by/art galleries
Karaka Bay;
Home to Lord of Rings cast/crew

Wellington - 15 minutes
Airport - 10 minutes

From city go though Victoria tunnel and follow signs to Seatoun. Turn left into Broadway, go through tunnel & turn left at coast. Continue to Karaka Bay.

If you don't need to be right in the middle of the city, staying at Edgewater among the waterfront homes of this historic seaside village is a very worthwhile experience. Seatoun has gained fame as the centre of Wellywood where Peter Jackson and other directors, cast and crew of King Kong live on Karaka Bay Road. Stella's unique home, with its distinctive white peaked roofs, won an architectural award when it was built in 1976 and still looks contemporary today. The four large guestrooms, with modern ensuites, are configured for privacy and are separated from the hosts' living quarters. My room at the rear of the house opened onto a sunny brick courtyard where I could have relaxed, but I decided instead to wander by the sea and drink coffee at the 'celebrity' Chocolate Fish Café down the road. At the table in the large open-plan lounge, with its white leather couches and wide views of the harbour, Stella served a breakfast of fresh fruit, stewed prunes and lemon, cereals and eggs Benedict. On request, she will also serve a superb three-course dinner of local produce. Stella also has a stylish self-contained cottage up the road called Villa Karaka Bay.

Accommodation available (NZ$)	👤	👥	＋👤	🛏	🛁	Family pets on site
1 Room	$170	$190		Q	EN	Breakfast: Special cooked
1 Room	$220	$250	$30	K/T	EN	Evening meal: $90pp
2 Rooms	$250	$290		SK	EN	Guest rooms:
1 S/C cottage	$300	$300	$100	K + 2S	EN	Ambience:
Two rooms have baths as well as showers.						Setting/location:

LOW   HIGH

Wellington by night.

Sunset over Ngarahoe.

Rotorua

Bistro 1284 1284 Eruera St,
Tel: (07) 346-1284. Award winning
restaurant. Great food, great service.
**Cableway Restaurant & Bar @
Skyline Rides** Fairy Springs Rd,
Tel: (07) 347-0027. Buffet style
food with 180 degree views of
Rotorua. Very popular.
Capers Café 1181 Eruera St,
Tel: (07) 348-8818. Large deli-style
café. Licensed.
Lime Caffeteria Café
Cnr Fenton & Whakaue Sts,
Tel: (07) 350-2033. Very modern
licensed café with a touch of retro.
Relish Café 1149 Tutanekai St,
Tel: (07) 343-9195. Wood-fired
food cooked in a manuka fire, all
day breakfasts. Licensed.
You and Me 1119 Pukuatua St,
Tel: (07) 347-0368. Silver service,
excellent menu.

Events
Enquire about the various Maori
cultural experiences available.
Rotorua Marathon
May - held annually

Lake Tarawera

**Tarawera Landing Restaurant &
Café** Lake Tarawera, 2kms past the
Buried Village, Tel: (07) 362-8502.
Idyllic setting to enjoy great food.
Open at 9am. Fine dining from 6pm.

Taupo

Bay Bar & Brasserie
703 Acacia Bay Rd, Acacia Bay,
Tel: (07) 378-8886. Wood fired
pizzas, bar.
Brew Juice & Espresso Bar
4 Marama Arc, Tel: (07) 378-5779.
Fully licensed. Great food and
coffee.
Pimentos 17 Tamamutu St,
Tel: (07) 377-4549. Intimate
atmosphere. Excellent food.
Plateau 64 Tuwharetoa St,
Tel: (07) 377-2425. Licensed.
A classic New Zealand meeting
place for locals and visitors alike.
The Bach 2 Pataka Rd, Lake Tce,
Tel: (07) 378-7856. Fine wine, fine
dining and wonderful lake views.
Villino 45 Horomatangi St,
Tel: (07) 377-4478. World class
cuisine, elegant atmosphere.
**Wairakei International Golf
Course - Clubhouse Café**
SH 1, Wairakei International Golf
Course, Tel: (07) 374-8152. Good
view of the 18th hole and cross
section of café fare available.

Zest Deli Café 65 Rifle Range Rd
Tel (07) 378 5397. A good place to
go if you want to sit in the sun.

Events
Ironman NZ Triathlon
March - held annually – one of NZ's
biggest sporting events of the year.

Taihape

Brown Sugar Café Huia St,
Tel: (06) 388-1880

Ohakune

Franz Alpine Cafe Cnr Clyde &
Miro St, Tel: (06) 385-9183.
Popular with the locals. Classic
European dinners.
**The Matterhorn Restaurant/The
Powderkeg** Bottom of the
Mountain Rd, Tel: (06) 385-8888.
Great for both fine dining and as
an après-ski venue.
Utopia Cafe 47 Clyde St,
Tel: (06) 385-9120. Good coffee,
food and music. Open fire. Licensed.

Tongariro River.

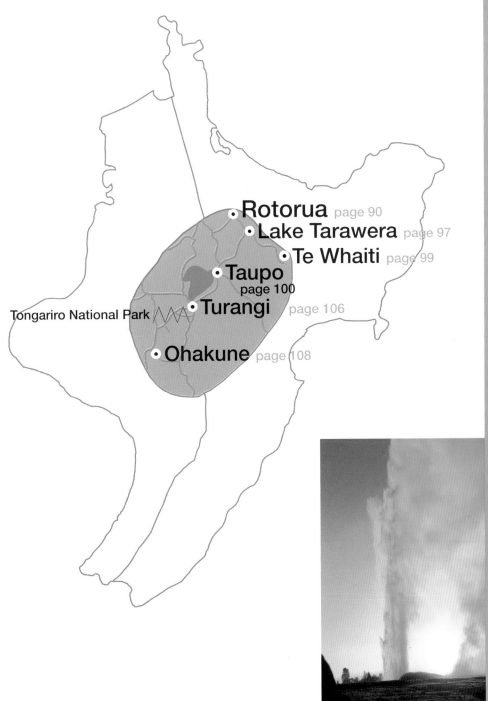

Rotorua

Lake Tarawera

Te Whaiti

Taupo

Tongariro National Park

Turangi

Ohakune

Sunset, Pohutu Geyser.

The Home of Hardy

Brent and Shirley Hardy
104 Parawai Road, Ngongotaha, Rotorua
Tel: (07) 357 4753   Mob: 021 959192
Fax: (07) 357 4758
shirley@hardy.co.nz
www.lodgings.co.nz/homeofhardy.html

Property features
Lakefront/spa pool
Cottages have courtyard/BBQ
Laundry plus own lounge
Petanque/croquet/gardens
Billiard table/guest lounge/Sky TV
High speed internet in cottages
Local features
Museum
Golf course
Thermal attractions
Kayaking/canoe

Ngongotaha - 5 mins drive
Rotorua - 10 mins drive

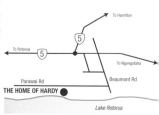

On SH 5 from Rotorua travelling north pass through lake roundabout Take second turn on right into Beaumont Road, second turn on right into Parawai Road.

In the guestbook at The Home of Hardy there is constant reference to the thoughtful touches - packaged picnics, fresh flowers, canoes, advice about places and tours, provided fishing equipment and Brent's freely offered advice from his own long fishing experience. But while the theme of the lodge is definitely trout fishing, with mounted trophies, artwork and rods providing much of the decoration, there are many reasons to stay in this delightful property set right on the lakes edge overlooking Mokoia Island. During a sumptuous breakfast cooked by Shirley and served on the sunny deck, thirty cormorants had lined up on the jetty from which a boat takes guests out onto the lake if they don't want to caste from the shore. A large wood burner in the comfortable guest lounge at the front of the house warmed the cooler evenings and guests gathered around the bar, played pool or watched television. On the other side of the dining room is a large lounge/library. Both open to the deck and the lawn. There are three ensuite bedrooms in the house and down the long paved driveway, set amongst tall trees are three, perfectly appointed, fully equipped, self-contained brick cottages each with a private garden and outdoor decking.

Family cat on site
Guest pets by arrangement

Accommodation available (NZ$)	👤	👥	+👤	🛏	🛁
2 S/C Cottages		$235	$30	Q+2S	EN
3 Rooms	$190	$220		Q	EN
1 Room	$220	$240		Q	EN
1 S/C cottage		$265	$50	Q + 2S	EN

Lunch also avail. for $30 please enquire. Cooked breakfast avail. $20pp.

Breakfast: Continental
Evening meal: $60pp
Guest rooms:
Ambience:
Setting/location:

LOW   HIGH

Property features
Lakefront position
Private fishing - Ngongataha River
Large established garden
Experienced fishing guide on site

Local features
Fly fishing-30 yards from cottage
Thermal pools
Farm Shows
Off-road 4x4 self drive
Luge and gondola

Trewillows
Dennis and Robyn Ward
6 Manuariki Avenue, Ngongotaha, Rotorua
Tel: (07) 357 4974   Mob: 025 2849889
Fax: (07) 357 4974
fishing@clear.net.nz
www.lodgings.co.nz/trewillows.html

Ngongotaha - 2 min walk
Rotorua - 10 minutes

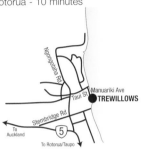

Ngongotaha is just off SH 5 to the
north of Rotorua. From Ngongotaha
township take Taui St towards the
lake. Turn right into Manuariki Ave,
Trewillows is at the end.

Trewillows is sited in an acre of established gardens, and located alongside the Ngongotaha Stream and Lake Rotorua. Of brick construction this cottage stands away from the hosts' home and seconds away from the lakefront and stream. The two bedrooms, full laundry facilities, well equipped kitchen including dishwasher, full size dining table and chairs and extensive garden - I thought it would be a great spot for a longer stay. There is good use of native timbers and modern amenities such as television, sound system and heating. The theme of the décor is hunting and fishing, which is fitting as Dennis is a professional fishing guide. I can just imagine setting up here, sending my partner off fishing and finding a shady spot under one of the large willows on the edge of the river to read my book. After such a strenuous day, the ideal conclusion would be a tall gin and tonic on the private verandah watching the world pass by. Comments in the guest book often refer to the generous hospitality of the hosts, an indication that you can be as private or as interactive with the hosts as you like. A quote from one Auckland guest ended with: 'Thank you for a memory that will last forever'.

Family pets on site	Accommodation available (NZ$)	👤	👥	+👤	🛏	🛁
Breakfast: Continental	1 S/C cottage	$195	$225	$25	Q+2S	PR

Guest rooms:
Ambience:
Setting/location:

Email/computer available in hosts home.

91

Nicara Lakeside Lodge

Heather and Mike Johnson
30-32 Ranginui Street, Ngongotaha, Rotorua
Tel: (07) 357 2105 Mob: 021 838424
Fax: (07) 357 5385
info@nicaralodge.co.nz
www.lodgings.co.nz/nicara.html

12

Property features
Lake views/lodge jetty
Security safe/trouser press in rooms
TV with DVD viewing
Refrigerator/tea/coffee facilities
Broadband internet connection
Kayaks

Local features
Tourist attractions
Trout fishing
Mud pools
Geysers

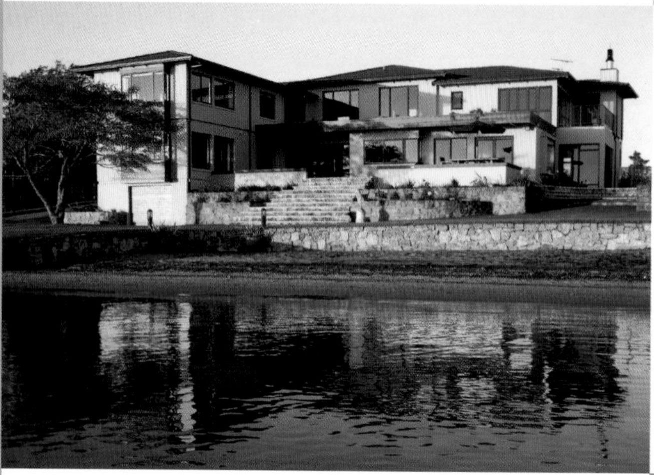

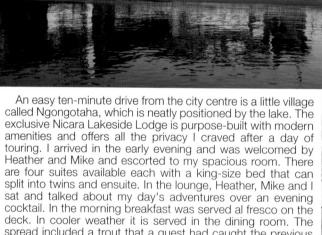

Ngongotaha - 3 minute drive
Roturua - 10 minute drive

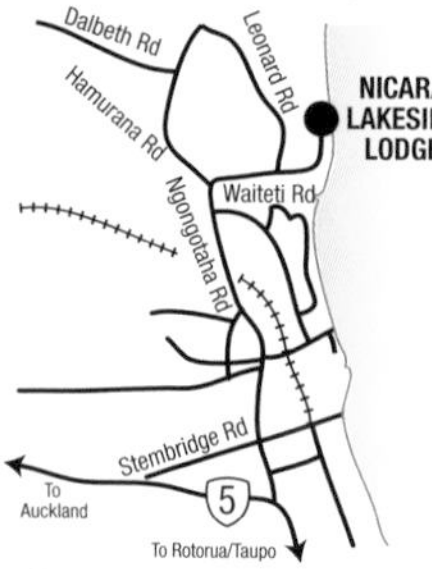

From Rotorua take SH5 to roundabout. Turn right to travel north through Ngongotaha. Cross railway line, turn right into Waiteti Road and then left at T junction into Ranginui St, Nicara is 0.5km on right.

An easy ten-minute drive from the city centre is a little village called Ngongotaha, which is neatly positioned by the lake. The exclusive Nicara Lakeside Lodge is purpose-built with modern amenities and offers all the privacy I craved after a day of touring. I arrived in the early evening and was welcomed by Heather and Mike and escorted to my spacious room. There are four suites available each with a king-size bed that can split into twins and ensuite. In the lounge, Heather, Mike and I sat and talked about my day's adventures over an evening cocktail. In the morning breakfast was served al fresco on the deck. In cooler weather it is served in the dining room. The spread included a trout that a guest had caught the previous day. It tasted superb and spurred me on to book a guided fishing trip for the next day. After dinner I sat outside absorbing the peace of the manicured gardens and in the distance a floatplane winged its way across the sky. My hosts told me that the plane can be hired if guests want to make a grand arrival at the lodge but, more commonly, people hire it to take a scenic flight and then be dropped off at the at Nicara's jetty.

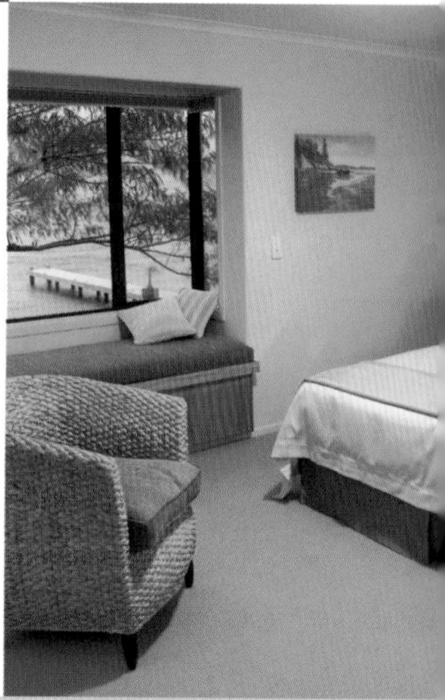

Accommodation available (NZ$)			+		
2 Rooms	$350	$400		K	EN
2 Rooms	$400	$450		K	EN

Family cats on site

Breakfast: Cooked

Guest rooms:
Ambience:
Setting/location:

LOW HIGH

Self contained cottage available on application.

Property features
Separate guest lounge
Rural and lake views
Deer and ostrich farm tour avail
Email/computer available
Petanque court and boules

Local features
Guided fishing trips arranged
Horse riding - farm and forest
Golf courses 5 within 20 mins
Traditional Maori hangi & concerts
Thermal attractions nearby

Clover Downs Estate
Lyn and Lloyd Ferris
175 Jackson Rd, Ngongotaha, Rotorua
Tel: (07) 332 2366   Mob: 021 712866
Fax: (07) 332 2367   Free: 0800 368753
reservations@cloverdowns.co.nz
www.lodgings.co.nz/cloverdowns.html

Ngongotaha - 5 minutes
Rotorua - 15 minutes

From Rotorua take SH5 to
roundabout. Turn right to travel north
through Ngongotaha. Cross railway
line, take third turn left into Central
Road and then first turn right into
Jackson Road.

On one side, the large, modern, brick home overlooks the green, gently rolling pastures of this six-acre lifestyle farm. On the other, is the distant blue spread of Lake Rotorua. The guest suites, which are in one wing of the house, are roomy and luxurious with pleasant views of the garden and the surrounding countryside. I was lucky enough to wake up to the sight of two graceful deer grazing in the paddock nearby. The layout of the house allows guests to be sociable or private. There is plenty of space, comfortable furniture, thoughtful touches and other amenities in the suites if you want to spend time alone, but there is also a charmingly appointed lounge dedicated to guest use and, at the front of the house, a very large communal bricked patio which is a wonderful spot to relax when the weather is warm and the sun shines. Breakfast might be served there or at the table in the dining room off the kitchen. I enjoyed the special treat of venison sausages made from meat produced on the farm. Don't miss the entertaining and informative tour around the lifestyle block and to watch a sheep dog working.

Family dogs on site
Guest pets by arrangement

Breakfast: Special continental

Guest rooms:
Ambience:
Setting/location:

	Accommodation available (NZ$)	🧍	🧍🧍	+🧍	🛏	🛁
	1 Room	$190-280	$205-300	$90	SK/T	EN
	2 Room	$220-320	$235-335	$90	SK/T	EN
	1 Room	$190-280	$205-300		K	EN

Off-season specials.

Country Villa

Anneke and John Van der Maat
351 Dalbeth Road, Ngongotaha, Rotorua
Tel: (07) 357 5893   Mob: 027 2726807
Fax:(07) 357 5893
countryvilla@xtra.co.nz
www.lodgings.co.nz/countryvilla.html

Property features
Sep guest lounge/piano/log fire
Quiet rural setting/views
Historic Victorian style home
Large landscaped gardens
Dutch spoken
Local features
Agrodome/Rainbow Fairy Springs
Golf courses nearby
White water rafting
Maori cultural activities
Thermal reserves

Rotorua - 12 minutes
Taupo - 1 hour

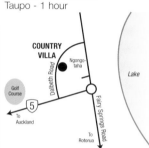

As you approach Rotorua on SH5
you can turn left into Dalbeth Rd at
Lake View Golf Course or turn left at
roundabout towards Ngongotaha and
left again over railway crossing into
Dalbeth Rd.

Anneke and John have lived in New Zealand for 38 years now, but throughout their new home there are decorative touches that indicate their Dutch origins. This large Victorian-style villa was built in Auckland in 1906, but it was in sad repair when, 90 years later, the couple bought it, transported it to a bare paddock on a hill close to Rotorua, and completely reconstructed it. Now, surrounded by a maturing garden, it looks as if it has never stood anywhere else. The interiors are comfortable and soothing and there is a gentle tempo about the place. Downstairs a guests lounge is cosily set up for cooler evenings with a comfortable semi-circle of settees around a large wood stove. The bedrooms are light and uncluttered with embroidered white linen and vases of fresh roses from the garden. The ensuites gleam with white tiling. Upstairs, accessed from one room in the two-bedroom suite, is a delightful hideaway alcove in a turret and adjacent to it a small attic-shaped room with television and coffee and tea-making facilities. Recently added is The Loft, a self-contained unit with open-plan living and a private entrance.   Anneke surprised me at breakfast with egg crepes, ham, mushrooms and Hollandaise sauce and spicy Dutch breakfast cake.

Accommodation available (NZ$)	👤	👤👤	+👤	🛏	🛁	
3 Rooms	$195-235	$215-255	$85	Q	EN	Breakfast: Cooked
1 Suite	$215-235	$235-275	$85	Q + 3S	PR	
1 S/C unit	$175-200	$175-200	$25	SK or 2S	PR	Guest rooms:

Two adjoining upstairs rooms can be booked as a suite.

Ambience:
Setting/location:

LOW   HIGH

Peppers On The Point - Lake Rotorua

David Smail
214 Kawaha Point Road, Rotorua
Tel: (07) 348 4868   Mob: 027 2451101
Fax:(07) 348 1868
onthepoint@peppers.co.nz
www.lodgings.co.nz/onthepoint.html

Property features
Private beach
Gymnasium
Tennis court
Massage therapy room
Billiard room
Local features
Maori culture
Geothermal wonders
Lakes/fishing
Numerous tourist attractions

Rotorua - 10 minute drive
Auckland - 3 hour drive

From Fairy Springs Rd, turn into Kawaha Point Rd. Follow the brown signs saying lodges, number 214, is at the very end. If the gate is closed ring the bell, drive in to the front of the house.

A short ten-minute drive from Rotorua, Peppers on the Point is luxurious accommodation with panoramic views over Lake Rotorua to Mokoia Island. I had the choice of staying in the Lake Cottage Suite, with a large deck and open-air spa bath; the Lake Villa, a four-bedroom home with extensive lake views; or one of the classic suites. I decided on one of the spacious classic suites, enticed by its large ensuite and spa bath and seeing myself enjoying a book and relaxing in the lovely surrounds. After settling in, I walked along the track, which winds through the native forest on the property and then headed for the private beach. Back at the lodge, I was tempted to indulge in a massage and beauty treatment in the on-site therapy room, but decided instead to relax on the deck in the sun. Dinner, prepared by the resident chef, was a good example of beautifully presented, New Zealand cuisine. From the underground cellar, where a wide range of the best New Zealand wines is stored, I selected my own bottle of wine. Peppers on the Point is a memorable retreat with everything guests need to celebrate the good things in life.

Family cat on site
Guest pets by arrangement

Breakfast: Cooked
Evening Meal: Included
Guest rooms:
Ambience:
Setting/location:

Accommodation available (NZ$)	♟	♟♟	+♟	🛏	🛁
1 Suite	$1175	$1564	$300	SK/T	EN
6 Suites	$1007	$1338	$300	SK/T	EN
2 Suites	$1007	$1338	$300	SK/T	EN
1 Lake Villa	$2812.50	$2812.50			PR

Lake Villa is priced for whole house (4 bedrooms, 2 bathrooms), B&B only.

Koura Lodge

David and Gina Wells
209 Kawaha Point Road, Rotorua
Tel: (07) 348 5868   Mob: 021 1191000
Fax:(07) 348 5869
stay@kouralodge.co.nz
www.lodgings.co.nz/kouralodge.html

Property features
Lakeside open-air spa pool
Finnish sauna/massage/gym fac.
Watercraft on site/canoes/windsurf
Guided boat & fly fishing by arrang
Complimentary green fees
On site astrograss tennis court

Local features
Airport - 15 minutes drive
Gondola and luge - 2 mins
Geothermal parks 10-30 mins
Maori culture and Hangis

Rotorua - 5 minutes drive
Tauranga - 45 minutes drive

Koura Lodge is located at Kawaha Point just 5 mins drive from the city centre and 15 mins from Rotorua Airport.

Koura Lodge is situated near the tip of Kawaha Point, a leafy peninsula on the western shore of Lake Rotorua. The Lodge is just five-minutes drive from the city centre, but secluded from traffic noise and sulphur fumes. This unique lake-front retreat nestles in a peaceful garden setting with panoramic views over the lake. It has a variety of accommodation from bedrooms with ensuite bathrooms, plus spa-bath options, to a self-contained family apartment. Guests can swim from the private beach, then warm up in the open-air spa by the lake. The Lodge also has a Finnish Sauna and massages available. The private jetty is an ideal starting point for floatplane and boating excursions. Complimentary green fees make a round of golf popular at the nearby 18-hole golf course. The breakfast buffet offers European breads, sliced meats, seasonal fresh fruit, cooked offering and more. Finnish soapstone fireplaces throughout ensure that Koura Lodge is warm and inviting in summer or winter. Koura Lodge can be booked exclusively for boutique weddings and small corporate functions and teambuilding.

Accommodation available (NZ$)	👤	👤👤	+👤	🛏	🛁	
3 Rooms	$195	$235		2K or 2S	EN	Breakfast: Special continental
1 Suite		$235-335	$50	Q+2S	EN	
3 Spa suites		$295		K	EN	Guest rooms:
1 S/C Apt		$395-495	$50	K+2Q	ENx2	Ambience:
						Setting/location:

LOW   HIG

Property features
Breathtaking lake & mountin view
Peaceful & tranquil lake retreat
Tennis/petanque/playground/spas
Trout fishing guide onsite
Local features
Buried village 5 min walk
Restaurants/cafés 5 min walk
Water taxi to Tarawera Falls walk
Scenic cruises of Lake Tarawera
Mountain bike/hiking trails
Rotorua Maori culture/geysers

Lake Tarawera Lodge

Jeff and Janine Oakes
19 Te Mu Road, RD5, Rotorua
Tel: (07) 362 8754   Mob: 027 2772676
Fax:(07) 362 8704
stay@laketarawera.co.nz
www.lodgings.co.nz/laketarawera.html

Rotorua - 15 mins drive
Taupo/Tauranga - 60 mins drive

Leave Rotorua on route 30, continue through the first set of traffic lights, turn right at the round-about, into Tarawera Road. 13km and 500m past Buried Village, turn left into Te Mu Road Lodge is at end.

Just an easy fifteen-minute drive from Rotorua, past lakes and dense native forest, the six cottages of Tarawera Lodge present an opportunity to experience some spectacular scenery of the North Island. The cottages, surrounded by native trees, are built on a five-acre, terraced section landscaped with natives and exotic trees planted in the 1800's when the property was a mission. Each cottage has been placed for privacy and the amazing view over the lake and looming bulk of the famous Mount Tarawera. Each has its own patio, undercover parking and barbecue area, with well-presented, functional interiors that have different sleeping configurations and are warm, comfortable and well-equipped. The lodge is suitable for couples, families, fishermen and those who like a wild environment served up with creature comforts. Jeff is a fly-fishing guide and can take you to the many fisheries around the area. Close by are all the attractions of the Rotorua area, but I preferred to stay on site and enjoy the tennis court, the forest walks, playground and spa pool. I could also have gone kayaking, fishing, or on a scenic cruise on the lake. The cottages are self catering but with prior notice and a small fee my hosts stocked the kitchen before I arrived.

Accommodation available (NZ$)	👤	👥	+👤	🛏	🛁
3 S/C cottages	$195	$225-255	$30	Q+4S	EN
2 S/C cottages	$195	$245-275	$30	Q+Q	EN
1 S/C cottage	$195	$245-275	$30	Q+K or 2S	EN

Breakfast: Provisions Extra $15pp

Guest rooms:
Ambience:
Setting/location:

LOW   HIGH

97

Pukeko Landing

Essence of New Zealand
6 Ronald Road, Lake Tarawera, Rotorua
Tel: 027 5424202
Fax: (07) 574 8096   Free: 0800 ESSENCE (3773623)
stay@essencenz.com
www.lodgings.co.nz/pukeko.html

Property features
Swim, fish & boat from own jetty
Private bushwalk & birdwatching
Sun facing view of tranquil lagoon
Petanque & picnic on lawn
Local features
Guided trout fishing
Scenic/fishing helitours
Scenic floatplane tours
Jet-skiing/natural hot pools
Hiking trails/volcanic tours
Buried Village/cultural experiences

Rotorua - 15 mins drive
Taupo - 1 hour drive

From SH33 (Te Ngae Rd) turn into Tarawera Rd. After approx 13 km's continue straight ahead into Spence Rd. Travel another 7 km's to Ronald Rd on your right. Pukeko Landing is 300m on the left.

As the road meandered closer to Pukeko Landing, I managed to catch a glimpse of beautiful Lake Tarawera between the hedgerows. Once there, I never wanted to leave! I enjoyed dining on the deck in the evening, looking across the water, listening to the surrounding bird song. The step-down deck area with a large extendable umbrella is perfect any time of day. From the house, guests can wander down the landscaped path to the water's edge and relax on the private jetty sipping a cool drink or play a game of petanque on the lawn. Clearwater Charter Boats are nearby for organising lazy days on the lake, trips to the thermal springs, or fishing, water skiing and wet biking for the more adventurous. This well appointed three bedroom lakeside cottage is perfect for a couple, a family or group of friends. Although the open plan kitchen, dining and indoor/outdoor living encourages gatherings, the bedrooms are private and chic. I must mention how I soaked in the master bedroom ensuite's bath, gazing out to the expanse of the lagoon. I had a truly memorable stay at this special place in a delightful and typically New Zealand environment.

Accommodation available (NZ$)	🧍	🧍🧍	+🧍	🛏	🛁
1 S/C house					
High Season	$1,114	$100	2SK/2S	EN	
Low Season	$889	$100	+2S	+PR	

Breakfast: Provisions provided
Evening meal: Enquire
Guest rooms:
Ambience:
Setting/location:

LOW   HIG

Chef available by prior arrangement. Charges apply. Tariff is for up to 4 people.

Property features
Indoor/outdoor spa pool
Panoramic views/farmland/rainforest
Deer, cattle and sheep on farm
Home grown vegetables/fruits
Native timbers in home & furniture
Local features
Whirinaki Forest Park
Te Urewera National Park
Bush walks/fly fishing/bird watching
Painting/photography sites
Professional guides available

Rotorua - 70 mins drive
Taupo/Whakatane - 80-100 min drive

Hukitawa Country Retreat
Lesley Handcock
Minginui Road, Te Whaiti, via Rotorua
Tel: (07) 366 3952
Fax:(07) 366 3950
lesley@hukitawa.co.nz
www.lodgings.co.nz/hukitawa.html

Directions will be forwarded when you make your booking.

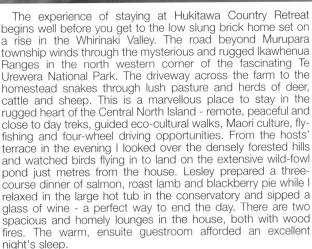

The experience of staying at Hukitawa Country Retreat begins well before you get to the low slung brick home set on a rise in the Whirinaki Valley. The road beyond Murupara township winds through the mysterious and rugged Ikawhenua Ranges in the north western corner of the fascinating Te Urewera National Park. The driveway across the farm to the homestead snakes through lush pasture and herds of deer, cattle and sheep. This is a marvellous place to stay in the rugged heart of the Central North Island - remote, peaceful and close to day treks, guided eco-cultural walks, Maori culture, fly-fishing and four-wheel driving opportunities. From the hosts' terrace in the evening I looked over the densely forested hills and watched birds flying in to land on the extensive wild-fowl pond just metres from the house. Lesley prepared a three-course dinner of salmon, roast lamb and blackberry pie while I relaxed in the large hot tub in the conservatory and sipped a glass of wine - a perfect way to end the day. There are two spacious and homely lounges in the house, both with wood fires. The warm, ensuite guestroom afforded an excellent night's sleep.

Accommodation available (NZ$)	👤	👤👤	+👤	🛏	🛁
1 Room	$280	$410		SK or 2S	EN
1 Room	$280	$400	$150	K or 2S	EN
1 Room	$280	$390		D	EN
1 Room	$280	$390		K/2S or 2S	GS

Guest pets by arrangement

Breakfast: Cooked
Evening Meal: Included
Guest rooms:
Ambience:
Setting/location:

LOW   HIGH

All meals, including lunch, are included in the tariff.

99

Paeroa Lakefront Homestay

Barbara and John Bibby
21 Te Kopua Street, Acacia Bay, Taupo
Tel: (07) 378 8449   Mob: 027 4818829
Fax:(07) 378 8446
bibby@reap.org.nz
www.lodgings.co.nz/paeroa.html

Property features
Lakefront location
Separate guest lounge
Flower filled garden
Private beach/dinghy available
Fishing charters
Local features
Taupo Hot Springs
Trout fishing/boat sightseeing
Tongariro National Park/walks
Jet boating/golf
Close to good restaurants

Taupo - 5 minutes
Rotorua - 1 hour

Just north of Taupo take Norman Smith St towards Acacia Bay. Take third street left into Acacia Bay Rd. When this road splits take left hand branch to stay on Acacia Bay Rd. First turn left is Te Kopua St.

Before moving to this stunning lakeside location, John and Barbara operated a farmstay for eighteen years - these two know what they are doing. The home could have been purpose-built as it works so well for guest accommodation. Spread over three levels are the penthouse suite, the guest wing on the second level or the ground floor that also contains a separate guest lounge. Elevated above the lake much of the house, including the three guestrooms, has panoramic views over Lake Taupo. There are several areas to relax in - a balcony, patio and the private courtyard - you should have no problem finding sun, shade or shelter. The penthouse room is probably my favourite. On the third floor it provides the most expansive views over Taupo township, the lake and the mountains and has a private patio, a spa bath and a super-king sized bed. Guests can meander through an established garden down to the lakefront where you are unlikely to be disturbed. Here you can find a shady spot under a tree, take the dinghy out for a quiet row, swim, sunbathe, take a fishing or sightseeing trip from the jetty or just admire the view.

Accommodation available (NZ$)	👤	👥	+👤	🛏	🛁			
1 Room	$200-250	$225-300		K	EN	Breakfast: Special cooked		
1 Room	$200-300	$225-300	$75	Q+S	EN	Evening meal: $45pp		
1 Room	$280-350	$280-350		K	EN	Guest rooms:		

Ambience:
Setting/location:

LOW   HIGH

Phone available in guest lounge. Evening meal by prior arrangement.

Property features
Swimming pool
Kitchen facility
Local features
Four golf courses - 10mins
Lake Taupo 5 mins walk
Guided river fishing
Charter boating and fishing
Walking and sightseeing

Karaka Cottage

Delia Barnes
42 Gillies Avenue, Taupo
Tel: (07) 378 4560   Mob: 027 4969432
Fax:(07) 378 4562
rugs@reap.org.nz
www.lodgings.co.nz/karakacottage.html

Taupo - 15 mins walk
Rotorua - 50 mins drive

From north on SH 1 turn left into Tamamutu St turn right into Rifle range Rd and turn left into Gillies Ave, 42 is on left around elevated corner.

This easily found cosy spot is a ten-minute walk away from the colourful and busy lakefront of Taupo, through what is known as the 'bird area' - where the streets are named after native birds. However guests may find it difficult to move on after enjoying the peace and quiet of sitting by the pool, smelling the roses and looking down to the lake and mountains in the distance. The cottage is perched on higher ground opening to a pool and is independent of the main house, where breakfast or dinner may be enjoyed by arrangement with Delia. Meals are always excellent as food is one of Delia's skills - but not the only one. Golf is second on the list and good local golfing can be organised for guests. She is also the diva of oriental rugs in New Zealand and you will find yourself surrounded by the interesting furniture and rugs. This comfortable character cottage has been purpose built for guests, I found all that I needed to help prepare my light dinner. There is an extra suite in the house if it is needed. Taupo has a variety of excellent restaurants, many outdoor pursuits and thermal spas, all within a short distance.

Accommodation available (NZ$)	👤	👥	+👤	🛏	🛁
1 S/C cottage	$250	$300	$40	K	EN
1 Room	$200	$280		K	EN
1 Room	$200	$280		Q	EN

Breakfast: Special cooked
Evening meal: $60pp+wine
Guest rooms:
Ambience:
Setting/location:

LOW   HIGH

Te Kowhai Landing
Essence of New Zealand
325 Lake Terrace, 2 Mile Bay, Taupo
Tel: 027 5424202
Fax: (07) 574 8096   Free: 0800 ESSENCE (3773623)
stay@essencenz.com
www.lodgings.co.nz/tekowhai.html

Property features
Full gourmet kitchen & alfresco dining
Dual living spaces, feature fireplaces
NZ contemporary art & sculpture
Spa pool/lake edge swimming
Row-boat/petanque/fly fishing
Lake views from every room

Local features
Guided trout fishing & hunting
International golf course
Water pursuits/aerial adventures
Restaurants/wine-tasting

Taupo - 35 mins walk/5 min drive
Rotorua - 45 mins drive

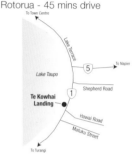

Te Kowhai landing is between the
lake edge and State Highway 1 at 2
Mile Bay, just north of the 'Sail
Centre'.

Approaching Te Kowhai Landing, which sits on the waters edge of Lake Taupo, I could not miss the striking road frontage that offers a barrier from the bustle of the road to the private haven within. Large entrance doors unveiled magnificent and intimate water views, through full-length double-glazed doors and windows. From here you either step upstairs where a bridge links two exclusive suites or down to the ground floor living that includes two separate living areas both with a fireplace, a full gourmet kitchen and indoor and outdoor dining spaces. The cosy underfloor heating was welcoming on a cool autumn day. I wished I had been able to stay here to enjoy the naturally inspired outdoor heated soak pool where you could listen to the water lapping and then cool off in the lake. The style and design detail of this purpose-built, self-contained lodge is exceptional and reminiscent of a typical New Zealand boatshed. Details include state-of-the-art wiring, which provides communications and conveniences with finger tip control. Stylish shops and restaurants are only a five-minute drive or 35-minute lake edge walk away. This is a wonderful base to access all that the Central Plateau of the North Island region has to offer.

Accommodation available (NZ$)					
1 S/C house					
High Season	$1,114	$100	2SK/Twin	2EN+1PR	
Low Season	$889	$100	2S in 2nd living room		

Breakfast: Provisions provided
Evening meal: Enquire
Guest rooms:
Ambience:
Setting/location:

Chef available by prior arrangement. Charges apply. Tariff is for up to 4 people.

LOW   HIGH

Property features
Lake views/terrace location
Sep guest lounge/fire/Sky TV
Spa baths/underfloor heating
Comp. Taupo airport transfer
Fishing tackle room/gear/tuition
Office facilities/loan mobile phone
Local features
Golf courses/thermal pools
Trout fishing guiding service
Guided walks/tours/lakesports
Restaurants/cafes - 5 mins

Albion Lodge

Susie and David Pierce
358 Lake Terrace, Two Mile Bay, Taupo
Tel: (07) 378 7788   Mob: 027 2159002
Fax: (07) 378 2966
boutique@albionlodge.co.nz
www.lodgings.co.nz/albionlodge.html

Taupo - 5 mins
Rotorua - 1 hour

From Taupo town centre follow SH1 along the lake side. After about 3.5 km you will see the Anchorage Motel on the left and the Albion signboard at the drive entrance - drive to the top.

Situated close to the lake's edge at Taupo, Albion is a fishing lodge if you want it to be and a great place to stay if you don't. The first thing I noticed was the alluring view over the water and town from the living area; the second was the interest Susie and David showed in my welfare. As I sat down to sip a glass of wine not long after my arrival, they helped me plan the days ahead. If I wanted to go angling, the lodge guide could take me or I could be taken on a guided tour around Taupo or Rotorua or the wineries of Hawke's Bay. They were happy to arrange any of the myriad of activities in the area. There are excellent golf courses nearby, including the Wairakei International Golf Course. The lodge cleverly combines comfort luxury and a relaxed ambience. When guests return at the end of the day (some had opted to do nothing at all) they gathered in the sumptuous lounge or the sheltered alfresco deck areas for drinks and to swap tales of their day's adventures. The companionable atmosphere begun around a fire and the pool table continued throughout the three-course dinner and well beyond.

Guest pets by arrangement	Accommodation available (NZ$)					
Breakfast: Cooked	3 Rooms	$175-255	$240-350	$75	SK or 2S EN	
Evening meal: $75pp	1 Room	$75	$100		SK or 2S GS	
Guest rooms:	Whole Lodge		$900 High			
Ambience:	Low Season		$700			
Setting/location:						

GS rm let in with 1 of the other rms. Rollaway bed & cot available.

LOW   HIGH

103

Lakedge

Tim and Leone Graves
14 Oregon Drive, Taupo
Tel: (07) 378 7834   Mob: 025 824404
Fax:(07) 378 7834
lakedge@reap.org.nz
www.lodgings.co.nz/lakedge.html

Property features
Purpose built/Italian tiled bathrooms
Lakeside uninterrupted views
Large deck overlooking lake
Kayaking from site
Local features
Three golf courses near
Hosts members Wairakei Int.
Many, varied outdoor activities
Thermal pools
Fly fishing

Taupo township - 5 mins drive
Rotorua - 50 mins drive

From the north take SH1 to Taupo.
Continue south on Lake edge and
turn right into Rainbow Drive. Turn
right again onto Oregon Drive.
Lakedge is No.14 on left. From
south take SH1 and turn left into
Rainbow Drive.

Tim and Leone demonstrate the warmth of New Zealand hospitality. As I explored this architecturally designed and purpose-built house, I discovered exciting views stretching across the lake to the Mt Ruapehu ski-field. Every modern comfort is provided in the spacious bedrooms which both have dressing rooms and lead from the upper floor to a deck where the moods of the lake can be observed in peace and quiet. Bathrooms are of a high standard with attractive Italian tiles and quality towels. Generous breakfasts are served in the dining room or alfresco on the decking. Three-course dinners are also available. Leone is an excellent cook and the menu may include smoked fish and seafood chowder followed by herb encrusted rack of lamb, accompanied by local wines. Tim and Leone are both golfing enthusiasts and are happy to either arrange games or play a round with guests at the Wairakei International Golf Course, where they are popular members. Swimming and walking can be accessed from the property which is on the lake edge, as the name suggests. You cannot be any closer to the water than this. Lake Taupo as a holiday venue grew famous because of spots like this.

Accommodation available (NZ$)				
2 Rooms	$230-260	$320-350	SK or 2S EN	

Breakfast: Special cooked
Evening meal: $60pp
Guest rooms:
Ambience:
Setting/location:

LOW   HIGH

Property features
Swimming pool/tennis court
Conservatory and courtyard
Three acres of garden
Petanque
Gazebo and pond
Separate guest lounge/dining
Complimentary laundry service
Local features
Lake activities/jet boats
Golf/hot pools/bungy jumping
Trout fishing

Taupo - 6 minutes
Rotorua - 1 hour

The Pillars

Ruth and John Boddy
7 Deborah Rise, Bonshaw Park, Taupo
Tel: (07) 378 1512
Fax: (07) 378 1511   Free: 0800 200983
enquiries@pillarshomestay.co.nz
www.lodgings.co.nz/pillars.html

South of Taupo township take SH 5 towards Napier. Drive approx. 6 kms and turn right into Caroline Drive. Turn left into Deborah Rise, The Pillars is on your right.

This modern country manor sits on five acres of park-like grounds with a rural view extending to the lake and mountains. There is also a lot of space in the house, a spacious lounge and conservatory, a large expanse of verandah and courtyard areas and guestrooms ranging from comfortable to huge. The décor is described as classical but certainly not so formal as to compromise comfort and relaxation. I stayed in the largest room which is very convenient for a long stay (but still delightful for just one night) with furniture such as a desk, lounge chair and couch, television and a huge ensuite bathroom with a dressing alcove. Ruth and John go the extra mile. Little extras like writing paper, herbal teas and plunger coffee, cookies, fruit, a choice of beverages and a complimentary bottle of wine in the room. As a guest I wanted for nothing. Taupo is just a short drive away but, like most people, I settled down here to take advantage of this mini-resort, which has a tennis court, swimming pool and large established gardens to wander through. An excellent breakfast was served in the dining room that looks out to the sunny and lavender-lined courtyard.

Family cats on site	Accommodation available (NZ$)					
Breakfast: Special continental	1 Room		$275		SK/T	EN
Evening meal: $65pp	1 Room		$375		CK/T	EN
Guest rooms:	1 Room		$475		CK/T	EN
Ambience:	1 Room		$275		K/T	EN
Setting/location:	Off-season discounts available. Internet sockets in 2 of the rooms.					

LOW   HIGH

Founders at Turangi

Peter and Chris Stewart
253 Taupahi Road, Turangi
Tel: (07) 386 8539   Mob: 025 854000
Fax: (07) 386 8534   Free: 0800 36863377
founders@ihug.co.nz
www.lodgings.co.nz/founders.html

Property features
Purpose built/all rooms ensuite
Guest lounge with open fire
Underfloor heating
Native flora in garden
TV lounge/library

Local features
Tongariro River - 5 min walk
Mt Ruapheu - 35 min drive
Tongariro Nat. Park - 10 min drive
Trout fishing/river & lake activities
Tramping/Tongariro Crossing walk

Turangi - 2 mins drive
Taupo - 40 mins drive

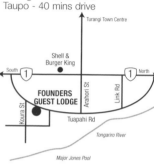

From Taupo, take SH1 to Turangi.
Turn left into Arahori St. At 'T'
junction turn right into Taupahi Rd,
travel 1km to lodge on left.

This purpose-built bed and breakfast is a good base from which to explore the Central Plateau and Taupo areas. During my stay, most guests were up early and off to hike the popular Tongariro Crossing track. Instead, I tried out the shorter Tongariro River walks, which are a five-minute stroll from Founders. From the bank of the river I watched anglers casting their fly-fishing rods against the backdrop of native bush and blue sky. Founders has underfloor heating throughout and the spacious lounge, with an open fire and comfortable seating I would imagine is cosy in winter when skiers return from the nearby ski fields of Mt Ruapehu. The wrap-around decking has a low-slung roof which is edged by a graceful wisteria vine. The deck leads into a garden full of New Zealand native plants. I enjoyed the friendly atmosphere as I sipped pre-dinner drinks with other guests and hosts, Chris and Peter. For dinner I headed for one of the nearby restaurants. The four, sound-proof, bedrooms are ensuite. Three have queen-size beds and one is a super-king or twin room. All doors open out to a deck. In the morning, Chris and Peter served a substantial, country-style breakfast from the large table in the kitchen. It fortified me for another day of action ahead.

Accommodation available (NZ$)	👤	👥	+👤	🛏	🛁	Family dog on site
3 Rooms	$120	$170		Q	EN	Breakfast: Special cooked
1 Room	$120	$170		SK or 2S	EN	

Guest rooms:
Ambience:
Setting/location:

LOW   HIGH

Property features
Well equipped fitness room
Admirals room - hot tub/TV/DVD
Broadband internet/Wi-fi
Air conditioning/SkyTV/DVD
Underfloor heating in bathrooms
Local features
Fly fishing - 2 min walk
Skiing/hiking
Golf/horse riding/swimming
Natural thermal pools - 10 min drive
Walking/kayaking/canoeing

River Birches

Gill Osborne
19 Koura Street, Turangi
Tel: (07) 386 0445   Mob: 027 4063650
Fax:(07) 386 0442
reservations@riverbirches.co.nz
www.lodgings.co.nz/riverbirches.html

Turangi - 2 mins drive
Taupo - 40 mins drive

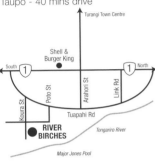

Turn into Arahori St opposite
Shell/Burger King, turn right into
Taupahi Rd. Second Rd on left is
Koura St. Cross the intersection.
River Birches is third house on left.

East meets west at this elegant single-level, cedar-clad lodge set along the banks of the Tongariro River. Native timbers, stone and concrete combine with soft natural hues and Eastern touches. Built and styled to meet every need of the discerning traveller, River Birches has three guestrooms, two lounge areas, a dining room and a dedicated fitness room. Named after nearby fishing pools: the Duchess Room looks out to a soothing water feature; the Major's Room is in a separate annex and has a patio area with a retractable roof making outdoor living possible, rain or shine; while the master bedroom, the Admiral's Room, is located at the other end of the lodge and has a private cedar hot tub and a Bali-style garden. All three guestrooms have private decks, spacious ensuites, underfloor heating, demister mirrors and heated towel rails, tea and coffee making facilities, IDD phone service, individual iPOD music stations and Wi-Fi and broadband internet access. From every room French doors open out to large decks and an expanse of country and native gardens. It is no wonder that fishing enthusiasts Zane Grey and the Duke and Duchess of York frequented this same location long ago, fly-fishing for trout in the world-famous Tongariro River at the doorstep.

Accommodation available (NZ$)	👤	👥	+👤	🛏	🛁
1 Room	$295	$325		K	EN
2 Rooms	$265	$295		K or 2S	EN

Breakfast: Special cooked
Evening meal: $50pp
Guest rooms:
Ambience:
Setting/location:

$750 for entire house.
Children permitted for single party bookings or by arrangement.

107

Cairnbrae House

Peter and Devon Mackay
140 Mangawhero River Road, Ohakune
Tel: (06) 385 3002   Mob: 027 2925491
Fax: (06) 385 3374
peterm@cairnbraehouse.co.nz
www.lodgings.co.nz/cairnbrae.html

(P) 👫 12 ✉ ♿   MasterCard VISA

Property features
View of Mt Ruapehu
Separate guest lounge with TV
Small Fallow deer farm
Tranquil setting
Local features
Mountain & scenic walks
Golf course
Tongariro crossing walk
Ski fields
Mountain biking/trout fishing
River rafting/kayaking/jet boating

Ohakune - 5 minutes
Taupo - 1 hr 30 mins

Turn west off SH49 in Ohakune towards Raetihi (at BP service station). Con't 7km. 100m past the Mangawhero Bridge turn right onto Mangawhero Rd. Travel 1km, Cairnbrae House is on right, after the bridge.

Peter and Devon extended me a warm welcome to their purpose-built, Cape Cod-style house surrounded by shrubs and flowers. Devon spent 14 years in the hospitality industry before coming to this part of the country and the couple run their four-bedroom accommodation with a good understanding of how to make people feel at home. The size and configuration of the bedrooms differ. Each has a rural or mountain outlook and is furnished in a practical manner with bathrooms that are light and roomy. A common guest lounge with views of the mountain is comfortably appointed with television, CD player, mini-bar and tea and coffee-making facilities, computer and fax - very snug after a walk in the alpine environment or a dip in the spa. In an enclosure behind the house the couple breed a herd of dainty fallow deer. Proximity to Tongariro National Park is also a big attraction and Peter takes guests to the Mangawhero River, which flows through property, to show them the good places to fish for trout. Devon cooks or smokes their catches. Unlucky fishermen have to make do with Devon's delicious venison, lamb or duck dishes, or steak barbecued under the willow trees down by the river.

Accommodation available (NZ$)	🧍	🧍🧍	+🧍	🛏	🛁	Family pets on site
1 Room	$120-130	$150-170	Q	EN		Breakfast: Special continental
1 Room		$160-180	K	EN		Evening meal: $50pp
1 Room	$120-130	$130-150	2S	PR		Guest rooms:
1 Room	$120-130	$140-160	D	PR		Ambience:
TV in guest lounge.						Setting/location:

LOW   HIGH

Lady in tube with snow capped volcanoes, Lake Taupo.

Coromandel

Peppertree Café & Bar
31 Kapanga Rd, Tel: (07) 866-8211.
Enjoy stylish dining in their
courtyard or verandah.
Try the mussel fritters.

Markets

The Bizarre 209 Kapanga Rd,
Tel: (07) 866-8948. On Friday
mornings this shop spills out
to the street becoming the local
produce market.

Whitianga

Café Nina 20 Victoria St,
Tel: (07) 866-5440. This 100-year
old miner's cottage serves great
food and strong coffee.

Colenso Café & Country Shop
Main Rd, Whenuakite,
Tel: (07) 866-3725. A must for
country cafe lovers, herbs straight
from garden. Just south of
Whitianga.

The Fire Place Restaurant
9 The Esplanade,
Tel: (07) 866-4828. Waterfront
location, great pizzas and seafood.

Tua Tua Restaurant & Bar
Upstairs 33 Albert St,
Tel: (07) 866-0952. Specialises in
seafood and tapas. Enquire about
live music.

Velocity 69 Albert St,
Tel: (07) 866-5858. Chic cafe with
great food and ambience.

Tairua

Shells Restaurant & Bar
Main Rd, Tairua, (07) 864-8811

Whangamata

Vibes Café 636 Port Rd,
Tel: (07) 865-7121. One of the top
spots for tasty counter food and
good coffee.

Waihi Beach

The Porch 23 Wilson Road,
Tel: (07) 863-1330. Casual
café/restaurant.

Hot Pipi Café
40 Beach Road, Waihi Beach, Tel:
(07) 863-5004. Beachy relaxed
café.

Sea kayaking - Cathedral Cove

Tauranga / Mt Maunganui

Astrolabe Café & Bar
82 Maunganui Rd, Mt Maunganui,
Tel: (07) 574-8155. Stylish with
good food, service and
atmosphere. Licensed.

Mediterraneo
62 Devonport Rd, Tauranga
Tel: (07) 577-0487

Sidetrack Café
Marine Pde, Mt Maunganui,
Tel: (07) 575-2145

Somerset Cottage Restaurant
30 Bethlehem Rd,
Tel: (07) 576-6889. Great service &
delicious food.

Gisborne

Verve Café 121 Gladstone Rd,
Tel: (06) 868-9095. A laid back café
serving excellent food & coffee.

Napier

Mission Restaurant 198 Church
Road, Greenmeadows, Napier
Phone: (06) 844-6048

Soak Café & Restaurant
42 Marine Parade,
Tel: (06) 835-7888. Enjoy the hot
saltwater pool complex, then dine
at the adjoining restaurant-café.

**Take Five Restaurant
and Jazz Bar** 189 Marine Parade,
Napier. Tel: (06) 835-4050

The Gintrap West Quay, Ahuriri,
Napier Phone: (06) 835-0199

Thorps Coffee House
40 Hastings St, Tel: (06) 835-6699.
A stylishly simple café, legendary
muffins.

Havelock North

Blackbarn Bistro Blackbarn Rd,
Tel: (06) 877-7985. The perfect
place to enjoy a light, fresh and
delicious menu.

La Postina Old Post Office,
Cnr Havelock and Napier Rds,
Tel: (06) 877-1714. European
cuisine with a New Zealand flavou

**Craggy Range Vineyards
Limited** 253 Waimarama Road,
Havelock North Tel: (06) 873-712€

Hastings

Te Awa Farm Winery Roys Hill Rc
SH 50, Tel: (06) 879-7602. A world
class wine and food experience.

RD1 & Mesa at Sileni Estates
2016 Maraekakaho Rd,
Tel: (06) 879-8768. Total food
and wine destination experience.

Vidal Estate Restaurant
913 St Aubyn Street East
Tel : (06) 876-8105. Open 7 days
for lunch and dinner as well as
brunch on Sunday

Markets

**Hawke's Bay Food Group
Farmers' Market** Every Sunday
8:30am-12:30pm. Hawke's Bay
Showgrounds, Kenilworth Rd,
Hastings, Tel: (06) 877-1001

Events

Brebner Print Art Deco Weeken€
February, Tel: (06) 835-0022.
A celebration of Napier's unique
Art Deco style.

Harvest Hawke's Bay
Early February. Tel: (06) 834-1919.
NZ's biggest and brightest
celebration of food and wine.

International Mission Concert
February, www.missionconcert.co.nz.
An outdoor concert held in a
natural amphitheatre at Mission
Estate.

Greytown

Salute 83 Main Street,
Tel: (06) 304-9825 Awarded
Wairarapas best restaurant 2003-
2004. Famous for its clean fresh
flavours from the Middle East and
Mediterranean.

Tastes Delicious 97 Main St,
Tel: (06) 304-8480. Excellent café
style food freshly prepared each day.

Wakelin House 123 Main St,
Tel: (06) 304-8869. Cuisine with a
classical Italian & French influence.

Martinborough

Café Medici 9 Kitchener St, Tel: (06) 306-9965. Great food, great coffee, great décor.
Coney Wines Drive River Road, Martinborough, Tel. (06) 306-8345 Cellardoor and vineyard café with outdoor courtyard. Open weekends and public holidays for lunch and tastings
Taste of Martinborough Cheese Shop 8 Kitchener St, Tel: (06) 306-8383. Perfect for lunch or to put together a picnic.
The French Bistro Kitchener Street, Martinborough, Tel. (06) 306-8863. Described by Cuisine Magazine as a real find offering "superb" cuisine & "the closest thing to a tiny family bistro in provincial France that we've visited in ages".

Mt. Maunganui Beach, The Bay of Plenty.

Driving Creek Villas

David Foreman
21A Colville Road, Coromandel Township
Tel: (07) 866 7755   Mob: 021 1166393
Fax: (07) 866 7753
reservations@drivingcreekvillas.com
www.lodgings.co.nz/drivingcreek.html

Property features
Private garden and reserve
Driving Creek Railway - 5 min walk
Fully equiped modern kitchen
TV/CD/DVD
Air conditioned/heated villas
Local features
Guided tour - Charles Rings house
Bush walks
Beautiful beaches
Restaurants/cafes

Coromandel - 5 mins
Thames - 1 hour

2km past the centre of Coromandel Township take the left hand fork to Colville. Driving Creek Villas is located 200 metres from here on your left.

Steeped in the history of its gold-mining past, Coromandel Township is located on a peninsula of land that sticks out like a thumb on the east coast of the North Island. The Coromandel itself is known in New Zealand for its spectacular beaches. These two new luxury villas are close to town and a short trip from the miniature Driving Creek Railway. The fully self-contained villas were purpose built and are colourfully decorated with Pacific Island colours. Each has large living areas, two bedrooms, and a sizeable bathroom. The villas are surrounded by native forest and rest beside a meandering stream. I particularly liked the punga logs that form a boundary around each private courtyard. Although the kitchen is fully equipped, the thought of the many restaurants just a five-minute's drive down the road proved irresistible. I also took the time to walk around the township and wander through the interesting shops and excellent art and craft boutiques. An alternative to eating out would have been to buy something from the Smoke Shop which has an exceptional selection of local seafood - a real treat if you like fish.

Accommodation available (NZ$)	👤	👤👤	+👤	🛏	🛁	
2 Villas	$175	$195-245	$25	1Q+2S	PR	

Breakfast: Extra charge $15pp
Evening meal: Enquire
Guest rooms:
Ambience:
Setting/location:

LOW   HIGH

Property features
Separate guest lounge
Historic places category 2
Historic home/antique furnishings
Local features
Historical significance
Coromandel stamper battery
Driving Creek railway and pottery
Art & craft galleries
Cafes and restaurants

Karamana (1872) Homestead

Judie and Ian Franklyn
84 Whangapoua Rd, Coromandel
Tel: (07) 866 7138
Fax:(07) 866 7138
reservations@karamanahomestead.com
www.lodgings.co.nz/karamana.html

Coromandel - 10 minutes walk
Whitianga - 45 minutes

On the coast road from Thames,
200 metres south of Coromandel
township, turn right into
Whangapoua Rd. Karamana is
approx. 1km on the right on a
sharp right-hand bend.

What a gem! This 1872 kauri villa has been passionately restored, lovingly furnished with antiques and is now an upmarket, intimate guesthouse. Karamana was transformed into bed and breakfast accommodation some years ago, and new owners, Judie and Ian, continue the theme. On the hot summer day I visited I enjoyed afternoon tea in the front garden under the sun umbrella. Inside, the old parlour is now the dining room, a light room overlooking the garden and a fitting venue for your silver service breakfast. Evening meals are available in the off-season and it is worth enquiring at other times, just in case. I have stayed in both double rooms and fell in love with the super-king, four-poster, Scottish antique bed in the middle room, although both have their own merits, personalities and access to verandahs and outdoor areas. Judie and Ian's quarters are separate and I was left to my own devices whenever I wanted. The cottage is in the old stables across the courtyard at the rear of the house - great if you want absolute privacy and can be semi self-catering. Karamana is an easy walk to Coromandel township which has an interesting history. It is recommended to take the hour tour of the Coromandel Gold Stamper Battery.

Accommodation available (NZ$)	🧍	🧍🧍	+🧍	🛏	🛁
1 Room	$110	$150-170		Q	EN
1 Room	$110	$150-170		SK	EN
1 Room	$110	$150-170		K/T	EN
1 Cottage	$110	$150-170	$30	Q+2S	EN

Breakfast: Special continental

Guest rooms:
Ambience:
Setting/location:

LOW   HIGH

Saltwater Lodge

John Phillips   Lesley Foote
4 Tui Terrace, Tairua
Tel: (09) 278 5006   Mob: 021 959921
Fax: (09) 278 9322
john@phillipsconsult.com
www.lodgings.co.nz/saltwater.html

Property features
CD stereo/selection classical CDs
VCR/selection of movies and DVDs
Full kitchens incl. microwave
Gas barbeques on deck
Broadband Internet
Panoramic river & harbour views
Own laundry facilities
Local features
Charter boats/fishing/diving/golf
Historic goldmine sites
Surf & family beaches/restaurants

Tairua - 5 mins walk
Whitianga - 40 minutes

From SH 1 south of Auckland drive east on SH 25 to Kopu. Continue on SH 25A over the hills to Hikuai, continue 9km to Tairua. Tui Tce is on your right approx. 1km before Tairua township.

Staying at one of these two spacious, semi-detached units set at a peaceful corner on the bank of the wide Pauanui/Tairua Estuary is like holidaying in a New Zealand bach (seaside cottage). One unit is at ground level and the other on the floor above. They are both tidy and spacious and overlook a stretch of tidal water to the conical peak of Tairua Head. The upstairs unit has two bedrooms and downstairs there are three. Both have sizeable lounges, dining areas, fully equipped kitchens, separate laundries and bathrooms, so they are ideal for families, couples and groups. They are presented in a simple style with everything guests need for a convenient and comfortable stay, including thoughtful details such as reading material, a petanque set, CDs, puzzles and games. Well-placed decks are ideal places to watch the small boats that ply the ever-changing estuary. A large flat lawn, accented by two huge pohutukawa trees and a variety of fruit trees, surrounds the house and is defined by a steep bank which drops off towards the water's edge. I was welcome to pick my own fruit from the small private orchard.

Accommodation available (NZ$)	🧍	🧍🧍	+🧍	🛏	🛁	
1 S/C unit	$90-175	$90-175	$20	Q+2KS	PR	Breakfast: Not available
1 S/C unit	$90-175	$90-175	$20	Q+3S	PR	

Surcharge of $40 charged for single night stays.

Guest rooms:
Ambience:
Setting/location:

LOW   HIGH

Coromandel Peninsula - Tauranga - Whakatane - Opotiki - Gisborne - Hawkes Bay - Wairarapa

Property features
Swimming pool/spa pool
Private patios for each guest room
Panoramic views of Tairua estuary/
Pauanui/Pacific Ocean/Slipper Island
All guest rooms are ensuite
Local features
Tairua Village - 15 min walk
White sandy beaches - 5 mins walk
Cathedral Cove - 1/2 hour drive
Hotwater Beach - 1/2 hour drive

Colleith Lodge
Maureen and Colin Gilroy
8 Rewa Rewa Valley Road, Tairua, Coromandel Peninsula
Tel: (07) 864 7970   Mob: 027 4721423
Fax: (07) 864 7972
welcome@colleithlodge.co.nz
www.lodgings.co.nz/colleithlodge.html

Thames - 35 mins drive
Auckland - 2 hour drive

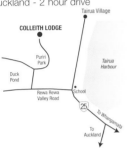

From Whangamata, take SH 25 north to Tairua. Just after the 50km sign, turn left into Rewa Rewa Valley Road. Turn right over cause-way and right into Puriri Park. Travel up hill to Colleith Lodge at top on left.

Set on a hill surrounded by one-and-a half acres of native bush, Colleith Lodge in the pretty seaside town of Tairua on the Coromandel Peninsula, has quality furnishings, comfortable spaces and tranquil surroundings. Sweeping panoramic views welcomed me from every room; Tairua Harbour, Pauanui, Slipper Island and the stretching Pacific Ocean. The green of New Zealand native bush and the green and blues of the Pacific Ocean were complimented by the honey-coloured hues of the kiln-dried, Hinuera natural stone that the lodge is built of. My queen-size bedroom with ensuite opened to a private patio, one of three bedrooms overlooking the swimming and spa pools and beyond to the ocean. In the early evening I sipped the New Zealand wine I'd chosen from the underground cellar and relaxed in one of the spacious living areas, before sitting down to a pre-arranged, three-course meal with Maureen and Colin. The following morning's breakfast included fresh tropical fruits grown on the property and an option of cooked dishes. For a day trip, Cathedral Cove and Hotwater Beach are both only a short 25-minute drive away. Colin is happy to arrange fishing trips for enthusiasts or guests are welcome to wander across the water in the two kayaks provided.

Family dog on site	Accommodation available (NZ$)	![person]	![two people]	+![person]	![bed]	![bath]
Breakfast: Special cooked Evening meal: $65 incl. wine	3 Rooms	$325	$350	$50	2Q+1SK 1 Rollaway	3 EN

Guest rooms:
Ambience:
Setting/location:

Phone in hall/TV available in guest room/evening meals all by prior arrangement/Wine from cellar available at extra cost.

Somerled Lodge

Mrs Valerie Palmer-Forbes   Dr Ian Forbes
442 Onemana Drive, Onemana, Whangamata
Tel: (07) 865 6200   Mob: 025 2227545
somerled@onemana.co.nz
www.lodgings.co.nz/somerled.html

Property features
Spectacular sea views
CD/stereo in guest rooms/laundry
Comp pre dinner wine & nibbles
One room has private courtyard
& kitchenette/BBQ/outdoor living
Lift to upper floor/VCR/TV
Local features
Swimming/diving/fishing/tramping
Quiet seaside village
Close to summer resort
Good restaurants nearby

Whangamata - 10 minutes
Thames - 45 minutes

Travel 6km north of Whangamata.
Take turnoff to Onemana. Continue
on to very top of road turning right a
T junction, then drive to top of cul-
de-sac.

Onemana is a small seaside village ten minutes north of Whangamata. It is a quiet, picturesque spot without the bustle of some of the bigger beaches of the Coromandel. Somerled Lodge is a large modern home located at the end of a residential cul-de-sac, with an elevated position overlooking Mayor Island, the Alderman Islands, and the Slipper Islands. These spectacular views are best seen from the spacious deck, and living areas upstairs. I stayed in the main guestroom, The Courtyard Suite, which is very roomy, with a private courtyard, kitchen facilities, barbecue, dining table, television, VCR, lounge furniture, a super-king-size bed (converts to twins) and a queen-size bed. It is very popular with couples, families and for longer stays. The Poseidon Room has a king-size bed, television and seating, and suits a shorter stay. Both guestrooms have sea-views and are privately located on the ground floor. Guests are welcome to wander upstairs to join their hosts or enjoy the spectacular views. In the morning on the deck I had an elegantly presented silver-service breakfast of fresh orange slices, strawberries, homemade muesli and French bread, croissants and muffins. With the view over ocean, islands and bright sky as a backdrop, it was a memorable event.

Accommodation available (NZ$)	♟	♟♟	+♟	🛏	🛁	Guest pets by arrangement
1 Room	Enquire	$275-295	$60	SK/2S+Q	PR	Breakfast: Special continental
1 Room	Enquire	$225-245		K	EN	

Bookings essential. Phone in hall. Enquire about childrens rates.
Discount applies for 2 nights or more.

Guest rooms:
Ambience:
Setting/location:

LOW   HIGH

Property features
German Black Forest style
Gourmet dining lounge
Massage and wellness
Treatments pre-book
Sauna$20pp/Spa$10pp
Glow worm grotto onsite
German & French Spoken

Local features
Bush-walks/river swimming
Golf-course 5 minutes
Surf/swimming beach

Whangamata - 10 minutes
Waihi - 30 minutes

**BUSHLAND PARK
NICKEL STRAUSSE**

Wentworth Valley Road
Across the river ford
To Tairua
Whangamata
Golf
To Waihi

Just south of Whangamata turn
right (at Golf course) into
Wentworth Valley Rd. Drive approx.
4km (100m past river ford) to the
lodge on your right.

Bushland Park Lodge & Nickel Strausse

Reinhard and Petra Nickel
Wentworth Valley Road, Whangamata
Tel: (07) 865 7468
bushparklodge@xtra.co.nz
www.lodgings.co.nz/bushland.html

Bushland Park offers its guests the opportunity of being pampered in a romantic escape and time to appreciate the five acres of beautiful New Zealand rainforest that surrounds the buildings. As only eight guests can be accommodated at any one time, this place is very restful and quiet. The owners and hosts, Reinhard and Petra, have blended European style with this very New Zealand environment at the base of the Coromandel Peninsula. Bushland Park has a European, old-world charm but also offers health-spa treatments and gourmet dining. My time was limited, and I had to choose between bush walking, resting beside the water lily pond or visiting the on-site, glow-worm grotto. If I'd wanted to leave the property, I could have found beaches and golf courses within a 10-minute drive. Guestrooms have a distinctive and elegant style. The two suites have separate lounges, televisions, fireplaces, private verandahs and stylish ensuite bathrooms. There are also two rooms, which have a shared balcony overlooking the bush-park, and suit guests who are travelling on a budget but don't want miss out the lodge's special atmosphere. Everything here has been done in empathy with the surrounding environment.

Breakfast: Special cooked
Evening meal: $75pp
Guest rooms:
Ambience:
Setting/location:

Accommodation available (NZ$)	👤	👥	+👤	🛏	🛁
2 Rooms	$200	$230		Q	EN
1 Room	$250	$300		SK/T	EN
1 Suite	$350	$380		SK/T	EN

Dinner: Set menu, special dietary or requests please pre-book
3 time finalists NZ Tourism Awards.

Waihi Beach Lodge

Greg Whyte   Ali Lawn
170 Seaforth Road, Waihi Beach
Tel: (07) 863 5818   Mob: 021 657888
Fax:(07) 863 5815
waihi.beach.lodge@xtra.co.nz
www.lodgings.co.nz/waihibeach.html

Property features
Sea and rural views
Many relaxing spaces/decks
2 minute stroll to beach
Email/computer available
Private guest entrances
TV and DVD's in all rooms
Local features
Handy to four café's
Karangahape Gorge walkways
Handy to golf courses
Mayor Island sightseeing/fishing

Tauranga - 40 minute drive
Auckland - 120 minute drive

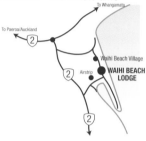

The Waihi Beach turn-off is off State
Highway 2 between Waihi and
Katikati. Wilson Road becomes
Seaforth Road which runs the length
of Waihi Beach.

Waihi Beach Lodge is an easy two-hour, scenic drive south of Auckland. Ali and Greg have created this new bed and breakfast 'beach getaway', which is located on the main road running parallel to the beach. It is a suitable staying place for anyone exploring the eastern coastline of the North Island, or for those who simply want to escape the city. The Beach Suite, on the ground floor at the rear of the house, is a simply decorated, studio-style unit. It has a queen-size bed, a pull-out couch, a dining table, television and DVD. There's also a small kitchenette, laundry and ensuite bathroom. Two private terraced areas catch the sun. There are also three guestrooms with ensuites, king-size beds, DVDs, televisions, and tea/coffee making facilities. The Matakana Room is upstairs inside the lodge. The Marlin and the Mayor Rooms are on the ground floor. They have doors leading out to private terraces and are styled in keeping with the beach theme. Breakfast is served upstairs in the dining room or al fresco on one of the patios that look out to Mayor Island and the Pacific Ocean. After a weekend at Waihi Beach Lodge and the beach walks, fishing, and great breakfasts, I left feeling relaxed and rejuvenated.

Accommodation available (NZ$)	👤	👥	+👤	🛏	🛁	
3 Rooms	$195	$195		K	EN	Breakfast: Special cooked
1 S/C unit	$195	$195		Q	PR	Evening meal: $50pp

Guest rooms:
Ambience:
Setting/location:

LOW   HIGH

Property features
Lounge/kitchenette/library
Stunning harbour/city/rural views
Unique garden/intimate weddings
Swimming pool/bbq/petanque
Tranquil private setting
Local features
Top golf courses/beaches
All water sports/fishing
Flying/gliding/parachuting
Beauty therapy/massage
Excellent restaurants/cafes

Tauranga - 15 minutes drive
Rotorua - 50 minutes drive

At Te Puna village, turn off SH2 into Minden Rd. Turn left into Dawn View Place. Then left into Elmwood Lane. Belvedere is at the end of the lane on the left.

Belvedere Boutique Accommodation

Suzanne and Russell Callander
Elmwood Lane, 7 Dawnview Place,
Minden, RD6, Tauranga
Tel: (07) 552 4838   Mob: 021 528062
Fax:(07) 552 4830
information@belvedere-web.com
www.lodgings.co.nz/belvedere.html

Belvedere, which in Italian means 'to view from a high place', is a romantic escape set on an acre of park-like gardens that overlook Mt Maunganui. This exclusive accommodation, nestled by native forest, can only be booked by one couple at a time. I was greeted warmly by Suzanne who gave me all the attention I needed and all the privacy I required. She took me through stable doors into a private garden, which led to my suite. There was a lot of detail in my room - even a choice of the pillow styles. Suzanne, who has travelled extensively, knows about personal comfort. I settled in, took a leisurely walk around the stunning gardens and then a dip in the pool. Later, I couldn't resist opening a bottle of Merlot from a local vineyard and, glass in hand, relaxed outdoors in the hammock provided. I didn't really want to leave the property for dinner but some of the restaurants in the area had been highly recommended. The next morning, I was alerted by the tinkling of a bell outside my door. At the entrance of the room I found a butler's trolley laid out with a wonderful breakfast. Belvedere was hard to leave.

Accommodation available (NZ$)					
1 Suite	$250	$350		SK or 2S PR	

Breakfast: Special cooked

Guest rooms:
Ambience:
Setting/location:

LOW   HIGH

Boscabel Lodge

Rosemary and Peter Luxton
98D Boscabel Drive, Tauranga
Tel: (07) 544 6647   Mob: 021 744441
Fax:(07) 544 6647
boscabellodge@yahoo.com
www.lodgings.co.nz/boscabel.html

Tauranga - 5 minutes drive
Rotorua - 1 hour drive

From SH 29 or SH 2 go towards Welcome Bay. Turn east into Welcome Bay Rd. Take the first right into Ohauiti Rd. Travel 3km and turn into Boscabel Dr. The lodge is towards the end down a shared drive.

The lodge is a large, modern mansion on a rise overlooking a sweep of rural and suburban land and the distant outline of the Kaimanawa Ranges, Mt. Maunganui and Mayor Island. Not long ago it was an avocado orchard. Rosemary and Peter and their two children are New Zealanders who have recently arrived back in the country and decided to put down roots in this sunny corner of the North Island. The house has many notable features. The colours and patterns of the Feng Shui tiling that covers the floors, patios and outdoor areas is integrated with the colourful drapes and furnishings. There are extensive spaces open to the sun and view and the ambience is cheerful and inviting. I stayed in one of the two family apartments, which are exceptionally roomy, with one double bedroom, one twin, a modern bathroom, fully furnished lounge and a kitchen with everything supplied. They are suitable for long-term stays. There is also a smaller suite for over-nighters. My apartment opened to a solar heated swimming pool, the spa pool and the extensive landscaped garden dotted with avocado trees. Special continental breakfasts are served to the apartments by arrangement. Staying here was a very pleasant experience.

Accommodation available (NZ$)	🧍	🧍🧍	+🧍	🛏	🛁	Family dog on site
1 Suite	$125	$150-160		Q	EN	Breakfast: Special continental
1 S/C unit	$145	$160-185		K+2S	PR	
1 S/C unit	$145	$160-185		Q+2S	PR	Guest rooms:
						Ambience:
						Setting/location:

Breakfast included in suite. Breakfast not included in S/C units, $10pp.

LOW   HIGH

Pohutukawa Beach B&B and Cottage

Jorg and Charlotte Prinz
693 State Highway 2, Pikowai
Tel: (07) 322 2182
Fax:(07) 322 2186
bnb@prinztours.co.nz
www.lodgings.co.nz/pohutakawa.html

Property features
Swimming pool
Finish dry sauna
Large garden
Organic cattle farm
Beach - 1 min walk
Local features
Active marine volcano, White Island
Swimming with dolphins
Te Urewera National Park
Game fishing/trout fishing
Rotorua Lakes/watersports

Whakatane - 25 mins drive
Te Puke - 25 mins drive

Our 35 acre lifestyle block is located directly on the Pacific Coast Hwy (SH2) at Pikowai; 8km west of Matata and 34km east of Te Puke. Look for signpost with blue B&B traffic signs.

I drove from the seaside highway up a short steep driveway to be met at the gate by a jubilant dog called Mystery. Smoke was drifting from the chimney of this renovated and redecorated farmhouse which has two comfortable and pleasantly decorated ensuite bedrooms for guests, a roomy lounge and dining area with large windows that face the sea. I immediately relaxed into the place, feeling as if I had come home. On the 34-acre hill farm, a small herd of organic cattle grazes and on the flat land, there is an orchard of citrus and feijoa trees and an organic vegetable garden. Much of my dinner that night was home grown. To one side of the house is an enclosed sunny courtyard with a swimming pool and sauna, and on the other side of that a well-appointed cottage which sleeps four. From the house and its extensive front garden there is a close view of sand dunes and sea through the spreading branches of a large pohutukawa tree. Sitting at breakfast guests can be lucky enough to see a pod of whales or dolphin slide by. Even orcas sometimes come close into shore. This place is a destination not just a place to overnight. It is better to stay more than one day if you can and consider joining Jorg's guided tour of the Bay of Plenty.

Family pets on site

Accommodation available (NZ$)	🧍	🧍🧍	+🧍	🛏	🛁
1 Room	$90	$110		K or 2S	EN
1 Room	$90	$110		Q	EN
1 S/C house	$150	$150	$30	Q+D	PR

Breakfast: Special continental
Evening meal: $35pp
Guest rooms:
Ambience:
Setting/location:

Capeview Cottage

Brian and Kathleen Young
167 Tablelands Road, Opotiki, Bay of Plenty
Tel: (07) 315 7877
Fax:(07) 315 8055   Free: 0800 227384
kyoung@capeview.co.nz
www.lodgings.co.nz/capeview.html

Property features
Spectacular views
Peace and tranquility
Outdoor hot-tub/satellite TV
DVD/home theatre stereo system
Fully S/C with kitchen & laundry
Local features
Golf course - 10 mins
Jet boating - 40 mins
Safe swimming beaches - 3 mins
Sea & river fishing/bush walks
White Island - volcano

Whakatane - 45 mins drive
Rotorua - 1hr 45 min drive

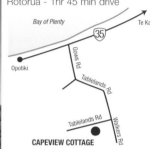

Follow the Capeview signs from SH
35 (Opotiki to Te Kaha). The cottage
is 4km from Opotiki.

Perched high on rolling hills with wide views of the East Cape mountains and the distant ocean, this self-contained retreat is best described as luxurious. The location is a great stopover en-route to Gisborne or East Cape. There comes a time in any long journey when it is right to take time out, cook your own food, catch up on the washing and take it easy for a day or two. What better way to do that than in this modern, purpose-built, secluded, fully equipped cottage? Inside I found a full kitchen (including a dishwasher), laundry facilities, bathroom (with bath) and a separate lounge/ dining area. Upstairs there are two, well-appointed, large bedrooms each with leather seating. Apart from views, the most memorable thing about the cottage is the comfort. Details, such as a coffee plunger, the sweet temptations, DVD player, Sky television and the well-appointed furnishings left me wanting for nothing. The cottage is only a short walk to the main home and so the seclusion is without isolation. One great way to spend an evening at Capeview Cottage is to admire the view and the star-filled night sky from the steaming hot-tub. You are guaranteed to feel refreshed strong and ready for the road.

Accommodation available (NZ$)						
1 S/C cottage	$130	$130	$30	2SK or 4S	PR	

Family pets on site
Guest pets by arrangement

Breakfast: Extra $15pp
Evening meal: $35pp
Guest rooms:
Ambience:
Setting/location:

Meals available on request.

LOW   HIGH

Property features
Private S/C family cottage
Open views of coast and sea
Fishing/crayfishing
Farm activities/tennis court
Fresh bread/crayfish on arrival
Farm and coastal walks
Mountain bikes for hire
Local features
Swimming and surfing beaches
Golf course
Hot pools/Marae visits

Gisborne - 1 hr 15 mins
Napier - 2 hrs 20 mins

Turn off SH 2 at Nuhaka, towards Mahia. At Opoutama don't cross railway line, but continue towards Mahanga Beach. Drive 2.5km past Mahanga. Take right fork to farmhouse - hosts will show you to The Quarters.

The Quarters

June and Malcolm Rough
Mahia
Tel: (06) 837 5751
Fax:(06) 837 5721
m.rough@xtra.co.nz
www.lodgings.co.nz/quarters.html

It was a great example of East Coast hospitality to arrive at the modernised shearers' quarters on this steeply-pitched, 1730-acre farm by the sea and discover in the fridge, a whole crayfish and a loaf of home-baked corn bread. The Quarters were relocated from their original site and placed to take advantage of the spectacular views of the ocean, Mahanga Beach and Mahia Peninsula. The cottage now perches like an eyrie on a ledge on the side of the hill, about 300 metres above sea level and a steep drive away from June and Malcolm's cliff top home. Well-appointed and self-contained it still retains, through its polished floors, wood burner, rustic timber furniture and rimu bench-top, the inviting feel of a New Zealand bush hut. There is one queen-size bedroom and a four-bunk room suitable for children or bunk-loving adults. From the verandah and from every room I was always confronted with the amazing water view. Extensive walks have been marked on the farm which take in spectacular coastal, farm and river views or perhaps you might like to try fishing for kahwai, snapper or kingfish from The Rock. I had heard great reports and was not disappointed.

Family dog on site
Guest pets by arrangement

Accommodation available (NZ$)			+		
1 S/C cottage	$125	$145-165	$25-30	Q+4S	PR

Breakfast: Extra $10pp
Evening meal: $20pp
Guest rooms:
Ambience:
Setting/location:

LOW   HIGH

Tunanui Station Cottages

Ray and Leslie Thompson
1001 Tunanui Road, Opoutama, Mahia
Tel: (06) 837 5790   Mob: 027 2402421
Fax: (06) 837 5797
tunanui@xtra.co.nz
www.lodgings.co.nz/tunanui.html

Property features
Well appointed s/c cottages
5000 acre working farm
Third generation farming family
Private river swimming hole/BBQ
Tennis court/horse riding
Trout fishing/walks/sea views
Local features
Morere hot mineral pools
Beaches/surfing/fishing
Marae dinners

Mahia - 10 minutes
Wairoa - 40 minutes

Travelling along SH 2 at Nuhaka, follow the signs to Opoutama. At Opoutama take Mahanga Rd for 2km. Turn left into Tunanui Rd. Tunanui Station is 4km on the right.

Tunanui is off the beaten track and well away from the city. To make the most of the experience, it is best to stay here several days if you can. "Two days planned - stayed three weeks. So hard to leave", one guest wrote in the guest book. Ray and Leslie own and run a 5000-acre, hill-country farm, which carries cattle, sheep and goats. The hundred-year-old cottage has been refurbished in an authentic country style. It's very cute and cosy, with three separate bedrooms and a living area of reasonable size. Leslie's flair for decorating along with polished floors, a stylish bathroom with double shower, a laundry and an open fire combine to make the cottage a comfortable sanctuary for a couple, a family or a small group of friends. It is a few minutes drive away from the homestead and surrounded by trees so guests' privacy is assured. The other accommodation available is The Farmhouse. This is set in its own private garden from where there is an excellent view over farmland, Mahia Peninsula and the Pacific Ocean. It is a modern home with four bedrooms to suit a group of people travelling together. Both cottages are well appointed and ideal for guests wanting to stay a few days and provide a unique opportunity for guests to stay on an authentic working farm.

Accommodation available (NZ$)	🧍	🧍🧍	+🧍	🛏	🛁	Family pets on site
1 S/C cottage	$195	$195	$20-50 Q+D+S	PR		
1 S/C house	$195	$195	$20-50 Q+D+4S	2PR		

Breakfast: Extra $15pp
Evening meal: $45pp
Guest rooms:
Ambience:
Setting/location:

LOW   HIGH

Property features
Petanque court and boules set
Semi self-contained
Own lounge area/patio to garden
Views from breakfast area
Guest pick-up available

Local features
Museum
Beach
Art-deco Napier
Vineyards/wineries
Gannet colony

Napier - 15 mins walk
Hastings - 25 minutes

From the city, follow Marine Parade toward the port. Turn left into Coote Rd, then right into Thompson Rd. Then turn left into Cobden Rd. Spence Homestay is on the right.

Spence Homestay

Stewart and Kay Spence
17 Cobden Road, Napier
Tel: (06) 835 9454   Mob: 025 2359828
Fax: (06) 835 9454   Free: 0800 117890
ksspence@actrix.gen.nz
www.lodgings.co.nz/spence.html

I was warmly welcomed into Spence Homestay by Kay and Stewart – an energetic retired couple who have moved into a home they have built on Bluff Hill which is next door to the 1880's villa they have lived in for the last 25 years. Everything here was inviting and immaculate. They have just one suite for guests so you can expect particular attention. Down stairs and opening onto a stone patio which leads to a walled garden is the guests lounge bedroom and bathroom area. The hosts live upstairs. The lounge, has a utility area with a microwave, refrigerator and sink. Breakfast is served up stairs at a dining area or, in summer, on the patio. From here there is a really great view over the sea and Westshore Beach to the Kaimanawa Mountains beyond, which, when I was there, were covered in snow. From Kaye's kitchen is another wonderful view across the Heretaunga Plains to the Havelock Hills. It's not difficult to feel at home in the pleasant ambience of Spence Homestay. And when you want to venture further afield, the centre of town, where you will find an art deco theme in the buildings, is just a ten minute walk away, although the walk back up the hill might take a little longer.

Accommodation available (NZ$)	👤	👥	+👤	🛏	🛁
1 Suite	$90-95	$135	$neg	Q+S	EN

Breakfast: Cooked

Guest rooms:
Ambience:
Setting/location:

LOW   HIGH

125

Mollie's Cottage

Shirley De Luca
21 Sealy Road, Napier
Tel: (06) 835 8573   Mob: 021 0477200
Fax: (06) 835 8573
delucamolliescottage@xtra.co.nz
www.lodgings.co.nz/molliescottage.html

Property features
Guest suite has private lounge
Close proximity to town
One group of guests at a time
Quiet and peaceful
Laundry facilities/fridge
Local features
Art Deco Napier
Vineyards/wineries
Beaches
Gannet colony
Historical walks/gardens

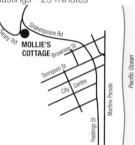

Napier - 5 mins walk
Hastings - 25 minutes

From Marine Parade, head into Hastings Street and continue north as the road changes it's name to Shakespeare Road. The entrance is at no. 64. Thereafter garage parking is available at 21 Sealy Road.

What a fantastic place to stay. When I am travelling, I always seem to have far too much luggage. The guest suite at Mollie's Cottage is large with a separate living area so that I could store all my luggage and have a bedroom that didn't look like a tornado had hit it as soon as I had opened one of my bags. The living room is complete with small dining table, lounge furniture, television, fridge with tea and coffee making facilities and elevated view - very comfortable for a longer stay. My host, Shirley, describes the accommodation as quintessential - the décor is romantic, plush and luxurious. This is certainly honeymoon territory. Breakfast can be served either in the dining room in the house or in your private living area where you won't be disturbed. The property has entrances from two streets. A walk down to Shakespeare Road means that you can be in the heart of Napier's city centre within minutes. I ate out at one of the many fine restaurants Napier has to offer and the walk back up the hill was welcomed. There is a lock-up garage available to guests on the street adjacent the house.

Accommodation available (NZ$)	👤	👤👤	+👤	🛏	🛁	
1 Suite	$130	$150		SK/T	EN	Breakfast: Special cooked/continental

Guest rooms:
Ambience:
Setting/location:

LOW   HIGH

Property features
- Personalised wine tours available
- Separate guest lounge
- Host speak French and Spanish
- Located in the city
- Opposite the ocean
- Gourmet breakfast

Local features
- Art deco Napier
- Beaches
- Vineyards/wineries
- Gannet colony/Aquarium

Napier - 5 mins walk
Hastings - 25 minutes

Heading south, coming into Napier, follow the port signs to Marine Parade. Mon Logis is opposite the ocean and near the aquarium.

Mon Logis

Gerard Averous
415 Marine Parade, Napier
Tel: (06) 835 2125   Mob: 027 4725332
Fax:(06) 835 8811
monlogis@xtra.co.nz
www.lodgings.co.nz/monlogis.html

This two-storeyed terrace house was built as a home in the 1860's, and as far back as 1915, became a private hotel. In 1991, it was revamped by its French owners and soon developed a reputation formidable. Now Gerard, who is also French, has taken over and continues its good name. 'Bon Jour. Comment ca va?' was his greeting, before he flicked into English and conducted me around this very pleasant four-bedroom accommodation. Downstairs is a cosy guest lounge with tea and coffee making facilities, CD player and television. Up a narrow flight of stairs are the bedrooms, which are all light and bright. Three have lace or damask bedspreads and antique brass bedsteads and two have views over the geraniums on the front balcony to Marine Parade and the sea. The fourth room is slightly different décor and has a private bathroom. I enjoyed the view over the rooftops of urban Napier. Breakfast in the dining room was brought to us by Gerard, who has travelled extensively and knows how to combine friendly interaction with discretion. The choice was between traditional French breakfast, with fresh fruit, croissants and breads, and traditional cooked English. The fresh coffee was, not surprisingly, great.

Accommodation available (NZ$)	👤	👥	+👤	🛏	🛁
2 Rooms			$140-$200	Q	EN
1 Room			$140-$200	2S	EN
1 Room			$140-$180	2S	PR

Breakfast: Cooked

Guest rooms:
Ambience:
Setting/location:

127

Olea Cottages

Martin Marshall   Joanna Neilson
101 Ru Collin Road, RD 4, Hastings
Tel: (06) 879 7674   Mob: 027 2299012
Fax:(06) 879 7630
oleacottages@xtra.co.nz
www.lodgings.co.nz/oleacottages.html

Property features
New self contained cottages
Quiet rural setting
Views over country side
Large garden
Widedecks/BBQ
Complimentary local wine
Local features
Many wineries - 5 min drive
Golf course - 5 min drive
Ten minute drive to Havelock North

Hastings - 10 minute drive
Napier - 30 minute drive

From North, follow Hastings /
Wellington expressway to very end,
turn at last roundabout, right at "T"
intersection, thru roundabout
(Pakipaki Rd) first right (Mangaroa R
2nd left is Ru Collin Rd

Located only a short drive from both Hastings and Havelock North, Olea Cottages are purpose built and set on ten acres of land planted with olive trees. Two cottages, named Leccino and Barnea after olive varieties, provide the accommodation. They are both spacious but Leccino has two bedrooms and Barnea just one. The lounges of both cottages have been pleasantly decorated and are presented to an impeccable standard. They are furnished with comfortable couches that look out to a field where calves and a pet sheep graze. Both cottages have large bathrooms, Barnea with a clawfoot bath. For cold New Zealand nights there are gas fires that warm the cottages. Martin and Joanna are the hosts. Breakfast provisions are also provided and I prepared mine in the fully-equipped kitchen and ate it at leisure. This was very enjoyable because I'd been on the road for some time. I would like to have had more that one day at Olea Cottages as there are so many activities in the Hawke's Bay, such as visiting wineries and vineyards, trout fishing or golfing on one, or both, of the two championship golf courses close by.

Accommodation available (NZ$)	👤	👤👤	+👤	🛏	🛁	
1 S/C cottage	$220	$220		Q	EN	Breakfast: Provisions provided
1 S/C cottage		$330	$25	2Q	EN+PR	

Guest rooms:
Ambience:
Setting/location:

LOW   HIGH

Property features
Extensive gardens
Antique furniture
Significant contemporary NZ Art
Full lifestyle sound system
Chip and putting green
Croquet sets/petanque court

Local features
The amenities of Havelock North and surrounding districts
Vineyards/wineries - 5 mins
Golf courses/beaches - 5 mins

Havelock North - 3 mins drive
Hastings - 8 mins drive

From roundabout in Havelock North village, take the Te Mata Road to the north-east. Turn right into Duart Road. Muritai is on the right.

Muritai

Denis and Margie Hardy
68 Duart Road, Havelock North
Tel: (06) 877 7588   Mob: 027 4443800
Fax: (06) 876 0275
endsleigh.cottages@xtra.co.nz
www.lodgings.co.nz/muritai.html

Up a winding driveway through weeping trees and rhododendron bushes is this historic, low-slung, weatherboard homestead which was one of several major houses established in the area in the 1890's. With its occupants this gracious dwelling, now restored and modernised, played an important part in the area's early history. A photograph taken in 1899 shows it surrounded by emptiness. Today it is in the middle of Havelock North's dress circle of homes. Ten guests can be accommodated in the four king-size ensuite bedrooms and the two single bedrooms with a private bathroom. All the larger rooms have their own entrance from the large verandahs that surround the house. The furnishings (much of it antique) and the décor are lavish and in keeping with the era the house was built in, but there are also modern paintings, central heating, hair driers, toiletries, Sky television and music systems to all the main rooms. Although the modern kitchen is set up for self-catering, outside caterers can easily be hired to prepare dinner for serving in the magnificent formal dining room or large outdoor patio, while guests relax in the spacious lounge. This is a wonderful place for a weekend house party.

Accommodation available (NZ$)	👤	👤👤	+👤	🛏	🛁
1 S/C house		$700			

Breakfast: Provisions provided
Evening meal: $50pp
Guest rooms:
Ambience:
Setting/location:

LOW   HIGH

Single party bookings $700 per night.

129

Endsleigh Cottages

Margie and Denis Hardy
Endsleigh Rd and Middle Rd, Havelock North
Tel: (06) 877 7588   Mob: 027 4443800
Fax: (06) 876 0275
endsleigh.cottages@xtra.co.nz
www.lodgings.co.nz/endsleigh.html

Property features
Petanque lawns
Croquet lawn/tennis court
Video and Sky TV
CD system
Mountain bikes
Antique cottage furniture
Cottage gardens
Local features
Trout fishing - guides available
Vineyards/wineries - 5 mins
Golf courses - 5 mins

Havelock North - 5 minutes
Hastings - 10 minutes

From Havelock North village, turn into Middle Road. Travel for 2km, and turn left into Endsleigh Rd. Endsleigh Cottages is the second drive on the right.

Margie and Denis provide self-contained, self-catering accommodation in three charming cottages situated in the Havelock North hills among gardens and trees on a semi-rural property, not far from the centre of the town. Each cottage reflects the style of earlier days but has all the comfort and convenience of today. Two cottages were brought to the site and restored using traditional methods and the third was built with recycled timber. The smaller cottage dates from the early 1900's; the larger cottages are really fully equipped houses with kitchen, laundries, bathrooms, separate bedrooms and attractive sitting rooms with comfortable sofas and open fires. The bedrooms are separate and one has an additional ensuite double bedroom. The main rooms in these cottages open onto wrap-around verandahs with rural views and are sunny and peaceful. In summer they are popular for barbecues and lunches or evening drinks. I stayed in the small cottage, which is big on charm and has a large bedroom and bathroom. It is great for a night or two and the larger cottages are more suitable for longer stay. Mountain bikes are provided if guests want to cycle around the village and hills and they are welcome to use the lawn tennis court.

Accommodation available (NZ$)	![person]	![two people]	+![person]	![bed]	![bath]
1 Cottage	$100	$100		Q	PR
1 S/C cottage	$150	$150	$50	Q	PR
1 S/C cottage	$200	$200	$100	Q+D	PR+EN

Family cat on site
Guest pets by arrangement

Breakfast: Provisions provided
Evening meal: $50pp
Guest rooms:
Ambience:
Setting/location:

LOW   HIGH

Property features
Rural setting/historic homestead
View over Pacific Ocean
Bush/farm/waterfall walk
Heated pool in season
Tennis/petanque courts
BBQ/brazier
Selection of wine for purchase
Local features
Swimming/surf beach - 5 min
Golf course - 15 min
Wineries/restaurants - 15 min

Havelock North - 20 minute drive
Napier - 40 minute drive

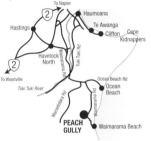

From Havelock Nth, follow signs to
Waimarama. After approx 20km,
you reach the crest of a hill and
below you is Waimarama beach.
From this vantage point, Peach
Gully is 500m, on the right.

Peach Gully Cottage

Craig and Kristal Foss
2006 Waimarama Rd, Waimarama Beach, Hawkes Bay
Tel: (06) 874 6009   Mob: 021 774755
cottage@peachgully.co.nz
www.lodgings.co.nz/peachgully.html

Every once in a while I found myself at a place that I
never wanted to leave. Peach Gully Cottage is one of
them. Tucked away on a large private section is a cute,
fairytale, one-bedroom cottage that is charming, luxurious
and full of character. Built in 1914, it has lately been
restored and re-decorated with contemporary furniture and
modern comforts. The bathroom of Peach Gully Cottage,
with its old clawfoot bath, is delightful and the kitchen has
all mod cons, including a microwave and dishwasher. The
great stretch of Waimarama Beach is only a short drive
away and the position of the cottage is ideal, not only for a
summer stay, but as a romantic winter retreat. Hosts, Craig
and Kristal, provide the fresh ingredients for breakfast but
guests provide any other meals for themselves. I stocked
up while I was in the township of Havelock North, which is
about a twenty-minute drive away. The large garden
surrounding the cottage is shared with the host's home
and set into it are a tennis court and a swimming pool. I
enjoyed a quick dip and then went for a short, fresh walk
across the farm.

Family dog on site	Accommodation available (NZ$)	👤	👤👤	+👤	🛏	🛁
Breakfast: Provisions provided	1 S/C cottage		$320		Q	PR
Guest rooms:						
Ambience:						
Setting/location:		Minimum 2 nights stay.				

Otawa Lodge

Del and Sue Trew
132 Otawhao Road, Kumeroa, RD 1 Woodville
Tel: (06) 376 4603   Mob: 027 2301327
Fax: (06) 376 5042
rest@otawalodge.co.nz
www.lodgings.co.nz/otawa.html

Property features
Historic homestead/mature garden
Guest sitting room & library
Native bush & hill walks
Central heating
Creative cuisine/selected wine list
Local features
Antique shops
Fishing/hunting/skydiving/tramping
Te Apiti/Tararua Wind Farm
Lavender farm visits/wind farm
Gottfried Lindauer Studio

Woodville - 15 mins drive
Dannevirke - 20 mins drive

4kms north of Woodville on SH 2 tu
right onto Hopelands Rd to Kumero
Travel 6.1 km, cross river and turn le
into Kumeroa Rd. At junction with
Totara Rd, Kumeroa Rd becomes
Otawhao Rd. Lodge on right just pa
Cemetery Rd.

A narrow road that snakes into the hills from the township of Kumeroa leads to this magnificent homestead in the Otawhao Valley. The large house is one of the finest examples of Art Noveau architecture in the country and captures all the style of the Edwardian era. Sue and Del have meticulously restored the old house to its original elegance. I really enjoyed the detail - the stained leaded glass windows, ceilings and walls of intricate plasterwork and timber panelling with Art Nouveau furnishings, tiling and door handles completing the decor. Guests have exclusive use of the north wing where the large comfortable sitting room with its own verandah overlooks the gardens and hills. Leading off this room is a sunny octagonal library. Accommodation is in two luxurious bedrooms with private bathrooms. The hosts live in the other wing of the house and dedicate their time to looking after their guests. The four-course dinners and the breakfasts are served formally in the dining area. Sue specialises in innovative fish dishes. By day visitors can enjoy the extensive garden with its mature trees, take a picnic to the old waterwheel or venture further afield to walk in the native bush, go fishing, or look for antique bargains in nearby Woodville.

Accommodation available (NZ$)	👤	👥	+👤	🛏	🛁		
1 Room	$195	$215-265		Q	PR	Breakfast: Special cooked
1 Room	$195	$215-265		K or 2S	PR	Evening meal: $70pp
						Guest rooms:
						Ambience:
						Setting/location:

LOW   HIG

Laptop connection available in sitting room/library. Phone in hall.

Property features
Heated swimming pool/petanque
Formal Italian-inspired herb garden
Set on 9 acres/mountain vistas
'House of the Year' award winner
Huge open fire/library/Sky TV
Local features
Walk to Greytown historic village
Fine restaurants/cafes/shops
Martinborough vineyards
3 golf courses/hot air ballooning
Horse trekking/adventure sports

Westwood Country House
Jill Kemp
82 West Street, Greytown
Tel: (06) 304 8510   Mob: 027 4716466
Fax: (06) 304 8610
westwood.kemp@xtra.co.nz
www.lodgings.co.nz/westwoodhouse.html

Greytown - 3 mins walk
Wellington - 1 hour drive

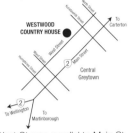

West St runs parallel to Main St (SH2) on the West side. From the south take first left into Humphries St and first right into West St. From the north take the first right into North St, first left into West St. Westwood Country House is number 82.

As I motored down the winding drive to Westwood Country House, I noticed the walled, Italian inspired, garden and made a mental note to explore it before dinner. A top category award winner for New Zealand House of the Year, Westwood was designed to blend and complement the backdrop of landscaped gardens, mature trees and stunning mountain vistas. This peaceful, nine-acre, rural property close to the Martinborough vineyards and wineries and only a three minute walk to Greytown's historic village and fine shops and restaurants, is a perfect stopover on a trip through the Wairarapa. Jill Kemp, Westwood's warmly-welcoming owner, encouraged me to make myself at home and enjoy the experience of staying in this lovely environment. I took in the quality, the attention to detail in décor and furnishings, and knew at once that this was going to be a memorable experience. I was taken to the guest wing and shown my room, which was a spacious bedroom, dressing room and large ensuite. Up to seven guests can enjoy these luxurious surroundings. I had breakfast alfresco and, for the rest of the morning, lazed in the sun or swam in the heated pool.

Accommodation available (NZ$)	🧍	🧍🧍	+🧍	🛋	🛁
2 Suites	$200-225	$225-250		SK or 2S EN	
1 Suite	$170-200	$195-220		SK or 2S PR	

Breakfast: Special cooked

Guest rooms:
Ambience:
Setting/location:

LOW   HIGH

For single room tariff - please enquire

The Old Manse

John and Sandra Hargrave
19 Grey Street, Martinborough
Tel: (06) 306 8599   Mob: 025 399229
Fax: (06) 306 8540   Free: 0800 399229
john@oldmanse.co.nz
www.lodgings.co.nz/oldmanse.html

Property features
Spa pool
Sky TV
Billiard room
Petanque
Local features
Golf course - 5 min drive
Wine tasting
Restaurants - 5 min walk
4WD quad bikes - 10 min drive
Cape Palliser seal colony - 45 min
Hot air ballooning - 15 min drive

Martinborough - 5 min walk

Take SH2 and 53 to Martinborough. Once in town, take the first right into Princess Street. Turn right at end of St and left into Roberts Street. The Old Manse corner of Roberts and Grey Streets.

Set beside a vineyard in Martinborough, is a lovely, historic house, built in 1876, and now restored and enhanced to offer guests a home away from home. Hosts, Sandra and John, made me feel like part of their family and my stay was extremely comfortable. The property is well situated for couples who want to visit some of the many vineyards in the area. It is also an ideal venue for weddings and group gatherings. There are six guestrooms in the house. Each has a private ensuite. When I arrived, other guests were sharing a bottle of one of the region's fine wines and swapping stories about their day's exploring. I joined in and then took a short walk to the centre of town where several restaurants had menus offering a good range of choices for dinner. I slept peacefully at the Old Manse that night and awoke to the quiet countryside and the enticing aroma of a cooked breakfast being prepared by John. At breakfast Sandra was busy organising a tour of the vineyards for other guests. Sadly, I had to move on. It felt a bit like leaving home; The Old Manse is a place I will particularly remember and return to.

Accommodation available (NZ$)	🧍	🧍🧍	+🧍	🛏	🛁	Family dog on site
5 Rooms		$170		Q	EN	Breakfast: Cooked
1 Room		$170		2S	EN	

Guest rooms:
Ambience:
Setting/location:

LOW   HIGH

Coromandel Peninsula - Tauranga - Whakatane - Opotiki - Gisborne - Hawkes Bay - Wairarapa

Property features
Historic buildings
Park like grounds/sunken garden
Tennis court
Petanque/croquet
Intimate weddings arranged
Conferences/private functions

Local features
Vineyards/wineries - 10 mins
Cafes/restaurants - 5 mins
Golf courses/walks
Seal colony/Pinnacle Rocks

Longwood and The Cottage Collection

Marguerite Tait-Jamieson   Garrick Emms
Longwood Road East, Featherston
Tel: (06) 308 8289
Fax:(06) 308 8189
longwood@xtra.co.nz
www.lodgings.co.nz/longwood.html

Featherston - 5 minutes
Wellington - 60 minutes

From Featherston follow signs towards Martinborough (SH 53). Turn right into Murphys Line then left into Longwood Rd. Longwood is on your right.

The Cottage Collection comprises three self-contained dwellings sited in the immense grounds of Longwood, which is one of the opulent, historic sheep-station homesteads of the Wairarapa. Two of the cottages have been designed in the great U-shaped, brick, stable complex and each has its own character. The Groom's Quarters is romantically rustic. There is a double bedroom, one with brass-bedhead bunks and above the dining room (once the tack room) a ladder leads to a loft with twin beds. Above the open fire in the sitting room is the cabinet in which grooms kept their keys. The Mews is larger with a lofty beamed ceiling, a large, light lounge, mezzanine and ground floor bedrooms and a modern kitchen and bathroom. The look is contemporary. The third cottage - The Gamekeeper's - is separated from the other two. It is a timber building of the 1850's, which was originally the cookhouse and is now decorated in a comfortable and understated colonial style, complete with potbelly fire, clawfoot bath and a fascinating antique kitchen stove. I stayed in this one but any of the three would have been an experience to remember. Stay as long as you can here. I loved it.

		Accommodation available (NZ$)	🧍	🧍🧍	+🧍	🛏	🛁
Family cat on site							
Guest pets by arrangement							
Breakfast: Provisions provided		1 S/C cottage	$168.75	$168.75	$33.75	D+4S	PR
		1 S/C cottage	$281.25	$281.25	$56.25	Q+2S	PR
Guest rooms:		1 S/C cottage	$168.75	$168.75	$33.75	2D	PR
Ambience:		Longwood Lodge	$781.85	$1,113.75		Q	EN
Setting/location:							

Luxury lodge tariff includes pre-dinner drinks, 4-course DB&B. 2 cottages have TVs.

135

Mussel bowl and Nelson Wine, Nelson

Farewell Spit

Farewell Spit Cafe & Visitor Centre, Tel: (03) 524-8454. Spectacular views of the Spit, be sure to sign the visitors book!

Takaka

Mussel Inn Bush Café
SH 60, Onekaka,
Tel: (03) 525-9241. Local brews, great food, live music, outdoor bonfire & a great crowd.

The Penguin Café & Bar
818 Abel Tasman Dr, Pohara,
Tel: (03) 525-6126.

Abel Tasman National Park

Awaroa Lodge Café Awaroa Bay, Tel: (03) 528-8758. This café has a fantastic setting & funky atmosphere in the heart of the Abel Tasman National Park.

Marahau

Hooked on Marahau
Sandy Bar, Marahau Rd,
Tel: (03) 527-8576. Great coffee and food and atmosphere. Licensed.

The Park Café
Harveys Rd, Tel: (03) 527-8270. Licensed, BYO. Blackboard menu. Eat in or take-away.

Tasman

Flax Restaurant & Bar Mapua Wharf, Mapua, Tel: (03) 540-2028. Modern New Zealand cuisine in a beautiful waterfront setting.

The Grape Escape Café & Winebar McShane Rd, Richmond, Tel: (03) 544-4341. Open for lunch, morning & afternoon teas.

Specialises in local tastes and flavours. Visit the cellar next door to sample the region's finest wines.
Riverside Cafe Moutere Highway, Tel: (03) 526-7447. Fresh local produce, hearty breakfasts, relaxed atmosphere.

Smokehouse Café Shed 3, Mapua Wharf, Mapua,
Tel: (03) 540-2280. Nelson winner of Huhtamaki best café of the year award 2003.

Waimea Estates Cellars & Café
22 Appleby Highway, Hope,
Tel: (03) 544-1791. Voted best Nelson vineyard café. A great café in a vineyard setting.

Nelson

In Vino Fides 136 Hardy St, Tel: (03) 548-8755. Tapas & full evening menu, great selection of local & old world wines & beers, live jazz.

Morrison St Café Cnr Morrison & Hardy Sts, Tel: (03) 548-8110. Solid reputation - Atomic coffee.

The Boatshed 350 Wakefield Quay, Tel: (03) 546-9783. Next to the water, enjoy great seafood in a busy café-style atmosphere. Licensed.

The Oyster Bar 115 Hardy St, Tel: (03) 545-8955. Unique and stylish. Sushi and oyster menu, complemented by a range of cocktails and imported beers.

Zest 5 Church St,
Tel: (03) 546-7064. Award winning café and deli. Worth a visit.
Events
The Arts Festival Winter.
Taste Nelson Jan-Feb.

Marlborough
Havelock

The Mussel Boys Restaurant
73 Main Rd, Tel: (03) 574-2824 Serving seafood cuisine. Mussels are harvested & cooked daily. Licensed.

Blenheim

CPR Cnr Main St & First Lan, Tel: (03) 579-5040. Small café in centre of town. Good food and coffee.
D'Urville Wine Bar & Brasserie
52 Queen St, Tel: (03) 577-9945. Stylish restaurant and bar serving French cuisine.
Figaro's Scott St,
Tel: (03) 577-7277. Yummy smells, good coffee and unpretentious cuisine.
Herzog 81 Jeffries Rd, Rapaura,

Tel: (03) 572-8770. Prize winning and exclusive restaurant serving Mediterranean cuisine.
Living Room Café and Lounge Bar Cnr Scott St & Maxwell Rd, Tel: (03) 579-4777.
Café and wine bar in the centre of Blenheim.
Terrace Café at Le Brun Terrace Rd, Renwick, Tel: (03) 572-9953. Casual ambience, indoor/outdoor seating with views of vineyard.
Events
Opera in the Vines July.
Selected Marlborough Vineyards.
Marlborough Farmers' Market Every Sunday 9am-12pm.
A&P Showgrounds,
Maxwells Rd, Blenheim.

Kaikoura Coast

Hapuku Café Hapuku Rd, Tel:(03) 319-6559. Open breakfast until dinner - enjoy superb food, coffee and ambience at this contemporary country café.
The Store Kekerengu
Tel: (03) 575-8600. Spectacular coastal location, great selection of food and well made coffee. Worth a stop.

Kaikoura

Finz of South Bay 103 South Bay Parade, Tel: (03) 319-6688.
Enjoy fresh seafood and wonderful mountain & sea views. Bookings essential.
Flukes Whaleway Station Rd, Tel: (03) 319-7733. Great for whale watching. Hearty, healthy breakfasts in a relaxed, friendly atmosphere.
Hislops Wholefoods Café
33 Beach Rd, Tel: (03) 319-6971. Organic food of a consistently high standard. Indoor/outdoor seating.
Events
Kaikoura Seafest First weekend of October, Tel: (03) 319-5641. Music, dancing, cooking, market, local produce and sea-based activities.

Love the Marlborough Sounds.

Awaroa Lodge

Allan Forsdick   Ivana Radulovic
Awaroa Inlet, Abel Tasman National Park
Tel: (03) 528 8758
Fax: (03) 528 6561
stay@awaroalodge.co.nz
www.lodgings.co.nz/awaroa.html

Property features
Abel Tasman Nat Park at door step
Beach/swimming/bird watching
Restaurant and bar on site/laundry
Sauna/organic vegetable garden
Conference & wedding facilities
Local features
Bush walks/native forest
Kayaking
Wetlands/tidal lagoons
White sand beaches/seal swim
Water taxi/light plane tours

Marahau - 90 mins water taxi
Nelson - 20 mins light plane

Access to the Lodge is by water taxi
from Marahau or Nelson. Alternatively
fly in from Nelson or Wellington.
Phone for further details.

Breathe – and that's what I did at this secluded eco-lodge in Abel Tasman National Park. Greeted off the water taxi, then checked in by friendly professional staff, I knew I was going to be well taken care of. I stopped in at my stylish studio-suite with its contemporary furnishings, modern fittings and nature-based colours. I'd arrived in the morning, which left me the whole day to wander the many tracks and beaches around the lodge. I dozed on the beach, settling into the pleasures that surrounded me – the fresh clean air, blue sky, turquoise water, fossicking oyster- catcher wading birds and the white sandy beaches. It felt like an island getaway. Keeping it simple is the focus of Awaroa Lodge. A distinct New Zealand ambience has been created with Pacific artworks, large open fireplaces and natural timbers. Guests are free to decide whether they want to sit and read a book or walk one of the numerous, well-marked tracks surrounding the lodge. Awaroa Lodge is a base from which you can explore the many natural aspects of Abel Tasman National Park or just relax in the magnificent environment of the lodge. The café and restaurant offer innovative cuisine at all hours of the day – decadent baked delights and an exceptionally good a la carte menu for breakfast, lunch and dinner.

Accommodation available (NZ$)	👤	👥	+👤	🛏	🛁		
12 Suites	$320-380	$320-380	$30	K+D	EN	Breakfast: Extra charge	
4 Suites	$235-280	$235-280	$30	K	EN	Evening meal: $55 average	
2 Suites	$235-280	$235-280	$30	K+D	EN	Guest rooms:	
4 Suites	$235-280	$235-280	$30	Q+S	EN	Ambience:	
4 Rooms	$245-290	$245-290	$30	3Q+2S	EN	Setting/location:	

LOW   HIGH

Abel Tasman Ocean View Chalets

Robert and Konstanca Palzer
Marahau Beach
Tel: (03) 527 8232
Fax: (03) 527 8211
o.v.ch@xtra.co.nz
www.lodgings.co.nz/oceanview.html

Property features
Individual timber chalets
Breakfast/packed lunch available
Activity booking on site
Sea views/BBQ available
Cots and high chairs available
Local features
Walk Abel Tasman Coastal Trek
Sea kayaking
Beach Walks
Horse trekking
Café/restaurant - 10 mins walk

Motueka - 20 minutes
Nelson - 1 hour

From Nelson follow signs to Abel Tasman National Park on SH 60. Approx 6km from Motueka, turn off to Marahau Beach. Ocean View Chalets is on the left, nearly at the end of the road.

Located on a 50-acre, coastal farm, each of these elevated self-contained Lawson Cyprus timber chalets has a view out to Marahau Beach and, in the distance, Tasman Bay, Fisherman Island, the Marlborough Sounds and Durville Island. There are three different styles of accommodation; open-plan studio, one-bedroom and two-bedroom chalets. Established native gardens surround each chalet ensuring guests' privacy, and the chalets are positioned to maximise the views. Each chalet has the same facilities including private parking, a fully equipped kitchen, television, phone, coffee/tea-making facilities, a balcony and a dining area. The interiors of the chalets are timber and they have been furnished in a simple, uncluttered way. Breakfast, served in the sunny dining room, is optional. Guests have a choice of Continental or European style, including cheeses and meats. As the chalets have been built into the side of a hill, some require a short walk down to the dining room. Ocean View Chalets are a favourite place to stay for guests embarking on adventures in Abel Tasman National Park where the native forests, beaches, clear waters, kayaking, hiking and all water activities are popular.

Family dog on site Guest pets by arrangement	Accommodation available (NZ$)	👤	👥	+👤	🛏	🛁
Breakfast: Extra $12pp	2 Studios	$108	$108		Q	EN
	5 S/C cottages	$138	$138		Q	EN
Guest rooms:	1 S/C cottage	$205	$205	$30	2Q	2EN
Ambience:						
Setting/location:						

LOW   HIGH

Abel Tasman Marahau Lodge

Robyn and Don Caird
Marahau Beach, Motueka
Tel: (03) 527 8250
Fax: (03) 527 8258
robyndon@abeltasmanmarahaulodge.co.nz
www.lodgings.co.nz/marahau.html

Property features
Native garden
Architecturally designed lodge
Evening meals available off-season
Room serviced
Sauna/spa pool/BBQ/laundry
NZ Tourism Award finalist, 1999
Local features
Abel Tasman Nat Park-5 mins walk
Sea kayaking/seal swimming
Bush walks/local restaurants
Water taxis/beaches

Motueka - 20 minutes
Nelson - 1 hour

From Nelson take SH 60. Follow Abel Tasman National Park signs after Motueka. At T junction to Collingwood turn left, then hard right into Marahau Sandy Bay Rd. Lodge is on left 500m before entry to park.

These semi-detached, modern units have the facilities of a quality motel but with a more personal feel. Robyn and Don love it here and know their guests will also enjoy this little 'slice of paradise'. Small extras – cheese, nibbles tray and chocolates to enjoy with your after dinner coffees. Robyn is happy to provide dinner when the two local, licensed restaurants are closed. Breakfast, although not included in the tariff, can be brought over to your unit at the time you choose. Packed lunches are available on request. There is a communal kitchen for the six studio units that do not have kitchen facilities, and guests are often found swapping travel stories while they cook their dinners. There is also an outdoor barbecue, plus a spa and sauna for people to relax in after their energetic excursions in the Abel Tasman National Park, which is just a one-minute drive away. I loved the way the local water taxi works. Robyn booked it and all we had to do was jump in the boat, which was towed behind a tractor, when it stopped at the gate for us. We didn't even get our feet wet. The spacious grounds and facilities make the lodge ideal for conferences and destination-style weddings.

Accommodation available (NZ$)	👤	👥	+👤	🛏	🛁	
4 S/C units	$160-200	$160-200	$20	SK+S	PR	Breakfast: Extra $10pp
8 Suites	$150	$150	$20	Q+S	PR	

Guest rooms:
Ambience:
Setting/location:

LOW   HIGH

Property features
Swimming pool/spa pool
Bird watching/bush walks
Guest lounges and log fire
Licensed dining on site
Local features
Abel Tasman National Park
Coastal, bush & mountain walks
Sea, estuary and river kayaking
Horse treks/cycling/sailing
Birding & eco tours
Wine and Art trails

The Resurgence
Clare and Peter
Riwaka Valley Road, RD 3, Motueka
Tel: (03) 528 4664
Fax: (03) 528 4605
info@resurgence.co.nz
www.lodgings.co.nz/resurgence.html

Marahau - 20 minutes drive
Nelson - 50 minutes drive

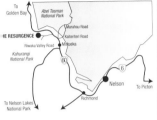

From Nelson follow SH6/SH60
through Motueka, Riwaka and past
turnings for Abel Tasman. After 2km
turn left down Riwaka Valley Road
(blue LODGE sign). Continue 6km on
right branch.

The Resurgence faces the splendid hills of Kahurangi National Park. Set at the end of the Riwaka Valley, the two chalets and the lodge are surrounded by a dense alpine wilderness. Named after the 'resurgence' where the Riwaka River flows out of a dark cave, the lodge is a wonderful place in which to find peace and privacy. I arrived in time for pre-dinner drinks and met two couples who were staying for a week. They shared their adventures with me: walks in the national park; kayaking the Abel Tasman; visiting vineyards and olive groves and relaxing by the lodge pool. Throughout the lodge, with its four guestrooms, native timbers have been used and the décor is warm and inviting. Down the drive are two cottages which are stylishly furnished and private. The cottages are self-contained and come with a 'welcome' basket of provisions for the first few breakfasts. The main lodge is on a dinner, bed and breakfast basis and cottage guests have this option too. I also recommend the dinners - four-course affairs made up of local products and Nelson wines. In the morning I sat on the sunny terrace outside my room listening to the calls of tui and bellbirds. It was truly a holiday.

Accommodation available (NZ$)	🧍	🧍🧍	+🧍	🛏	🛁
2 Rooms	$230-330	$245-395		Q	EN
2 Rooms	$200-380	$295-445		QorQ+D	EN
2 S/C cottages	$245-395	$245-395		Q/SK/2S	EN

Breakfast: Special cooked
Evening meal: Included
Guest rooms:
Ambience:
Setting/location:

LOW   HIGH

Lodge room tariffs include Dinner, B&B. Meals available for cottages.

Wairepo House

Joyanne and Richard Easton
Weka Road, Mariri, Coastal Highway, Nelson
Tel: (03) 526 6865   Mob: 027 4357902
Fax:(03) 526 6101
joyanne@wairepohouse.co.nz
www.lodgings.co.nz/wairepo.html

Property features
Landscaped woodland garden
Grass tennis court/garden chess
Heated swimming pool
Next to 150 acre apple/pear orchard
Paeonies grown on site
CD player and fridge in rooms
Local features
Abel Tasman & Kahurangi parks
Golf courses/trout fishing
Beaches/kayaking
Wine & craft trails/next to vineyard

Motueka - 10 minutes
Nelson - 40 minutes

From Nelson travel towards Motueka on SH 60. Weka Rd is the second road on the left past Tasman Village. Wairepo House entrance is approx. 200m along Weka Rd on the right.

I drove through apple orchards and fields of peonies to arrive at Wairepo, which was a cheerful introduction to this stylish country home set in a meticulously landscaped garden, on a 150-acre orchard. Joyanne has created four comfortable suites in the house and entertains guests as if they were long-time friends. I loved the atmosphere; sophisticated but not the least bit pretentious. All the rooms are large, have a good deal of privacy, and open to the garden, the heated swimming pool or deck. To sleep here and wake up to the garden with its delightful abundance of flowers and silver beech and scarlett oak trees, to pass the tennis court and walk to the summer house or play chess with the life-size set, or petanque in the back garden was the perfect antidote to urban overload. I was there in the autumn and the trees were dressing in their reds and yellows. If weather had permitted, I would have had breakfast in the summerhouse or on the patio. But it was cool, and we ate in the dining room, which still visually includes the outdoors. Joyanne created a superb breakfast including meats and nuts, and choice of avocado, mozarello and bacon or pikelets, caramelized bananas, bacon and maple syrup - a hard choice.

Accommodation available (NZ$)						Family dog on site
1 Suite	$320	$355		SK	PR	Breakfast: Special cooked
1 Suite	$365	$395		SK	EN	
1 Suite	$565	$595	$55	SK+SK/T	EN	Guest rooms:
1 Suite	$465	$495	$55	SK/T	EN	Ambience:
						Setting/location:

LOW   HIGH

Property features
Stunning 360 degree views
Peaceful and private country stay
High speed internet
Comfortable guest lounge
Petanque and croquet
Local features
Restaurants and village - 6 mins
Two golf courses - 10 mins drive
Golf clubs for loan
Personalised day trips organised

Clayridge House

Marion and Peter Copp
53 Pine Hill Road, Ruby Bay, Nelson
Tel: (03) 540 2548 Mob: 027 4472099
Fax: (03) 540 2541
info@clayridge.co.nz
www.lodgings.co.nz/clayridge.html

Motueka - 15 mins
Nelson - 25 mins

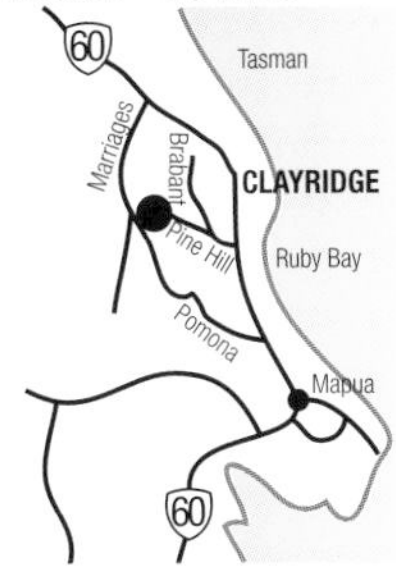

From Richmond drive 20 mins towards Motueka on SH60. At Ruby Bay, drive 100m past Ruby Bay store, turn into Pine Hill Rd. Clayridge House sign is .5 km on left.

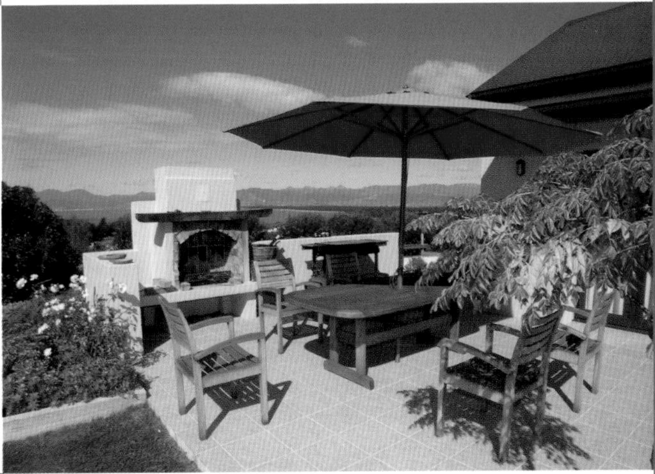

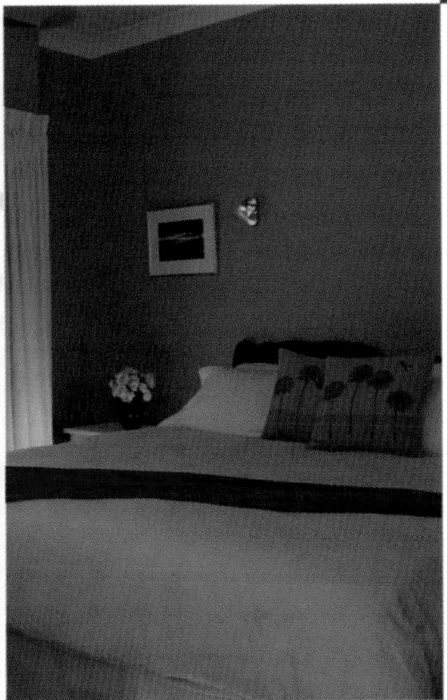

Located high on a ridge above Nelson's popular Ruby Bay and the quaint seaside village of Mapua, Clayridge House has spectacular 360-degree views. From almost anywhere on the property, I was able to admire the wide blue expanse of Tasman Bay with Nelson city and Rabbit Island in the distance. Inland, the view is across rolling pasture, orchards, vineyards and small lakes to the distant mountains. You can watch this ever-changing picture-postcard view from either of Clayridge's two immaculate, ultra-modern, self-contained cottages. Each has two bedrooms. A shell pathway meanders to the nearby home of hosts, Marion and Peter Copp, where a further two bedrooms (one with an ensuite) are available for bed and breakfast guests. Both Marion and Peter have creative interests. Marion is a keen photographer, Peter is a hobby artist and many of their fine works are on display. Breakfast, was a sumptuous affair served at a sunny table. Wide, corner-opening windows in the room let in the fresh air and allowed a good view of the rose gardens where some 90-odd varieties grow. I could also have been served outside if the weather was right or in the dining room. Guests mingle in a spacious guest lounge with an open fireplace and comfortable leather couches.

Family pets on site
Guest pets by arrangement

Breakfast: Continental

Accommodation available (NZ$)					
1 Room	$110	$175		SK or 2S	EN
2 Cottages	$140	$140	$20	K+Q	PR

Guest rooms:
Ambience:
Setting/location:

LOW HIGH

Cottages have a breakfast option available - extra charge.

Old Schoolhouse Vineyard Cottage

Pam Robert   David Birt
Dee Road, Kina Beach
Tel: (03) 526 6252   Mob: 025 2812425
Fax: (03) 526 6252
kinabeach@xtra.co.nz
www.lodgings.co.nz/schoolhouse.html

Property features
Vineyard setting/outdoor seating
Views over Tasman Bay
Character schoolhouse building
Fully self-contained/BBQ
Private peaceful environment
Local features
Vineyard tours
Art & craft trails
Walking/beaches
Golf course 5 mins
Cafes nearby

Nelson - 30 minutes
Motueka - 15 minutes

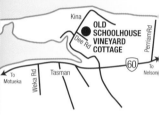

From Nelson take the coastal highway (SH 60) towards Motueka. Turn right at Tasman into Kina Beach Rd then first right into Dee Rd. The cottage is the first driveway on your left.

Even from the road, the cottage in its picturesque setting among rows of grapevines, draws comment and it was no disappointment when I arrived there. The building is still easily recognised from the outside as an old schoolhouse. It was built in 1931, and recently moved ten kilometres to its present site and renovated by Dave and Pam into this romantic retreat, which has light, space and enchanting views over the vineyard and out to Tasman Bay. The old school bell hangs on one side of the door but the only thing you have to learn here these days is how to relax. I loved the simplicity of the cottage's décor - cream walls, a glowing timber floor, the cosy wood-burning fire, comfortable chairs and a CD player issuing a background of classical music. The kitchen and bathroom are modern and fully equipped and at the front of the cottage is a deck with a barbecue. You could tuck into the cottage for several days and have complete privacy if you wanted it, but the hosts are happy to help with any information you need or to demonstrate the workings of a small vineyard.

Accommodation available (NZ$)						Family pets on site
1 S/C cottage	$200	$200-250	$25	Q+S	PR	Breakfast: Provisions provided

Breakfast provisions are complimentary for 2 days.
TV available on request.

Guest rooms:
Ambience:
Setting/location:

144

Property features
Petanque/tennis court
Historic setting/estuary shoreline
Airport pick-up available: $30
Dinghy/canoe/windsurfer
Gardens/boutique vineyard
Heated saltwater lap pool
Local features
Wineries/arts & crafts
Abel Tasman National Park
Nearby beaches/golf course
Award winning restaurants

Bronte Lodge
Bruce and Margaret Fraser
Bronte Road East, Off Coastal Highway 60, near Mapua
Tel: (03) 540 2422   Mob: 025 2807654
Fax: (03) 540 2637
margaret@brontelodge.co.nz
www.lodgings.co.nz/bronte.html

Nelson - 30 minutes
Richmond - 15 minutes

Turn onto SH 60 from SH 6 on the southern side of Richmond. Travel for approx. 10 minutes along Coastal Hwy 60 to Bronte Road East. Turn right into this road and travel 1.5km to the gate.

The water at high tide lapped just feet away from the deck of my secluded hideaway. Four luxury units sit on the water's edge, each with private decks and magnificent views of the Waimea Inlet. It is quiet and peaceful, and yet only 30 minutes from Nelson. Margaret and Bruce seem to have thought of everything when they designed the interiors of these suites and villas. They are modern, crisp and stylish, with a relaxing ambience and lack nothing in detail including robes, local art, binoculars, pre dinner drinks, cookies and an extensive range of bathroom extras. Each contains a king-size bed, kitchenette, comfortable living space with lounge chairs and coffee table. The bathroom is modern and built for luxury. After a day's adventure you can soak any stress away in the spa bath or enjoy a Chardonnay on the deck, listening to the lapping water and songbirds at sunset. Breakfast is special at Bronte – the food and the setting. The diverse menu may include local fruit juices, croissants, a variety of waffles and omelettes, free-range eggs and the freshest local fruits; and espresso made from locally roasted beans. Bronte has its own small vineyard, a 13-metre heated swimming pool and a tennis court.

Family pets on site	Accommodation available (NZ$)	👤	👤👤	+👤	🛏	🛁
Breakfast: Cooked	1 Suite	$425	$440		K	EN
	1 Suite	$425	$440		SK/T	EN
Guest rooms:	1 Suite	$525	$540		K	EN
Ambience:	1 Suite	$525	$540		SK/T	EN
Setting/location:	Drivers room available. Helicopter landing site.					

145

Aporo Pondsiders

Marian and Mike Day
Permin Road, Tasman, Nelson
Tel: (03) 526 6858   Mob: 027 2403757
Fax: (03) 526 6258
marian@aporo.co.nz
www.lodgings.co.nz/aporopondsiders.html

Property features
Farm and Woodland walk
Birdwatching
Rowing boat on lake
Views to lake/farmland/mountains
Secluded peaceful location
Local features
Walks/wineries/arts/crafts
Beaches/golf courses nearby
Abel Tasman National Park

Motueka - 10mins drive
Nelson - 30 mins drive

From Nelson travel on SH 6, turn onto SH 60. Travel approx 20 mins. Turn right into Permin Road. Aporo's drive is first left.

As I left the main road I wondered what I might find and discovered, to my delight, three very chic modern villas built literally over an ornamental pond. Marian welcomed me aboard. How cool and pleasant it was walking onto the decking and into the pondsider. The next best thing to being on a boat, except no rocking. Each villa has been cleverly staggered to give privacy. From the balconies, which are accessed from large sliding doors, you can watch the bird life, ducks cruising in and out of the rushes, or the views of mountains and farmland. Marian and Mike have planted many native shrubs and trees to enhance the pond. The interiors, carefully chosen, give a very contemporary feeling, using fabrics, textures and colour in great harmony. Underfloor heating and all the latest equipment for easy living is here. Interesting hamper breakfasts or provisions are provided. The fresh fruit and flowers, homebaking and port just topped it off. I was delighted by all that has been achieved here. This place is very near the Abel Tasman National Park and only 30 minutes from Nelson. A very central spot for all this region has to offer.

Accommodation available (NZ$)	♦	♦♦	+♦	🛏	🛁	
2 S/C units	$250	$270	$30	K or 2S	EN	Breakfast: Special cooked
1 S/C unit		$270	$65	2 K/T	GS	

One party booking only in second unit. There are 3 Pondsiders in total.

Guest rooms:
Ambience:
Setting/location:

LOW   HIGH

The Last Straw Cottage

Jon and Lynne Young
Mt Heslington Road, Brightwater, Nelson
Tel: (03) 542 3575 Mob: 025 6862926
laststraw@ts.co.nz
www.lodgings.co.nz/laststraw.html

Property features
BBQ and braziers, rural setting
Petanque court/own garden
Potager garden with produce
Mountain bikes available
Horses and sheep on property

Local features
Steam museum - 5 mins.
Award winning cafes
Restaurants/potteries/wineries
Abel Tasman National Park
Rivers/beaches/market

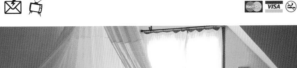

Richmond - 10 mins drive
Nelson - 20 mins drive

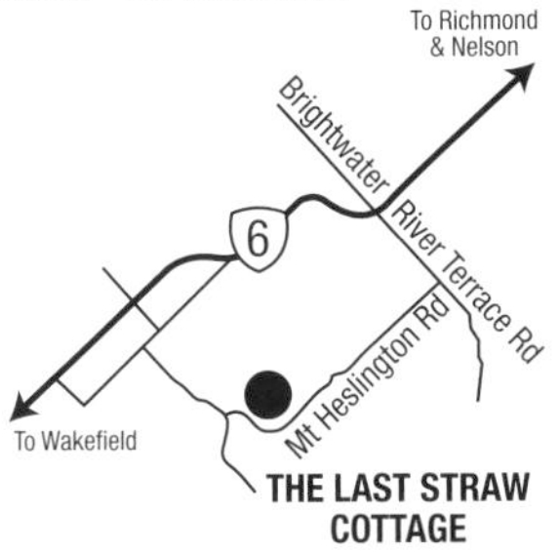

Take SH6, at Brightwater Motor Inn turn left onto River Terrace Rd for 1.5km then first right onto Mt Heslington Rd. After 3.5 km look for black and white sign on right.

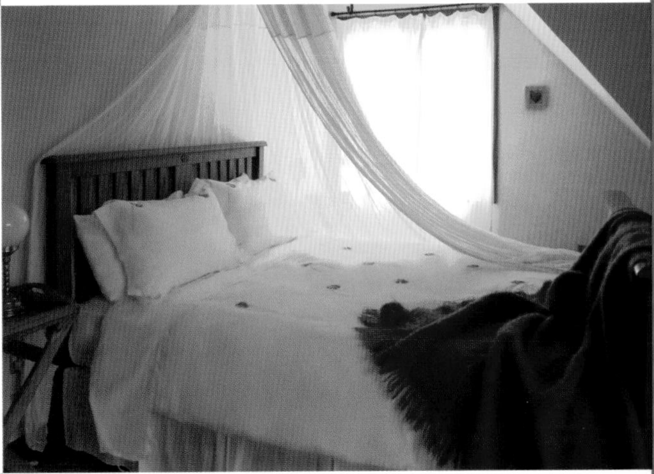

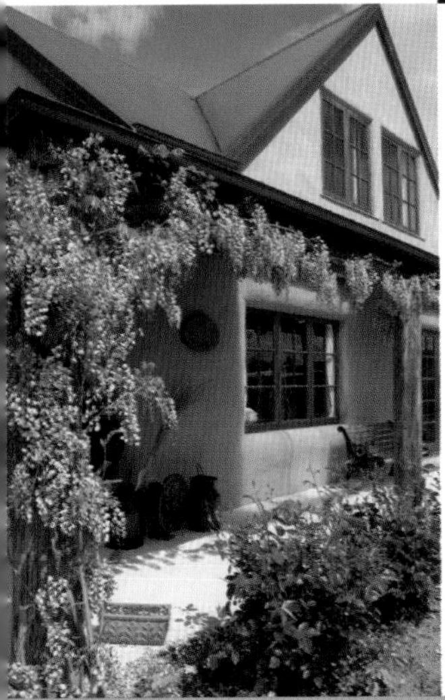

After leaving the main road I soon arrived in a picturesque valley where Jon and Lynne have built this masterpiece, straw-bale cottage. The name suggests character, and I was not disappointed. Set on a 16-acre farmlet, The Last Straw has the balance and space it deserves. The garden, neatly landscaped, has a small stream meandering at its edge, and beyond are sheep and horses. Lynne is a keen horsewoman and has an arena over the fence where she schools her horse. Inside, the thick walls give a very insulated feeling. Smart country furniture and many attractive embellishments along with an open fire create a very welcoming ambience. Linen is fresh and crisp, and everything you need to be comfortable away from home has been thought of. The spaces are generous, the kitchen well equipped and there are good laundry facilities. All windows have small outlooks to fields and hillsides. Jon and Lynne live across the fields and are there should you need them, but you can be totally private if you want to relax on your own in this quiet country environment. This region has many interesting activities and the cottage is an easy place from which to explore.

Family cats on site
Guest pets by arrangement

Breakfast: Provisions provided

Accommodation available (NZ$)	Single	Double	+ Extra person	Beds	Bath
1 S/C house	$230-285	$230-285	$55	2Q+2S	

Guest rooms:
Ambience:
Setting/location:

LOW HIGH

The Wheelhouse Inn
& Captain's Quarters

Ralph and Sally Hetzel
41 Whitby Road, Nelson
Tel: (03) 546 8391   Mob: 027 4493380
Fax: (03) 546 8391
wheelhouse@ts.co.nz
www.lodgings.co.nz/wheelhouse.html

Property features
Spectacular views of harbour & bay
Quiet bush surroundings
Privacy and total independence
Private BBQ area/deck
Mountain bikes avail
Décor with nautical theme
Local features
Pottery & craft galleries
Beaches/walks
Abel Tasman National Park
Vineyards/wineries

Nelson - 5 minutes
Motueka - 40 minutes

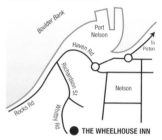

From Nelson drive towards Tahunanui via waterfront (Rocks Rd). About halfway between the port & Tahunanui turn left up Richardson St. Go straight ahead on to Whitby Rd - continue to end.

This view took my breath away. In this highly elevated position, the outlook over Tasman Bay is magic. The Wheelhouse and the adjacent Captain's Quarters are multi-level houses and at $130-$190 for a whole house is good value. The fronts of the buildings are mostly glass so there is no shortage of light or access to the view. With the skilled use of timber and quality furnishings, the décor is comfortable and uncluttered. The nautical theme using pictures and old boating paraphernalia adds interest, even for landlubbers. Both houses have well-equipped, kitchens (no dishwasher but everything else) lounges with great views, televisions, CD players and DVDs. The Wheelhouse, on three levels, has one bedroom and its own barbecue area on a patio adjacent to the kitchen. I stayed at the The Captain's Quarters (10 metres away) which is on two levels and, off the lounge, has a balcony that overlooks the bay. It also has a small extra bedroom with 'boat-cabin' bunks. The hosts live up the drive, but they make an effort not to interrupt your stay. Just five minutes from the heart of Nelson and located up on a hill that is surrounded by trees and shrubs, it is very peaceful and the waterfront is not far away.

Accommodation available (NZ$)	♦	♦♦	+♦	🛏	🛁	
1 S/C house	$130-190	$130-190	$15	Q+S	PR	Breakfast: Extra $15pp
1 S/C house	$130-190	$130-190	$15	Q+2S	PR	

Sofabed avail. in each unit plus extra bed in Wheelhouse lounge.

Guest rooms:
Ambience:
Setting/location:

Property features
Stunning sea and mountain views
Beautifully restored colonial villa
Private verandahs
Original work by local artists
Jenny's handpaints textiles
Kitchen/breakfast provisions
Local features
Walk to waterfront cafes - 5 mins
Arts/crafts/galleries/vineyards
Easy access to three National Parks
Beaches/rivers/walks

Villa 10 Waterfront Apartments

Jenny and Graham
10 Richardson St, Nelson
Tel: (03) 548 4619
Fax: (03) 545 6110
info@villa10.co.nz
www.lodgings.co.nz/villa10.html

Nelson - 5 minutes
Blenheim - 2 hour drive

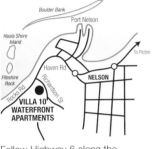

Follow Highway 6 along the waterfront. Turn up the hill into Richardson Street at the intersection opposite Haulashore Island and the Harbour entrance. Villa 10 is signposted, second on the right.

Jenny and Graham have done a fantastic job converting their large family home, built in 1908, into two separate, self-contained villas. Both have unobstructed views out to Haulashore Island and beautiful Tasman Bay. The Loft, which is the upstairs villa, is ideal for a couple looking for romance. The walls reflect the colour of the sea, and bold, coloured textiles, made by Jenny, add to the ocean theme. I really enjoyed this place; the attention to detail and comfort as well as the views. The Loft has a king-size bed, which is overhung by an amazing canopy imprinted with glowing stars. The Westwing Villa, which has been kept in its original form, is decorated with warm colours and has two generous-sized rooms that lead onto a Victorian verandah. Even relaxing in the bath, I could still see the view. Both villas are filled with original art and many of Jenny's own creations. They are fully self-contained but instead of eating in, I walked down to the waterfront where I found many award-winning restaurants. And there was no need to worry about stocking up for breakfast. The pantry and fridge in the villas were filled with a variety of fresh produce for breakfast.

Accommodation available (NZ$)	♦	♦♦	+♦	⤸	🛁
1 S/C Apartment	$190-240	$190-240	$25	Q+2S	PR
1 S/C Apartment	$190-240	$190-240	$25	K+D	PR

Breakfast: Cooked

Guest rooms:
Ambience:
Setting/location:

LOW   HIGH

Te Puna Wai Lodge

Richard Hewetson   James Taylor
24 Richardson Street, Nelson
Tel: (03) 548 7621   Mob: 021 679795
Fax: 021 789669
stay@tepunawai.co.nz
www.lodgings.co.nz/tepunawai.html

Property features
Sea/mountain view/eclectic art
Historic building circa 1857
Es,De,Fr,Pt,Dk spoken
WIFI/LAN/high speed internet
Central heating
Tea/coffee fridges in all rms
Local features
Walk to restaurants/beaches
Galleries/WOW centre
Vineyards Wineries
National parks

Nelson - 5 minutes
Picton - 2 hours

TE PUNA WAI LODGE

Follow Hwy 6 until it becomes the waterfront. Richardson St is the only major intersection on this road. Follow Richardson St up hill & through turn to the left. Te Puna Wai is second drive on the right.

This three-storeyed villa in the Port Hills has an unparalleled view over Tasman Bay and Haulashore Island from two of its suites, which have been developed by Richard into luxurious, designer accommodation, made interesting with antiques and collections of local art. Built in the middle eighteen hundreds the house was, for 30 years, occupied by photographer William Tyree who is renowned for freezing on film, scenes of Nelson's early history. The Haulashore Apartment is spacious with an open fire, chic marble ensuite and a small modern kitchen with a view out to the island. Double glass doors open to a verandah and Mediterranean-style walled terrace. I sat out here in the evening and watched the moon light up the bay. On the same floor is the Wakatu Room, a smaller and more modest suite which is still of an excellent standard, but has no view. But the Fifeshire Suite on the third level up a narrow staircase is where I could have stayed a week. It's a loft-like room with folding windows that encompass a knockout view to Fifeshire Rock. It has a smaller second bedroom and a bathroom with character in its marble washstand and clawfoot bath. On the second floor is a delightful lounge/dining area where Richard and James enjoy entertaining their guests.

Accommodation available (NZ$)	👤	👤👤	+👤	🛏	🛁	Family pets on site Guest pets by arrangement
1 S/C Apart.	$190	$260		Q	EN	Breakfast: Cooked
1 Room	$120	$160		Q	EN	
1 Suite	$165	$210	$50	Q+D	PR	Guest rooms: Ambience: Setting/location:

LOW   HIGH

Te Puna Wai was included in the NBR 'Top 100 Houses of NZ' list.

Property features
Historic innercity cottage
Quiet and tranquil
Antiques/clawfoot bath
Sunny balcony/office/2 lounges
2 TV's
Local features
Art/pottery galleries
Restaurants/cafes/shops-3 mins
Beaches/wineries/museums
Abel Tasman National Park

The Little Manor

Angela Higgins
12 Nile Street West, Nelson
Tel: (03) 545 1411   Mob: 021 2471891
Fax: (03) 545 1417
the.little.manor@xtra.co.nz
www.lodgings.co.nz/littlemanor.html

Nelson CBD - 2 mins
Richmond - 15 mins

From Nelson's main street, Trafalger St, turn right at the church steps, then first left, then first right onto Nile St West. The Little Manor is at No 12 opposite the Rutherford Hotel.

Built in 1863, this delightful small house is today passionately and lovingly cherished by Angela. It is just two minutes walk from all that is central to Nelson City. I passed through the front door and a true hideaway unfolded. Separate dining room and very small kitchen in which, I believe, many great meals have been produced. The kitchen was even fully equipped with breakfast provisions. Everything you could possibly need has been thought of here and for those who are fussy about pillows, there are 18 different options in the bedroom area. One bedroom has a king-size and the other a queen-size bed. A double sofabed is also available. The upper floor flows out to a private deck which gives cool shade on hot summer afternoons. In winter a coal burning fire gives cheer. A colourful history is evident in The Little Manor and the building is aptly named. Angela has all the history, dating back to the 1860's, on tape. The manor is an elegant, charming and secluded place set away from the bustle of the city. Books, magazines, games and videos are plentiful and there's a washing machine and dryer if you want to catch up with laundry.

Accommodation available (NZ$)	🧍	🧍🧍	+🧍	🛏	🛁
1 S/C cottage	$195	$195-240	$40	K+Q	PR

Breakfast: Provisions provided

Guest rooms:
Ambience:
Setting/location:

Sofabed also available for guest use.
Pantry fully stocked with provisions on guest arrival.

South Street Cottages

Peter and Jeanette Hancock
1, 3 and 12 South Street, Nelson
Tel: (03) 540 2769   Mob: 027 4363858
Fax: (03) 540 2769
info@cottageaccommodation.co.nz
www.lodgings.co.nz/southstreet.html

Property features

S/C Historic cottages built in 1864
In oldest preserved street in NZ
Fully equipped kitchen & laundry
Privacy in enclosed courtyards
Quiet central city location

Local features

Pottery and craft galleries
Restaurants/cafes 3 mins walk
Vineyards/wineries/Museum 3 mins
Beaches/3 golf courses
Abel Tasman National park

Nelson - 3 mins walk
Richmond - 15 minutes

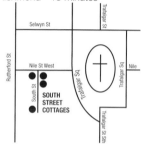

On entering Nelson take Rutherford St (west of town centre). Turn into Nile St West, South St is the first on your right. Also accessible from Trafalgar St (to the right) via Selwyn Pl, Trafalgar Sq and Nile St.

South Street is reputed to be the oldest preserved street in New Zealand. Biddle, Briar and Dillon cottages are three of a number of charming homes restored to capture the atmosphere of 130 years ago. The cottages are just a three-minute walk from the heart of Nelson, perfect for travellers who want to explore the city on foot and who enjoy their privacy. However, don't let the proximity to town lead you to think it's noisy here. The cottages are surprisingly quiet. They have two bedrooms leading off lounges, which have wood-burning stoves and French doors opening to a private courtyard. The kitchens are fully equipped and include fridges, stoves, coffee plungers and a range of teas. There are also full laundry facilities. In addition to the cottages, there is a new apartment available in the same street. It is not in a big complex, but in a well-designed, two-storeyed building which offers your own entry and all the trappings you would expect in a quality, modern unit. The hosts live off-site on their vineyard in Ruby Bay. Breakfast is self-service but includes Jeanette's homemade preserves. These are romantic little hideaways, which offer privacy and independence in the city.

Accommodation available (NZ$)	🧍	🧍🧍	+🧍	🛏	🛁	Guest pets by arrangement
2 S/C cottages	$160-185	$160-185	$40	Q+D	PR	Breakfast: Provisions provided
1 S/C cottage	$160-175	$160-175	$40	2D	PR	
1 apartment	$180-195	$180-195	$40	Q+D	EN	Guest rooms:

Ambience:
Setting/location:

LOW   HIGH

Property features
Fully self contained mod urban
inner city retreat above health centre
Quiet/views/two balconies/BBQ
All day sun/spabath/central heating

Local features
Art/pottery/glass galleries
Restaurants/café/shops 2 mins
Beaches/wineries/museum
WOW centre/gardens
Abel Tasman National Park
Golf courses

Nelson CBD - 2 min walk
Richmond - 15 mins

From Nelson's main street,
Trafalger St, turn right at the church
steps, then first left, then first right
into Nile St West. The Little
Retreat is at No 22 opposite the
Rutherford Hotel.

The Little Retreat

Angela Higgins
Level 1/ 22 Nile St West, Nelson
Tel: (03) 545 1411   Mob: 021 2471891
Fax: (03) 545 1417
the.little.retreat@xtra.co.nz
www.lodgings.co.nz/littleretreat.html

"A Little Retreat indeed" and "Little piece of paradise" are both quotes I read from the guest book. Located in the heart of Nelson with views of the Nelson Cathedral is a well appointed apartment. Ideally situated above a natural health centre called Being which is run by the host Angela. It is only a short few minutes stroll into town. The decor is ultra-modern with up-to-the-minute amenities and a fully equipped kitchen and laundry. The Little Retreat has one bedroom with a king-size bed, spa bath and other luxuries such as bathrobes and nice toiletries. There is also a day bed in the living room for an extra guest or a place to relax while watching the LCD television. There are two private decks, one with a barbeque. I spent my first day at the retreat reading quietly, and then booked myself in for a soothing shiatsu massage downstairs at Being. As I was there on a Sunday I awoke to the ringing of bells from the Cathedral. I sat on the front deck and watched people pass by on their way to church or to the various activities in the town. Angela had left me provisions, including fresh fruit, breads and eggs etc. and enjoyed breakfast al fresco while I warmed myself in the sun.

Accommodation available (NZ$)			+		
Breakfast: Provisions provided	1 S/C unit	$195	$195-240	$25	K+D	PR

Guest rooms:
Ambience:
Setting/location:

LOW   HIGH

153

Manuka Cottage

Alison Phillips   Robin White
3 Manuka Street, Nelson
Tel: (03) 548 9418
Fax:(03) 548 9418
manukacottage@xtra.co.nz
www.lodgings.co.nz/manukacottage.html

Property features
Charming fully restored cottage
Quiet private and tranquil
Modern kitchen/laundry/TV/DVDs
French doors to sunny deck & BBC
Delightful cottage garden
Local features
Pottery/crafts/art galleries
Restaurants/cafes and shopping
Cathedral & school of music
Queens gardens/markets/theatre
All 5 to 10 mins walk

Nelson CBD - 3 mins walk
Richmond - 15 mins drive

From Nelson's main street, Trafalge
St, turn left at the church steps, the
right at the lights onto Collingwood
St, after the roundabout, take first l
onto Manuka St, Manuka cottage is
No 3.

Manuka Cottage is a spacious, fully-restored, 19th century cottage, artistically refurbished and furnished with a slightly oriental flavour. The master bedroom, with a king-size bed, is splendid with its black velvet curtains, rich fabrics and quality linens. Up a spiral staircase can be found a sunny, bright loft bedroom with a queen-size bed and king single bed plus two special Ming dynasty chairs. The modern kitchen which is partly timber and partly a cheerful blue colour, is well stocked with all the basics. Croissants, bread and fresh fruit are left for breakfast, which you can prepare for yourself. The open plan living and dining area has French doors opening to a deck and a bricked barbecue area that catches the sun all day. A few steps further took me out to the back lawn and a cottage garden overflowing with roses and herbs. This is a real little home away from home with all conveniences, such as dishwasher, washing machine and dryer, Internet access, television, DVD and sound system at hand. Features include totara and kauri floorboards, clawfoot bath, wood burner and gas barbecue.

Accommodation available (NZ$)						
1 S/C cottage	$200-250	$200-250	$30-50	K+Q+S	PR	Breakfast: Provisions provided

Guest rooms:
Ambience:
Setting/location:

Phone and TV in main bedroom.

Property features
1.5 acres of private garden
Views of Nelson City & Tasman Bay
Historic home - circa 1936
Local features
Golf course - 5 min drive
Art gallery/shops/cafes - 10 min
River walks - 5 min walk
Centre of NZ walkway
Boat harbour/boat ferry/beaches
National Parks - Abel Tasman
Botanic gardens/tennis courts

Long Lookout Gardens

David and Yvonne Trathen
60 Cleveland Terrace, Nelson
Tel: (03) 548 3617
Fax:(03) 548 3127
enjoy@longlookoutgardens.co.nz
www.lodgings.co.nz/longlookout.html

(P) ✉ 📺 ✆ ♿   MasterCard VISA

Nelson - 8 minute walk
Blenheim - 2 hour drive

Take SH6 to Nelson, turn onto
Trafalgar St, take first left onto Wainui
St then right onto Collingwood St,
left onto Nile St, right into Mayroyd
Tce and right into Cleveland Tce.
Long Lookout on left.

This luxury bed and breakfast is set on one-and-a-half acres of established English-style gardens, in the foothills of Nelson, with views out over nearby Nelson city to Tasman Bay and Abel Tasman National Park. Yvonne and David are passionate about their gardens and many beautiful white roses line the driveway. Native trees are planted throughout the property; there's a small apple, pear and citrus orchard, olive trees, bluebells (which are a carpet of colour in September) and a huge acorn tree framing the view out to sea. The historic home was built in 1864 and rebuilt in 1936. Beautiful antiques and exquisite fabrics have been used throughout the interior. There are two elegant guestrooms both with large modern ensuites. The Hunter-Brown Room is decorated in gold and black furnishings with Asian-style accents. It has a super-king-size bed, flat screen television, a private patio and views out to the garden and the sea. Downstairs, the more spacious Richmond Room has a private entrance and views out to the garden. The bed is queen size and the room is elegantly decorated in blue and gold. I spent a lot of time examining the original artworks that hang on the walls throughout the house.

Family dog on site

Breakfast: Special cooked
Evening meal: $65pp
Guest rooms:
Ambience:
Setting/location:

RECOMMENDED BOUTIQUE LODGINGS
★★★★
LOW   HIGH

Accommodation available (NZ$)	👤	👤👤	+👤	🛏	🛁
1 Room	$295	$350		Q	EN
1 Room	$295	$350		SK	EN

Dinners by prior arrangement. Children welcome by prior arrangment.

155

Warwick House

Nick and Jenny Ferrier
64 Brougham Street, Nelson
Tel: (03) 548 3164   Mob: 021 688243
Fax:(03) 548 3215   Free: 0800 022233
enquiries@warwickhouse.co.nz
www.lodgings.co.nz/warwickhouse.html

Property features
Magnificient old victorian home
Views over Nelson city to water
5 min walk to cathedral and city
Private/quiet location
Experienced and helpful hosts
Very spacious/home comforts
Local features
Close to beaches/rivers/city/walks
Wine tours/golf/pottery nearby
Fishing/skiing/kayaking/biking
Markets/antiques/museums

Nelson - 5 minute walk
Abel Tasman - 35 minute drive

Take SH6 to Nelson roundabout, tu
into Trafalgar St. Take first left onto
Wainui St, then first right onto
Collingwood St. Follow to Brougham
St and turn left to Warwick House a
end on right.

"The Castle" as it is known to the Nelson locals, is a large,1854, mansion which had been designed for entertaining. Jenny and Nick have done a great job restoring this lovely building and re-creating the spaces to serve their original purposes. Because it is situated on a hill above Nelson city, the views are fantastic. The house has three grand guestrooms and a large ballroom which can be used for small weddings or other occasions. The Bayview Suite has views over the city and a four-poster bed. The Peacock Garden Suite, which I recommend for a special occasion, offers guests exclusive use of the spa pool. I stayed in the Tower Suite which has a Victorian theme and a queen size bed. The large tower, after which it is named, is now a sitting room. I slept like a princess in this quiet place and in the morning Jenny welcomed me into the ballroom for a wonderful breakfast of homemade muesli followed by herb scrambled eggs. It was a grand affair with flickering candles and soft opera music - an elegant way to start the day.

Accommodation available (NZ$)	![person]	![two people]	+![person]	![bed]	![bath]	
1 Suite	$355	$395	$45	K+2S	EN	Family dog on site
1 Suite	$310	$350	$45	Q+1S	EN	Guest pets by arrangement
1 Suite	$280	$320	$45	SK	EN	Breakfast: Cooked

Breakfast: Cooked
Evening meal: Enquire
Guest rooms:
Ambience:
Setting/location:

Breakfast available between 7-10am.

LOW   HIG

Abel Tasman National Park - **Nelson** - Nelson Lakes - Marlborough Sounds - Blenheim - Kaikoura

Property features
Quiet yet close to city centre
Heat pumps/air conditioning
Interior design includes local art
Guest lounge/CD/VCR/books
English garden/pond/seating
Suite has a kitchenette
Local features
Walk to restaurants/cafes
Art & craft galleries/vineyards
City/bush walks
Beaches & public gardens

Shelbourne Villa

Val and Wayne Ballantyne
21 Shelbourne Street, Nelson
Tel: (03) 545 9059   Mob: 027 4474186
Fax: (03) 546 7248
beds@shelbournevilla.co.nz
www.lodgings.co.nz/shelbourne.html

Nelson - 5 mins walk
Picton - 2 hours

From SH 6 drive down Trafalgar St (main street in town centre) towards the cathedral. Take the last road left (Selwyn Pl) then second right (Shelbourne St). Shelbourne Villa is number 21 on your left.

This adapted villa, recently taken over by Val and Wayne, is tucked away in a quiet corner of Nelson, just five minutes walk from the city centre. The designed wood and metal gates opening to the property are an indication of the theme of the house which is decorated and furnished with the work of local artists, many of whom live nearby. I could have wallowed in the comfort of the guest lounge and admired its leafy outlook, but I preferred to wander the house and garden to find among the sculptures, paintings and ceramics, works from Jane Evans, Grant Palliser, Bill Burke and Christine Boswijk. The upstairs suite with a balcony and view over the town is furnished in a slick contemporary style incorporating the excellent metal designs of Glenn van der Leij. Of particular note are the geometric fireplace surround and the innovative wardrobe. The three other rooms, two at ground level and one downstairs are very spacious with sleigh beds, writing desks, televisions, lounge chairs, stocked bookshelves, art work and extra-large ensuites all immaculately presented. The large colourful garden is dominated by birch trees and has several attractive sitting areas on different levels.

Accommodation available (NZ$)	👤	👤👤	+👤	🛏	🛁
Breakfast: Cooked					
1 Room	$175	$195		K	EN
1 Room	$245	$265		K	EN
Guest rooms:					
1 Room	$275	$295		SK	EN
Ambience:					
1 Suite	$190	$210	$50	K	EN
Setting/location:					

Muritai Manor

Jan and Stan Holt
48 Wakapuaka Road, Wakapuaka RD 1, Nelson
Tel: (03) 545 1189   Mob: 027 4370622
Fax:(03) 545 0740   Free: 0800 260662
stay@muritaimanor.co.nz
www.lodgings.co.nz/muritaimanor.html

Property features
Colonial architecture
Swimming pool/spa pool
Separate guest lounge/dining
Complimentary refreshments
Mature garden with sea views

Local features
Vineyards/wineries
Pottery/craft galleries
Three National parks
Restaurants/cafes - 5 mins
Golf course/beaches

Nelson - 5 minutes
Blenheim - 1 hr 30 mins

From Nelson, take SH 6 towards Blenheim. Travel for approx. 5 mins. Muritai Manor is on the right after Clifton Terrace school and Allisdair S

If you drive toward Picton from Nelson for five minutes you will arrive at this impressive example of colonial architecture. Climbing roses cover the balconies, and established trees in the large garden provide shelter and shade. Muritai Manor was built in 1903, and some years ago was converted to a bed and breakfast. The renovations are sympathetic to the original design. Heavy drapes in the front guestrooms frame the view through the sash windows of Nelson Haven, Abel Tasman National Park and Rabbit Island. Other rooms have views over the swimming pool with some harbour and rural views. Jan and Stan make an extra effort to operate their bed and breakfast in a professional way. Thoughtful touches in the guestrooms such as chocolates, lollies and herbal teas and the table/desk and chair for writing letters home (or maybe work) make it clear that this is more than just a business for the hosts. I am sure that other guests appreciate their efforts as much as I did. The formal dining room and guest living areas offer the same style and comfort. Even though it is an older home I found Muritai Manor to be bright and sunny and a very pleasant place to stay.

Accommodation available (NZ$)	👤	👤👤	+👤	🛏	🛁	Family dog on site
1 Room	$160	$195		Q	EN	Breakfast: Special cooked
1 Room	$160	$195		Q	EN	
1 Room	$175	$215		K	EN	Guest rooms:
1 Room	$175	$215		SK/T	EN	Ambience:
1 Cottage	$200	$240	$70	SK/T+S	EN	Setting/location:

Property features
Native birdlife/sunny decks
Onsite companion fishing
House exclusively for guests
Beech forest surroundings
Local features
Rivers, bush & alpine walks
Fly fishing/boating/kayaks
Local cafes/bike rentals
Rainbow skifield/lake based activities
Marlborough/Nelson vineyards
Nelson Lakes National Park

Nelson - 60 mins drive
Blenheim - 60 mins drive

St Arnaud House

Debbie and Justin Murphy
Cnr Bridge, Holland & Lake Road, St Arnaud
Tel: (03) 521 1028   Mob: 027 2418523
Fax: (03) 521 1208
retreat@st-arnaudhouse.co.nz
www.lodgings.co.nz/starnaud.html

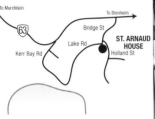

From Nelson take SH 63 to St Arnaud. Before the bridge turn into Bridge St. St Arnaud House is on the left at the corner of Holland and Lake Rds.

Justin and Debbie have travelled extensively and have named their rooms after various destinations they have travelled to in Nepal, Vietnam, Ireland and New Zealand – all have king, queen or twin-size beds, pure wool underlays, electric blankets and pretty views out to the surrounding beech-tree forest and the St Arnaud Ranges. This peaceful sub-alpine retreat is a Frahmos House – nail free with pine interlocks. Nature is on the doorstep – tuis, robins, bell birds, fantails and other native birds are abundant. On the summer morning I visited, 'Mr Robbie' and a small family of robins showed up on schedule for their breakfast. Justin is a keen trout fisherman and happy to accompany anyone who would like the company of a local in the know or can arrange a professional local guide. There is a spacious, casual guest lounge downstairs with comfortable couches, an extensive collection of books, CDs and records to play, as well as regional information. The house is kept cosy from the wood-burning fireplaces in the dining room and lounge. Justin and Debbie live in the cottage next door, so the house is exclusively for guests. There is much to do in the Nelson Lakes region; world class fly-fishing, skiing, lake and alpine walks and boating activities.

Accommodation available (NZ$)	👤	👥	+👤	🛏	🛁
1 Room	$150	$185	$55	Q+S	EN
1 Room	$150	$185		Q	EN
1 Room	$125	$150		2+KS	PR
1 Room	$185	$215		K	EN

Breakfast: Special cooked
Evening meal: $45pp
Guest rooms:
Ambience:
Setting/location:

LOW   HIGH

Children welcome by prior arrangement.

159

Owen River Lodge

Felix Borenstein
Owen Valley East Road, Murchison, Nelson Lakes
Tel: (03) 523 9075
Fax:(03) 523 9076
enquiries@owenriverlodge.co.nz
www.lodgings.co.nz/owenriver.html

Property features
2 lounge areas/TV/video player/DVD
Onsite chef
On-site fly fishing equipment
Absolute river frontage
16 acres of gardens/farmland
Surrounded by National Park
Local features
Golf/horse riding/wine tasting
Rafting/canoeing/tramping/hiking
Cycling/mountain biking/fishing
Hot air ballooning/skydiving/gliding

Murchison - 20 minute drive
Nelson - 1.5 hour drive

From Nelson, drive south on SH6 towards Murchison. Approx 110kms from Nelson turn right into Owen Valley East Road (before Owen River Bridge) Lodge is 2 km down rd on left.

The first thing I noticed as I drove down the long drive to Owen River Lodge was the sweet smell of manuka trees in bloom. The lodge, set on the banks of the Owen River, is completely secluded and luxurious and from all rooms, views of the Mt Owen Ranges are apparent. There are four guest suites, all generous sizes. They are situated in a separate wing from the main part of the house and their design manages to be both contemporary and charming at the same time. Dinner at the lodge is prepared by the onsite chef and can be enjoyed in the main lodge or, if weather permits, on the deck which looks over the garden. The lodge has top-of-the-line fishing equipment and Felix, who is the lodge's host, arranges guided fishing expeditions for guests who need help. But many guests simply like to enjoy the lodge and its peaceful surroundings. It is a wonderfully unruffled place, inviting guests to slow down and relax. After a sightseeing trip around the attractive Nelson Lakes area, which is close by, I enjoyed a quiet time in the lounge before dinner, sipping a cocktail made at the well-equipped bar.

Accommodation available (NZ$)			+		
4 Rooms	$425	$660		SK or 2S EN	

Breakfast: Special cooked
Evening meal: Included
Guest rooms:
Ambience:
Setting/location:

LOW   HIGH

Property features
- Secluded romantic bungalows
- Intimate candelit outdoor baths
- Four poster beds/luxurious linen
- Moss covered candlelit terrace
- Very nice selection of wines

Local features
- Private walkway/great views
- Kayaks/rowboats/fishing gear
- Swimming/windsurfing
- Queen Charlotte track
- Eco/Sounds tours

The Lazy Fish

Rosie and Steve George
Kahikatea East Bay, Queen Charlotte Sound, Picton
Tel: (03) 573 5291
relax@lazyfish.co.nz
www.lodgings.co.nz/lazyfish.html

 16

Picton - 20 mins by boat
Blenheim - 20 mins boat + 20 mins drive

Bay of Many Coves

Queen Charlotte Walkway

Queen Charlotte Sound ferry route

THE LAZY FISH

Picton

Catch either The Cougar Line or a water taxi from Picton.

A trip to The Lazy Fish on Queen Charlotte Sound was a highlight. This is about as near to paradise as you could find. Being on the water is, of course, what I love best, so having to catch a ferry to get there, seeing the dolphins cruising beside me and anticipating The Lazy Fish was a great start to the day. A wooden jetty stretches out into the water from the centre of this tiny bay. Steve and Rosie greeted the ferry and doubled as boat fender. Immediately you know this place is delightfully relaxed. The crystal clear water, just a stones throw from the verandah of the main building, is astonishing. Set in lush green gardens, the separate and private cottages each have their own charm. Outdoor baths, with hot water on tap and lit by candlelight, appealed to me. It was impossible not to feel very spoiled to be here, with its fresh flowers, private sun terraces and hammocks on the verandahs. The furnishings and decoration is soothing and stylish. Meals can be served in your own cottage or in one of the very attractive settings around or inside the main building. An interesting moss-covered, walled terrace has water trickling over it in the summer. I was aware artistic talent had a strong presence at The Lazy Fish and, for the active, there is plenty to do.

Family pets on site	Accommodation available (NZ$)	👤	👤👤	+👤	🛏	🛁
Breakfast: Special cooked	4 studios	$445	$495	$100 Q+S		EN
Evening meal: Included						
Guest rooms:						
Ambience:						
Setting/location:		All meals included.				

LOW   HIGH

Sherrington Grange

The Harper Family
Mahau Sound, RD 2, Picton
Tel: (03) 574 2655
Fax: (03) 574 2655
info@sherringtongrange.co.nz
www.lodgings.co.nz/sherringtongrange.html

Property features
Antique/art/musical instruments
400 acres with private wharf
2km deserted coastline
Over 10km walking tracks
Beekeeping/perfume/cheese
Local features
Area of great natural beauty
Kayaking onsite or 10 min drive
Queen Charlotte track - 10 min drive
Wineries - 50 min drive

Picton - 50 minutes
Blenheim - 50 minutes

Turn up Kenepuru Road at Linkwater
and after approx 20 minutes, take the
signposted driveway (first road after
the cattle stop).

At this farm house I stepped back into the way things used to be. The Harper family invited me to join in with their everyday routine but also offered me the options of walking, kayaking or fishing. Instead, I spent the day walking around the property with Lisa, the family's botanist, who introduced me to some of the species in their native forest. This farm is set on 400 acres and located right on Mahau Sound in the South Island's beautiful Marlborough Sounds. The Harpers are an amazing family whose warm welcome makes guests feel right at home. Sherrington Grange has two guestrooms, each with a water view. The larger room has a king-sized bed and the smaller one, a queen-size. The bathroom is guest shared. I joined the family for dinner that night and enjoyed hearing them talk about their lives, which is very different from those in a city. They talked of their experiences with beekeeping, travel, the family's history and the old farming techniques some of which they still use today. This was a great place to get back to basics and I felt a long way away from the busy world.

Family pets on site

Accommodation available (NZ$)	👤	👤👤	+👤	🛏	🛁	
1 Room	$120	$150	$N/A	Q	GS	
1 Room	$140	$180	$40	SK	GS	

Breakfast: Special continental
Evening meal: $30pp
Guest rooms:
Ambience:
Setting/location:

Property features
1886 Heritage-registered villa
5 acre private setting
Short stroll to Picton's amenities
Luxurious character apartments
Courtesy transfers/internet
Local features
Queen Charlotte track & cruises
Marlborough vineyard tours
Sailing/kayaking/mountain biking
Dolphin/bird/wildlife cruises
Gift shops/restaurants/beaches

Picton - 5 mins walk
Blenheim - 20 mins drive

Oxford Street runs off Nelson Square in Picton.

Sennen House

Richard and Imogen Fawcett
9 Oxford Street, Picton
Tel: (03) 573 5216   Mob: 021 0359956
Fax: (03) 573 5216
enquiries@sennenhouse.co.nz
www.lodgings.co.nz/sennen.html

Richard and Imogen warmly welcomed me to Sennen House. Built in 1886, this restored Heritage-registered, colonial villa offers three elegant apartments and one suite set in spacious grounds at the foot of a bush-clad hill. It is evident that the couple are accomplished landscape architects as the house and gardens combine contemporary style with historic charm. Sennen House is well positioned for those who wish to explore Picton, the Marlborough Sounds and Marlborough's wine-growing region. Each apartment has its own distinctive character, with a private entrance, a lounge and ensuite. The Cook's Apartment, has a king-size bed, separate lounge with open fire, full kitchen and private verandah with views to the sea and hills. Banks' Apartment has a queen-size and single bed, separate lounge with kitchen, a shared balcony and views to native bush. With similar views to Cook's, Victoria Apartment has a queen-size bed and a spacious and sunny, shared balcony. The suite has two bedrooms and guests have exclusive use of the formal lounge and entrance. Breakfast hampers, complimentary tea, coffee, and evening drinks are provided. The house is quiet and yet it is only a short walk from the town centre and ferry terminal.

Family cat on site

Breakfast: Special continental

Guest rooms:
Ambience:
Setting/location:

LOW   HIGH

Accommodation available (NZ$)	♠	♠♠	+♠	🛏	🛁
1 S/C unit	$225-265	$245-295		Q	EN
1 S/C unit	$225-295	$275-325	$60	Q+S	EN
1 S/C unit	$315-365	$345-395	$75	K	EN
1 Suite	$265-295	$295-695	$75	K+SK/T	EN+PR

163

Old Saint Mary's Convent Retreat

Christine Webber
776 Rapaura Road, Blenheim
Tel: (03) 570 5700   Mob: 021 405603
Fax:(03) 570 5703
retreat@convent.co.nz
www.lodgings.co.nz/saintmarys.html

Property features
Separate guest library/Sky TV
Park-like garden/rural setting
Bikes available for guests
Verandahs and balconies
Local features
Wineries - 2 mins
Grass tennis court next door
Trout fishing
Art & craft galleries

Blenheim - 10 minutes
Picton - 20 minutes

From SH 1 turn west into Rapaura Rd at Spring Creek township. The convent is 5km on your left. If comir from Nelson, Rapaura Rd is on your left shortly after crossing the Wairau River before reaching Renwick.

This is a stunning building. What used to be the Saint Mary's Convent built in 1901 is now an up-market guest accommodation. This huge building, with its many verandahs, houses Christine, the host, as well as seven large suites for guests. The elegantly appointed living areas include a dining room and, because the Convent has recently been renovated, guests are provided with all modern luxuries in an environment that reflects the original use of the building. The honeymoon suite which is a replica of the original house chapel, is beautifully, copied and furbished with such care, will take your breath away. The Convent is located on 20 acres of immaculately landscaped, formal lawn and gardens which are surrounded on all sides by vineyard and olive groves. My bedroom was spacious and light with a huge bathroom complete with a unique, deep, oval bath. All ensuites have claw-foot baths as well as showers and feature beautiful toiletries. Breakfast was fresh fruit, yoghurt and cereals and a full cooked selection, all elegantly served. There is an historic, deconsecrated church on the property that is mostly used for weddings and functions.

Accommodation available (NZ$)	👤	👥	+👤	🛏	🛁		
1 Room		$550		SK	EN	Breakfast: Cooked	
1 Room		$500		Q	EN		
1 Room	$350	$450		SK/2S	EN	Guest rooms:	
2 Rooms	$350	$450		Q	EN	Ambience:	
2 Rooms	$350	$400		Q	EN	Setting/location:	

LOW   HIGH

Property features
Solar heated pool
Lawn tennis court
Petanque court/citrus orchard
Farm animals/birds
Local features
Malborough vineyards 5-10 mins drive
Malborough Sounds 20 mins drive
Bush walks 20 mins drive
Beaches 20 mins drive

St Leonards Vineyard Cottages

Jeanette and Steve Parker
18 St Leonards Road, Blenheim
Tel: (03) 577 8328   Mob: 025 6861636
Fax: (03) 577 8329
stay@stleonards.co.nz
www.lodgings.co.nz/stleonards.html

Blenheim - 5 mins drive
Nelson - 90 mins drive

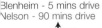

From Blenheim railway station take left at roundabout, (from Picton go right) onto Nelson St (beginning of SH 6). Go through Blenheim towards the airport, 2km out is St Leonards Rd on right.

Located on five acres of land in the heart of the Marlborough wine country, only a few kilometers from the town of Blenheim and surrounded by vineyards, are five charming cottages. Four are for guests and one is the home of hosts, Steve and Jeanette. Each cottage is as fabulous as the next. The Annex is quaint and was once the external kitchen of the old homestead, but now it has been redecorated into intimate and cosy accommodation. The original stables have also been renovated and would be a great choice for a romantic weekend as it is set well apart and has a fireplace to cuddle up in front of. As it was, I spent a delightful weekend in The Woolshed, the largest of the cottages, which has two bedrooms decorated with memorabilia from the old sheep-shearing days. The newest addition is simply called The Cottage and it has been designed to reflect the style of an old cob cottage. I enjoyed an early morning wander through the property among the fruit trees (I was encouraged to pick the fruit) and admiring the domesticated and friendly horses, sheep and chickens. Although there are five cottages they are positioned so that guests' privacy is assured.

Family pets on site
Guest pets by arrangement

Breakfast: Continental

Guest rooms:
Ambience:
Setting/location:

Accommodation available (NZ$)	👤	👤👤	+👤	🛏	🛁
1 S/C cottage	$160	$160		Q	EN
1 S/C cottage	$100	$100		Q	EN
1 S/C cottage	$190	$190		Q+S	PR
1 S/C house	$270	$270	$50	Q+3S	PR

165

Cranbrook Cottage

Ian and Keren Mitchell
145 Giffords Road, Rapaura, Marlborough
Tel: (03) 572 8606   Mob: 027 4352354
Fax: (03) 572 8707
stay@cranbrook.co.nz
www.lodgings.co.nz/cranbrook.html

Property features
Guest pick-up available
Vineyard setting
Fishing guides can be arranged
White linen breakfast delivered
Fully S/C character cottage
Local features
Vineyards/wineries
Trout fishing/golf courses
Bush walks/horse riding
Art & craft galleries
Gourmet tours with Keren

Blenheim - 12 minutes
Picton - 25 minutes

From Blenheim take Middle Renwick Rd towards the airport. Turn right into Jacksons Road which becomes Giffords Road. Cranbrook Cottage is down a long drive near the end of the road.

If Cranbrook Cottage was in the dictionary, I'm sure it's definition would be 'peaceful, romantic hideaway'. An elegant breakfast delivered by tray, the netting draped over the linen covered bed, the flowers climbing the front of the verandah, tasteful decoration with numerous period touches combine with modern facilities. Take some relaxing music and a glass of wine and you won't want to leave. The cottage has two bedrooms - one double and one twin, and is located on a vineyard a short drive from a selection of good restaurants and cafes. Set well away from Ian and Keren's interesting earth-brick home, the cottage provides all the privacy you would want on a holiday or honeymoon. It's almost worth getting married for. The interior is rustic, with lots of rough-sawn timber and a genuinely colonial atmosphere. My breakfast was a superb collection of home-made preserves, a selection of interesting breads, platter of fresh fruit, juice and a light egg soufflé. Visitors from Florida wrote: 'This epitomises all the wonderful things we hoped to find in New Zealand'. I couldn't agree more and it is good value for money.

Accommodation available (NZ$)	👤	👤👤	+👤	🛏	🛁	
1 S/C house	$110	$180	$40	Q+2S	PR	

Family dog on site
Guest pets by arrangement

Breakfast: Special cooked

Guest rooms:
Ambience:
Setting/location:

LOW   HIGH

Property features
Vineyard setting
Swimming pool/petanque
Open fire/underfloor/central heating
Airport/ferry transfers arranged
Complimentary port/sherry
Local features
Vineyards/wineries
Trout fishing
Bush walks
Golf course/tennis courts
Art & craft galleries

Stonehaven Vineyard Homestay

John and Paulette Hansen
414 Rapaura Rd, RD 3, Blenheim
Tel: (03) 572 9730   Mob: 027 6821120
Fax: (03) 572 9730
stay@stonehavenhomestay.co.nz
www.lodgings.co.nz/stonehaven.html

Blenheim - 10 minutes
Nelson - 1 hr 30 mins

From SH 1 turn west into Rapaura Rd at Spring Creek. Stonehaven is after Jacksons Rd on your left. If coming from Nelson, Rapaura Rd is on the left shortly after the Wairau River and before Renwick.

When I arrived at Stonehaven Vineyard homestay I was immediately struck by the house and its surroundings. This near-new, large stone-and-cedar house is right in the middle of premium sauvignon blanc vineyards in Marlborough - a stunning setting. John and Paulette settled me into my immaculately presented room with its magnificent views across the extensive lawns and gardens and the vineyard to the rugged Richmond Range. Mine was the 'Nikau' Room, offering every comfort, from quality bed linen, a large ensuite, tea and coffee making facilities and a choice of port and sherry, to heated floor and towel rail and television. I was served coffee and delicious home baking in the casual lounge and shown the menu for a three-course dinner. This included fresh, home-grown vegetables. The evening meal exceeded expectations and afterwards I relaxed around the fire, discussing winery tours and four-wheel driving, just two of the many activities on offer. Breakfast in the summerhouse had a special ambience. We overlooked the swimming pool and the other guests and I reflected on the great company, wonderful food and relaxing comfort that is Stonehaven.

Family pets on site	Accommodation available (NZ$)	🧍	🧍🧍	+🧍	🛏	🛁
Breakfast: Cooked	1 Room	$200	$220		K	EN
Evening meal: $50pp	1 Room	$175	$195		Q	EN
Guest rooms:	1 Room	$110	$135		2KS	PR
Ambience:						
Setting/location:						

LOW   HIGH

Le Grys Vineyard Cottage and Homestay

John and Jennifer Joslin
Conders Bend Road, Renwick, Blenheim
Tel: (03) 572 9490   Mob: 021 313208
Fax: (03) 572 9491
stay@legrys.co.nz
www.lodgings.co.nz/legrys.html

Property features
Includes glass of Le Grys wine
Mudblock construction
Indoor solar heated swimming pool
Vineyard setting
Local features
Vineyards/wineries/olive groves
Trout fishing
Horse and trap winery tours
Sailing/mailboat trips
Golf courses
Horse riding/walks

Renwick - 4 minutes
Blenheim - 15 minutes

On SH 6 from Blenheim to Nelson,
Renwick is approx 8 minutes from
Blenheim. From Renwick, drive 2km
and turn left into Condors Bend Rd.
Le Grys is the third drive on the left.

A glass of fine Marlborough chardonnay, enjoyed on my own private deck of a self-contained cottage amongst the vines is something I often dreamed of. In John and Jennifer's romantic vineyard setting, in the heart of Marlborough's wine-growing region, it became a reality. The wine could have come from the vines just a few metres away. The earth-brick cottage is quite private from the main home and has been finished to an impeccable standard. All the fabrics, furniture and appliances have been stylishly woven together to create a romantic base from which to enjoy the vineyards. This cottage has two bedrooms, kitchen facilities, barbecue on the deck, a lounge/dining area and bathroom. There is also homestay accommodation in the Le Grys Homestead that has been finished to the same high standard as the cottage. The homestead features earth-brick walls, topped with trusses from the old Picton Railway Station, which provide a feeling of solidarity and character. Having travelled widely, these two experienced voyagers are now turning their energies into providing the kind of comforts they found sometimes hard to find in their travels. They also make quality, award winning wine.

Accommodation available (NZ$)	👤	👤👤	+👤	🛏	🛁	Family dog on site Guest pets by arrangement
1 S/C cottage	$250	$250	$50	Q+2S	PR	Breakfast: Provisions provided
Homestay	$150	$150		Q	PR	

Cooked breakfast available at homestay. Self prepare in cottage.
TV in cottage. Socket for laptop internet connection avail in homestead.

Guest rooms:
Ambience:
Setting/location:

LOW   HIGH

Property features
- Feature garden with potager
- Rammed earth construction
- Guest pick-up available
- Open fire in winter

Local features
- Vineyards/wineries
- Golf course
- Trout fishing
- Horse and wagon trips
- Gardens/museum
- Olive groves

Renwick - 2 minutes walk
Blenheim - 12 minutes

Broomfield Garden Homestay

Kaye and Gary Green
35 Inkerman St, Renwick
Tel: (03) 572 8162
kay.gary@xtra.co.nz
www.lodgings.co.nz/broomfield.html

To Blenheim & Airport

Renwick Village

Inkerman St

BROOMFIELD

To Nelson

From Blenheim take Middle Renwick Rd to Renwick. Turn into Inkerman St on your right, Broomfield is 150m on your left.

This rammed earth building and separate cottage have been built overlooking the spectacular garden to the hills surrounding the Marlborough plains. A mix of simplicity and design flair has resulted in a cosy, intimate, comfortable surrounding. Kaye and Gary are keen helpful hosts but their enthusiasm is tempered with an understanding that guests require their privacy. On the patio at dusk, the rural setting, the lime-washed walls of the house and the large formal gardens all fostered a wonderful feeling of relaxation. Here I enjoyed a glass of wine from a bottle I had chosen during the day. Within the house there is just one large guestroom, which is private from the hosts and has been decorated with the same flair as the rest of the house. The newly appointed two-bedroom cottage offers fresh country comfort and is beautifully decorated. It is located at the bottom of the garden and ideal for those seeking extra privacy. The hosts are garden enthusiasts and their thought and planning over many hours is evident. There is an abundance of colour, fragrance and creativity - not to mention food - in the adjoining potager. I eyed the attractive ripening fruit on espaliered vines and sucked on snatched berries as I wandered through.

Family cat on site	Accommodation available (NZ$)	▮	▮▮	+▮	🛏	🛁
	1 Room	$100	$150-160		K	EN
	1 Cottage	$200	$200-240	$50	K + D	PR

Breakfast: Special cooked

Guest rooms:
Ambience:
Setting/location:

LOW   HIGH

Antria Boutique Lodge

Phil Sowman   Kathryne Fleming
276 Old Renwick Road, RD 2, Blenheim
Tel: (03) 579 2191
Fax: (03) 579 2192
stay@antria.co.nz
www.lodgings.co.nz/antria.html

Property features
Luxurious beds and linen
Extensive NZ art collection
Private lounge/Sky TV/open fire
Great selection local wine
Petanque and tennis court
Local features
Walkways/Marlborough Sounds
Vineyard dining nearby
Golf courses
Art galleries/traditional Maori art
Vineyard tours

Blenheim - 5 mins drive
Nelson - 70 mins drive

From Picton turn right after bridge
before Blenheim approx 4km to gate.
From Nelson turn into Raupara Rd
right at Jackson's Rd, left into Old
Renwick Rd. Antria is on left approx
2km.

Driving down the driveway to Antria, I was first impressed by the dominating gothic, copper doors. The entrance is spectacular and opens into a Mediterranean- style house inspired by one that Phil and Kathryne fell in love with when they were in Greece. Antria offers guests two suites, each in a private wing and decorated with lively colour and original art. They have super king-size beds and double walk-in showers. The hosts warmly welcomed me and a note written in the guest book reinforced the hospitable attitude of the couple: "You are both very special people and have a way of making your visitors feel like long lost friends," it stated. Surrounded by vines, Cloudy Bay the nearest winery, Antria is an excellent place to stay if you want to tour the area. Phil is on hand to arrange a guided tour. Breakfast was a magnificent experience. I enjoyed corn fritters topped with Kathryne's delicious chilli plum sauce. As the weather was pleasant, I was able to sit outside in the courtyard, defined by old railway bridge beams. I was soothed by the sound of water rippling across the courtyard's unique water feature while I enjoyed a local Sauvignon Blanc. In the distance the mountains began to change their colours as the day unfolded.

Accommodation available (NZ$)	👤	👤👤	+👤	🛏	🛁	Family pets on site Guest pets by arrangement
1 Room	$295-305	$335-395		K	EN	Breakfast: Special cooked
1 Room	$295-305	$335-395		SK or 2S	EN	

Guest rooms:
Ambience:
Setting/location:

LOW   HIGH

Property features
Swimming pool/petanque
2 hectares gardens/paddocks
Sheep and horses on property
Baby grand piano
Italian hospitality
Guest lounge with open fire
Earth block cottage
Local features
Vineyards/wineries nearby
Golf courses/gardens
Trout fishing/walks

Uno Piu Homestead and Cottage

Gino and Heather Rocco
75 Murphy's Road, Blenheim
Tel: (03) 578 2235   Mob: 021 1744257
Fax: (03) 578 2235
stay@unopiu.co.nz
www.lodgings.co.nz/unopiu.html

Blenheim - 5 minutes
Airport - 5 minutes

From Blenheim drive towards
Nelson/Blenheim Airport on SH 6.
Turn right into Murphys Rd.
Uno Piu is 600m on the left.

Gino and Heather have turned one half of their elegant home over to guests. Two bedrooms at the front of the house have spacious ensuites (one with a claw foot bath). I found my room inviting and comfortable with thoughtful extras, such lots of spare pillows, a television, a fridge with complimentary beverages and a good tea and coffee-making facilities. Gino is Italian. Nearly twenty years ago he came to Blenheim and set up the successful Roccos Restaurant. So it is no surprise that meals are a feature here. He changes his Italian-influenced dinner menu daily and is happy to consult about guests' preferences. Breakfast was served in the enormous lounge/dining room, which has an open fireplace and a baby grand piano. We relished the berries and crepes with maple syrup and lemon and the platter of cheese, anchovies, sun-dried tomatoes olive and artichokes. I had to have a vigorous swim in the 10-metre pool to work it off. If you were looking for something a little less active you can play a game of chess on the new outdoor set. Also available on this five-acre property is an charming two-bedroom, earth-block cottage which is self contained and in a large private garden of its own. It is a favourite with honeymooners.

Family pets on site Guest pets by arrangement	Accommodation available (NZ$)	![person]	![two people]	+![person]	![bed]	![bath]
Breakfast: Special 3 course	2 Rooms	$190-290	$210-350		K+SK or 2S	EN
Evening meal: $70pp	1 S/C cottage	$240-380	$240-380	$60	SK+Q+S	PR
Guest rooms:						
Ambience:						
Setting/location:		Children in cottage only.				

171

Straw Lodge Boutique Vineyard Accommodation

Nettie Barrow   Jane Craighead
17 Fareham Lane, Wairau Valley, Marlborough
Tel: (03) 572 9767
Fax: (03) 572 9769
strawlodge@xtra.co.nz
www.lodgings.co.nz/strawlodgeboutique.html

Property features
Private vineyard setting
Straw bale construction
Complimentary wine tasting
Guests spa/BBQ courtyard/kitchen
Bikes/golf clubs
Local features
River access/fishing/swimming
Vineyards/wineries
Wilderness/walking
Professional guiding/advice

Blenheim - 15 minutes

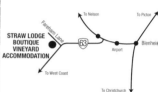

From Blenheim take SH6 towards Nelson. Pass airport then turn left into SH63 towards West Coast/Wairau Valley. Travel approx. 7.5km & turn right into Fareham Lane. Straw Lodge 200m on left.

As I rode a bike, provided by the lodge, through the 22 acres of Sauvignon Blanc and Pinot Noir vines, I admired the mountain views that rose up in all directions. The lodge, which is constructed out of straw bales, is fascinating. Nettie and Jane showed me photographs of the long and hard building process. There are three private suites available for guests each a little different, but all with an outlook that opens to individual courtyards which then leads to a huge lawn and the vineyard. In the evening guests were treated to a formal wine tasting of the vineyard's wines. I enjoyed learning about the grapes that grow on the site. Dinner is provided on request and on warm evenings this can be eaten al fresco while looking out over the vines. Meals are a specialty at Straw Lodge. I recommend dining in at least one night during a stay. I enjoyed locally caught salmon served on kumara mash with a spinach, hazelnut and blue cheese topping. Delicious! Both Jane and Nettie are also Department of Conservation guides so they know a lot about the area and will even take guests on a separately arranged guided tour.

Accommodation available (NZ$)	🧍	🧍🧍	+🧍	🛏	🛁	Guest pets by arrangement
2 Suites	$195-255	$225-295	$60	K or 2S+D EN		Breakfast: Special cooked
1 Suite	$195-255	$225-295		K or 2S EN		Evening meal: $75pp incl. wine

Internet socket in rooms, Sky TV in lounge.
Sounds bach also available – please enquire.

Guest rooms:
Ambience:
Setting/location:

LOW   HIGH

Property features
Privacy/seclusion
BBQ/country picnics/DVD
Sea views/beach & bush walks
Open wood fire/African Hammock
Local features
Café - 5 mins
Sawcut Gorge
Woodside Gorge - 3 hour walk
Golf course/wineries/gardens
Fishing/rafting/seal colony
Horse riding

Woodside Cottage

Nick and Jock Clouston
Kaikoura Coast, Marlborough
Tel: (03) 575 6819   Mob: 025 349951
Fax:(03) 575 6419
woodsidecottage@xtra.co.nz
www.lodgings.co.nz/woodside.html

Blenheim - 45 minutes
Kaikoura - 45 minutes

Situated between Blenheim and
Kaikoura on SH 1. From Blenheim
travel 60km - approx 5 minutes
south of stone church. From
Kaikoura travel 60km - approx 5
minutes north of 'The Store'
road sign.

This delightful 1950's blade-shearers' cottage is close to the wild shore of the Kaikoura coastline. It is sited on Benmore sheep and cattle station comprising five thousand acres of land that climbs from sea level to 1200 metres. Woodside has been rescued and freshened with artistic empathy, so that the original period style is not lost. There are many modern touches (the heated towel rail, toaster kettle) which, with good quality bedding and an open, brick fireplace with wood provided, makes a stay very comfortable. I felt very much at home in this cottage, which has such a close relationship to the tussocky sand dunes around it. Swinging on the African Hommock on a quiet evening, I hoped I would be lucky enough to see dolphins out on the sea. Hidden as I was from the rest of the world, I could have easily stayed here for a restorative week or more. Breakfast provisions are left in the fridge - muesli, bacon, eggs and tomatoes or freshly caught fish, homemade muffins and preserves. Nick also sells her own jams and preserves. People write in the guest book that they are very pleased to have discovered this place. So am I.

Guest pets by arrangement	Accommodation available (NZ$)			+		
Breakfast: Provisions provided	1 S/C cottage	$100	$165	$25	K+Q+2S	PR

Guest rooms:
Ambience:
Setting/location:

Breakfast provisions are for continental and cooked.

The Factory

Leanne French   Greg Keith
Factory Road, Hapuku, RD 1, Kaikoura
Tel: (03) 319 6999   Mob: 021 1384586
Fax: (03) 319 6997
reservations@thefactory.co.nz
www.lodgings.co.nz/thefactory.html

Property features
Historic cheese factory
3 minute walk to beach
Majestic mountain views
Only one group of guests at a time
Self contained with kitchen/lounge
Courtyard/outdoor bath
Local features
Whale/dolphin/seal watching

Kaikoura - 10 minute drive
Blenheim - 1.5 hours drive

Head north from Kaikoura on SH1. After 10kms you will see Factory Road on the right. Go all the way to the end and turn right at The Factory sign.

Between the mountains and a wild stretch of coast just north of Kaikoura, this near-derelict cheese factory has been rescued, turned into a home with self-contained accommodation, and filled with exuberant colour and art. Driving down the road, I was greeted by resident pukeko native birds who followed me to the impressive looking building. The interior of The Factory is also impressive. River rocks line the living room floor, Leanne and Greg's artwork cover the walls and other interior details have been creatively recycled to reflect the building's past or make reference to the railway line which runs down the coast behind the house. The accommodation is to one side of the main house and has three bedrooms. The room designed for children was my favourite. It has two high beds (I had to use a step to get into mine) and scattered around are stuffed animals, and dress-up fairy and pirate costumes. Much of the wonderful furniture throughout the house has been built by Greg from wood from the original cheese factory. A short track leads through long grass to a beach where some days you may not see another soul. I was so inspired I found myself creating my own bit of artwork as I signed the visitor's book, and I noticed that other guests had done the same.

Accommodation available (NZ$)	🧍	🧍🧍	+🧍	🛏	🛁	Family cat on site Guest pets by arrangement
S/C unit	$250-295	$250-295	$100	K+Q+2S	PR	

$70 for extra child charge - 15 and under. Maximum 6 people.

Breakfast: Provisions provided
Evening meal: Enquire
Guest rooms:
Ambience:
Setting/location:

Property features
Claybird shooting
Tennis court/croquet/petanque
Mountain bikes available
Black Escorial sheep
Bonnie the Sheepdog for demo's
Minature angus cattle
Local features
Maori tours
Quad biking
Whales and dolphins
Kaikoura night sky tours

Kincaid Lodge
Helen and Judith Costley
611 Main North Road, RD1, Kaikoura
Tel: (03) 319 6851
Fax: (03) 319 6801
helen@kincaidlodge.co.nz
www.lodgings.co.nz/kincaidlodge.html

  12

Kaikoura - 5 mins drive
Christchurch - 2 hours drive

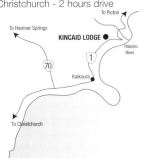

Kincaid Lodge is located 6km north of Kaikoura on SH 1, on the left (mountain) side of the road.

Backed by snowcapped mountains and views to the Pacific Ocean, the historic Kincaid homestead has stood for 100 years. Kincaid Lodge sits in the relaxed, private ambience of the countryside and is only six kilometres from the award-winning attractions and restaurants of Kaikoura. Kincaid Lodge is a perfect place to unwind and feel pampered. The homestead has four charming guest suites each with ensuits. They are spacious and luxuriously appointed and I felt both indulged and at home. Homemade biscuits, chocolates and complimentary port all added to my pleasure. The lounge had an inviting open fire, piano, guitar, wine list, bookcase and a selection of games. For the more energetic, there is a game of tennis perhaps, or croquet, claybird shooting, mountain biking or golfing. In the evening Helen was happy to drop me into town for dinner and it was only a short taxi ride home. Helen and Judith, a mother and daughter team, are New Zealanders with farming backgrounds. They have both travelled extensively and with their friendly sheep dogs, look forward to sharing their piece of paradise. Before I left, I enjoyed an extensive breakfast on my private verandah, then strolled through the large landscaped garden of native and English plantings.

Family dog on site
Guest pets by arrangement

Accommodation available (NZ$)					
1 Room	$495			SK or 2S	EN/spa
1 Room	$495			SK or 2S	EN
2 Rooms	$495			Q	EN

Breakfast: Special cooked

Guest rooms:
Ambience:
Setting/location:

TV's available on request.

Dylans Country Cottages

Mike and Maureen Morris
Postmans Road, Kaikoura
Tel: (03) 319 5473
Fax: (03) 319 5425
dylans.cs@clear.net.nz
www.lodgings.co.nz/dylans.html

Property features
Outdoor bath
Lavender farm
Lavender shop on site
Display gardens
Local features
Whale watching
Seal colony
Swim with dolphins
Fishing
Golf course
Bush walks

Kaikoura - 10 minutes
Blenheim - 1 hr 30 mins

From SH 1 turn into Postmans Rd,
which is just north of Kaikoura
township. Continue past Mt Fyffe Rd
to Dylans on your right.

Nestled at the foot of Mt Fyffe, Dylans offers two rustic cottages, each with French doors, lots of exposed timber, a creative individual style and a large dose of country atmosphere. Both cottages are two storied, with queen beds upstairs and lounge/dining, kitchenette and bathroom downstairs. The Kowhai cottage has a funky bathroom with a spa bath, while the Mahoe cottage offers an outdoor bath and shower in addition to the usual bathroom facilities. Breakfast is a freshly made loaf of bread, homemade preserves and free range eggs. Dylans cottages are an integral part of a 5 acre working lavender farm and display gardens. There is also an onsite lavender shop with a wide range of products related to relaxation and well being. With all that Dylans has to offer it is guaranteed that your stay will be restful and provide a unique experience. These cottages are designed for your privacy but friendly hosts are only a few steps away. Kaikoura township is only a short 10 minute drive away where I found numerous local shops, cafes and restaurants. Whale watching tours are famous at this quaint seaside town.

Accommodation available (NZ$)	🧍	🧍🧍	+🧍	🛏	🛁	Family pets on site
1 S/C unit	$150	$150	$15	Q+S	PR	Breakfast: Continental
1 S/C unit	$150	$150	$15	Q+S	PR	

Both units also have fold out double divan beds. Enquire for children's tariffs.

Guest rooms:
Ambience:
Setting/location:

LOW   HIGH

Property features
Hungry Nun Café/Chocolate shop
Swimming pool
Separate guest lounge
Croquet lawn
Mountain range views
Free use of bicycles
Local features
Whale watching
Swimming with dolphins
Seal colony
Bush walks

The Old Convent

Judith & Jenny Hughey   Gordon Cockerell
Mt Fyffe Road, Kaikoura
Tel: (03) 319 6603
Fax: (03) 319 6690
o.convent@xtra.co.nz
www.lodgings.co.nz/oldconvent.html

Kaikoura - 4 minutes
Blenheim - 1 hr 30 mins

From Kaikoura town centre cross
Beach Rd (SH 1) and continue down
Ludstone Rd. Take Mt. Fyffe Rd on
your right and continue to the corner
of Mill Rd. Off-street parking is
accessible from Mill Rd.

The convent of Our Lady of the Missions was built in 1911, and has since been converted into guest accommodation. It retains much of its original charm and features. The guest lounge is the old Chapel and there is a hidden staircase once used by a priest to get into the confessional without intruding on the nuns. There are now 17 guestrooms housed in both the convent and the adjacent schoolhouse, which gives the place a rambling, casual ambience that is suitable for groups. Many of the upstairs guestrooms enjoy views over the often snow-capped mountains and all have pleasant rural views over the land and surrounding farms. A significant feature of The Old Convent is the dinner, which features crayfish and New Zealand meats. My favourite menu included a seafood flan, followed by blue cod with a prawn sauce and finished with an apple tart with almond cream and calvados. I have always been a sucker for seafood. A stay at The Old Convent is an opportunity to meet fellow travellers, enjoy the peace and tranquility of a rural stay in an historic building and indulge in fine food. Kaikoura township is just a four minute drive.

Guest pets by arrangement	Accommodation available (NZ$)	♂	♂♂	+♂	🛏	🛁
Breakfast: Cooked	2 Rooms	$85			S	EN
Evening meal: Menu Choice	5 Rooms	$100-145	$155	$30	D/T	EN
Guest rooms:	5 Rooms	$140	$140-185	$30	K/Q/T	EN
Ambience:	2 Family Suites		$210-230		K/Q/T	EN
Setting/location:						

Glacier Country, Lake Matheson reflections.

Westport

Bay House Café 41 Beach Rd, Tauranga Bay, Tel: (03) 789-7133. Enjoy great kiwi cuisine, awesome scenic views & friendly West Coast hospitality.

Freckles Café 216 Palmerston St, Tel: (03) 789-8270. We have been told the pies are second to none.

Punakaiki

Nikau Coffee Shop
SH 6, Tel: (03) 731-1813
Good coffee and healthy snacks.

Barrytown

Rata Café
State Highway 6,
Tel: (03) 731-1151. Good lunch menu and coffee.

Greymouth

Bonzai Bakery & Pizzeria
31 MacKay St, Tel: (03) 768-4170
Café 124 on Mackay
124 Mackay St,
Tel: (03) 768-7503. Great lunch. Near railway station with nice gift shop behind café.
Steamers Carvery & Bar 58 Mackay St, Tel: (03) 768-4193. Excellent seafood. Good selection of wine and beer.

Hokitika

Café de Paris 19 Tancred St, Tel: (03) 755-8933. Good food, popular with the locals.
Stumpers Bar & Café 2 Weld St, Tel: (03) 755-6154. Good service, very West Coasty.
Events
Wild Food Festival
Early March - held annually.

Pukekura

Puke Pub Lake Lanthe, Tel: (03) 755-4008. Unique, fun 'road kill' menu. Great hospitality.

Franz Josef Glacier

Alice May Cron St, Tel: (03) 752-0740. Relaxed casual dining. Guinness and Kilkenny on tap.

Fox Glacier

Café Neve Main Rd, Tel: (03) 751-0110. Good place to stop for a snack, meal or coffee. Good pizzas.

South Westland

The Salmon Farm Café
SH 6, Paringa, Tel: (03) 751-0837
Specialises in salmon dishes. Licensed. Feed the salmon.

Haast

McGuires Lodge
SH 6, Tel: (03) 750-0020. Last stop for a bite or coffee before heading through Haast Pass to Queenstown or first stop after coming through the Pass. Friendly operators.

Walking a West Coast beach.

Glacier Country, Okarito clouds reflecting on lagoon.

Breakers Seaside Bed & Breakfast

Jan Macdonald
9 Mile Creek, SH6, Coast Road, Greymouth
Tel: (03) 762 7743
Fax: (03) 762 7733   Free: 0800 350590
stay@breakers.co.nz
www.lodgings.co.nz/breakers.html

Property features
Views from all rooms of Tasman Sea
Mountain views/2 acre gardens
Private beach access
West coast sunsets
TV/tea/coffee facilites in all rooms
Local features
Paparoa National Park
Hiking/biking/caving/rafting
Arthurs Pass National Park
Jade carving/wood turning
Glass blowing

Greymouth - 10 mins drive
Punakaki - 20 mins drive

The Breakers is located on the Coast Road, (State Highway 6) at Nine Mile Creek, 14kms North from Greymouth.

The name says it all because from every room in the house I could hear the waves of the Tasman Sea crashing below. This New Zealand style accommodation is set above one of the West Coast's amazing beaches. Breakers has four guestrooms, two of which are in the house. Both have ocean views, queen-size beds and access to a large balcony. The other two rooms are away from the main house in a separate wing and have views over Mussel Point. These two rooms are more modern but still in keeping with the New Zealand 'bach' (small seaside cottage) theme. I stayed in one of the newer rooms called the Sunset Room, which had a large king-size bed where I lay in the morning with the curtains and door open to enjoy the water view while I had a cup of tea in bed. The house is surrounded by piles of driftwood and river rocks which have been collected from local beaches and I was amazed by the amount. Jan prepared a lovely breakfast and gave me advice about the sort of activities I might enjoy during the day. She loves the outdoors and had many walks to recommend.

Accommodation available (NZ$)	👤	👤👤	+👤	🛏	🛁	
						Family dog on site
						Guest pets by arrangement
1 Room	$150			Q	EN	Breakfast: Special cooked
1 Room	$210		$30	Q+S	EN	Evening meal: $60pp
1 Suite	$235		$30	SK+S	EN	Guest rooms:
1 Suite	$235		$30	K	EN	Ambience:
						Setting/location:

Property features
Incl. breakfast & 4-course dinner
Incl. 2 guided farm/nature activities
6180 acres range/forest/river/lakes
DOC Licence CA 15048
Working sheep station/guided walks
Sheep shearing/kayaking
Local features
Beech forest & alpine tracks
Arthur's Pass National Park
Wild rivers and high country lakes
Fishing - trout and salmon

Arthur's Pass - 15 minutes
Christchurch - 2 hours

Wilderness Lodge Arthur's Pass

David Webster and Kathy Dunn
State Highway 73, Arthur's Pass
Tel: (03) 318 9246
Fax: (03) 318 9245
arthurspass@wildernesslodge.co.nz
www.lodgings.co.nz/wildernessap.html

The Lodge is 16km east of Arthur's Pass township on Highway 73. Transfers from train station can be arranged. Shuttle bus stops at lodge.

Nestled in a mountain beech forest clearing in the heart of the Southern Alps, this 24-four room lodge is surrounded by Arthur's Pass National Park. Each of the spacious guestrooms have superb views and feature New Zealand timbers. Recent additions to the lodge are the four Alpine Lodges, which are separated from the main lodge and have been stylishly furnished with a super-king-size bed, a lounge and balcony that looks out to landscaped gardens and the mountains. This is a high quality, professionally run operation. Maps help guests to explore the 20 kilometres of easy walking tracks on their own, or they can join in the Lodges guided nature adventure programme. Included in the tariff is a daily program of shorter, guided, nature and farm tours including mustering and sheep shearing, canoeing on high country lakes and exploring beech forest and tussock lands to look for birds and alpine plants.I was amazed at how much there was to learn about the environment, even in the immediate area around the lodge. This lodge is associated with Wilderness Lodge Lake Moeraki in the rainforests of South Westland. Both are designed to show that well managed ecotourism can both protect the environment and provide employment to small communities.

Guest pets by arrangement	Accommodation available (NZ$)	👤	👤👤	+👤	🛏	🛁
Breakfast: Cooked	20 Rooms	$330-430	$460-660		Q+S	EN
Evening Meal: Included	4 Lodges	$590-690	$780-980		SK/T	EN
Guest rooms:						
Ambience:						
Setting/location:		Tariff incl. 4 course dinner, breakfast, 2 guided short nature activities daily.				

Kapitea Ridge

Trixie and Murray Montagu
Chesterfield Road, 5 km south of Kumara Junction
Tel: (03) 755 6805
Fax: (03) 755 6895
stay@kapitea.co.nz
www.lodgings.co.nz/kapitea.html

12

Property features
Clay bird shooting/petanque
Sheltered garden jacuzzi/spa
Overlooks panoramic seascapes
Fishing guide & massuese avail
In house marriage celebrant
Gold panning/mountain bikes
Helipad: scenic/hunting/fishing

Local features
Golfing/rafting/canoeing
Glacier/Mt Cook/Milford flights
3 Nat Parks/Pancake Rocks/beach

Hokitika - 15 minutes
Greymouth - 15 minutes

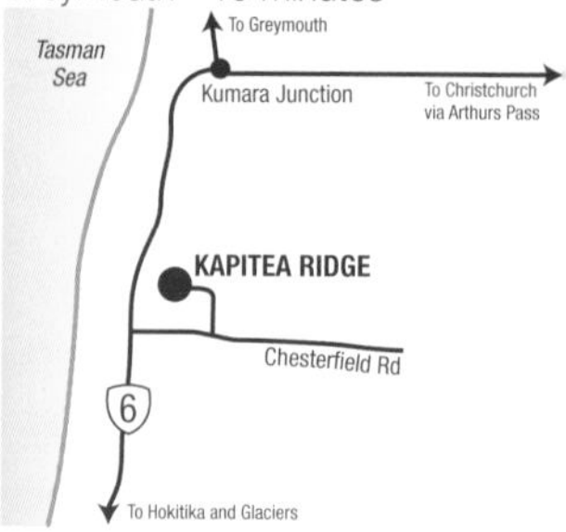

From SH 6, just south of Kumara Junction, turn into Chesterfield Rd (approx. 23km south of Greymouth or 17km north of Hokitika). Cross railway line and take first driveway on left.

The view up the coast disappearing into the sea mist way in the distance remains etched in my memory. This fresh modern property is elevated and several rooms take full advantage of the views, some from their own balconies where you can observe the many moods of the coast. The lodge was purpose-built and there has been no compromise on guest comfort. All rooms are finished to a high standard of fittings and furnishings, televisions and good heating. The spacious lounge has a log fire and the dining room is in the conservatory - an area very well used because of its views over the garden and out to the ocean. "Kapa Wahine" an interesting copper sculpture stands here. There is a covered spa pool just a few metres from the lodge, among native ferns and shrubs and, depending on the weather, you can hear the ocean crashing against the shore. Murray has an in depth knowledge of Maori culture and is able to speak Maori. Self-guided or interpretive guided beach walks are offered as part of your stay at Kapitea Ridge and you will be sure to leave the area well informed and satisfied that you have been given all the options for exploring the region.

Accommodation available (NZ$)					
2 Rooms	$495	$495-555	$80	SK/T	EN
4 Rooms	$385	$385-455		SK/T or Q	EN

Breakfast: Cooked
Evening meal: $35 - 75pp
Guest rooms:
Ambience:
Setting/location:

LOW HIGH

Property features
2.5 acres of native garden
Outside spa in bush setting
Canoes/vintage cars on site
Eco friendly
Peaceful private setting
Local features
Helicopter flights from homestead
3 National Parks/beach
Fishing guides arranged
Glow-worm tour
Jade/glass/gold/crafts

Hokitika - 10 mins drive
Greymouth - 20 mins drive

From SH 6 just south of Kumara
Junction, turn into Stafford Rd at
Awatuna (approx. 25 km south of
Greymouth, 12km north of Hokitika).
Cross railway line, Awatuna
Homestead is first on the left.

Awatuna Homestead

Pauline and Hemi Te Rakau
9 Stafford Road, Awatuna, RD2, Hokitika
Tel: (03) 755 6834
Fax:(03) 755 6876   Free: 0800 006888
rest@awatunahomestead.co.nz
www.lodgings.co.nz/awatuna.html

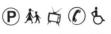

This coastal retreat set beside the tranquil Waimea River has a peaceful and relaxing environment. Pauline, Hemi and family have lived here for over 30 years and combine the warmth of a family atmosphere with the luxury of a boutique lodging. The homestead is set among plantings of native trees and shrubs which foster bird-life. Nature and culture come together because many of the plant varieties are steeped in Maori tradition. It's a special experience to relax in the spa pool that is set among native trees and listen to the roaring of the sea, a five-minute walk away. Hemi, a retired cultural advisor to the Department of Conservation, speaks Maori and is willing to share his knowledge of the Pacific navigators, language, customs and traditional stories of his people during the evening. The ambience of the homestead is complemented by an open fire in the guest lounge, a room in which guests relax in the evening after a full day and a meal of country cuisine for which Pauline is renowned. There is so much adventure and excitement in this region and this is a good place to base yourself while you explore the options, as Awatuna is situated between Greymouth and Hokitika.

Family pets on site	Accommodation available (NZ$)	♦	♦♦	+♦	🛏	🛁
Breakfast: Cooked	1 Room	$175	$190		2S	EN
Evening meal: $55pp	1 Room	$230	$230		1Q	EN
Guest rooms:	1 Room	$300	$300		SK or 2S	EN/Spa
Ambience:	1 S/C unit	$200	$200	$25	Q,D,2S	PR
Setting/location:	Single bed for children: $15. S/C unit: breakfast is $18pp extra.					

183

Rimu Lodge

Helen and Peter Walls
33 Seddons Terrace Road, Rimu, Hokitika
Tel: (03) 755 5255   Mob: 025 6487060
Fax:(03) 755 5237
rimulodge@xtra.co.nz
www.lodgings.co.nz/rimulodge.html

Property features
Large stone open fireplace
Large outside deck
Spectacular river and bush views
Local features
Golf course nearby
Trout fishing tours
Glaciers/ Mt Cook
Milford Sound flights
Punakaiki - pancake rocks

Hokitika - 10 mins drive
Greymouth - 40 mins drive

From Hokitika, travel south across Hokitika Bridge, turn first left into Arthurstown Rd. Travel 4km to intersection, turn right into Woodstock-Rimu Rd. At Rimu, turn left into Seddons Terrace Rd. Rimu Lodge is 300 metres on left.

Rimu Lodge is elegant and intimate and overlooks the Hokitika River and distant alpine peaks. The building has a steeply pitched roof which fits in with the mountainous surroundings and the views from the property are unparalleled. It was once a family holiday home but hosts, Helen and Peter, felt it was too good to keep to themselves. The guest lounge has cathedral-like ceilings and I enjoyed sitting in this space, in front of a roaring fire, before evening drinks and hors d'oeuvres were served. There are four guestrooms, each with queen-size beds and spacious ensuites. They are decorated with modern, good taste and have plenty of room to spread out in. I woke up in the morning and through my window was a surreal view of the mountain peaks rising majestically out of the mist. Breakfast was served on the deck where Helen offered me wonderful home-made muesli and the option of a cooked breakfast. She recounted interesting stories about the area and gave me advice on what to do during my stay. Rimu Lodge is well-placed if guests want to explore the region, but it is also a treat to relax and enjoy the lodge.

Accommodation available (NZ$)	👤	👤👤	+👤	🛏	🛁	Family dog on site
3 Rooms	$175	$275		Q	EN	Breakfast: Special cooked
1 Room	$175	$225		Q	EN	

Guest rooms:
Ambience:
Setting/location:

LOW   HIGH

Property features
Tranquil rural setting
Extensive gardens/outdoor area
Large spacious bedrooms/living
Superior comfort beds
Elk farm tour
Trout fishing guides
Local features
Glow worms
Pack track walkway
Glaciers - 45 min drive
White heron sanctuary - 45 min

Hari Hari - 5 minute walk
Hokitika - 50 minute drive

Located one hour south of Hokitika,
take SH6 to Harihari. Wapiti Park
Homestead is just south of Harihari,
on the west side of the highway.

Wapiti Park Homestead

Grant and Beverleigh Muir
State Highway 6, Hari Hari, South Westland, West Coast
Tel: (03) 753 3074   Mob: 021 385252
Fax:(03) 753 3024   Free: 0800 927484
wapitipark@xtra.co.nz
www.lodgings.co.nz/wapitipark.html

The comfortable and unpretentious Wapiti Park Homestead is located just out of Hari Hari on the South Island's dramatic West Coast. This country-style luxury lodge is set among award-winning gardens, on a deer farm where over a hundred Rocky Mountain Elk (Wapiti) graze. Downstairs is a dining room where guests can enjoy gourmet delights, that change daily, and premium New Zealand wines. There's a comfortable guest lounge, and a trophy and games room containing a small billiard table. A neat row of gumboots lined up on the outside terrace, tempts guests to go fly-fishing or hunting, to explore the 50-acre farm, or go on a farm tour and feed the Wapiti. Of the five guestrooms the Oak Room was my favourite. It has an antique four-poster king-size bed, comfortable armchairs and a patio with stairs that lead to the garden. From the patio I looked over the garden pond, which is crossed by a small bridge and set among a native garden of toetoe bushes and cabbage trees. Wapiti graze in the nearby paddocks. There are many activities in the area, such as rainforest walks, heli-flights to Fox and Franz Josef glaciers, visits to the White Heron Sanctuary, or sailing on the paddle vessel, Tamati, on Lake Lanthe.

	Accommodation available (NZ$)	👤	👥	+👤	🛏	🛁
Family cat on site						
Breakfast: Special cooked	3 Rooms	$300	$375	$95	SK+1S	EN
Evening meal: $75pp	2 Rooms	$200	$275		SK or T	PR
Guest rooms:						
Ambience:						
Setting/location:		Dinner rate includes pre-dinner drink and nibbles.				

185

Westwood Lodge

Bill and Janet Gawn
SH 6, Franz Josef, Westland
Tel: (03) 752 0112
Fax:(03) 752 0111
westwood@xtra.co.nz
www.lodgings.co.nz/westwood.html

Property features
Dinner available - bookings essential
Guest lounge and bar/snooker tble
Mountain and bush views
Fridges/tea/coffee in rooms
Local features
Glacier flights/horse riding
Bush walks/helihikes/kayaking
Fishing - lake and river
White heron sanctuary
Guided glacier walks/rafting

Franz Josef - 2 minutes
Greymouth - 2 hours

Tasman Sea
To Hokitika
Lake Mapourika
6
WESTWOOD LODGE
Franz Josef Township
To Fox Glacier
To Franz Josef Glacier

From Franz Josef village travel 2km north along SH 6. The lodge is on your right.

The exposed timber walls of these large, brightly decorated suites and their attached bathrooms are exactly what you might expect in a mountain landscape. All eight rooms overlook forest and farmland or the mountains and several small side glaciers. Bed covers and hangings are fabric art that is made or designed by Janet, and throughout the lodge, hang landscape photographs taken by Bill. The extensive living areas include a room with a full-size snooker table, a spacious and inviting lounge that looks to the view and a dining area with seating for 18 people. Stay here and you will have luxury and excellent food dished up with the alpine environment. Bill and Janet are natural hosts who like to give individual attention to their guests; and so you will find your car thoughtfully parked for you. They are also happy to share their local knowledge and help arrange activities such as helicopter rides. The mood that the hosts have created is relaxed and congenial. Guests can usually be found at the bar before sitting down to lodge-style dining, which is a three-course set menu of West Coast produce such as fish, venison or beef. Bookings essential.

Accommodation available (NZ$)	👤	👤👤	+👤	🛏	🛁	Family cat on site
8 Rooms	$295	$395	$150	K/T	EN	Breakfast: Cooked
1 Suite	$395	$495		K/T	EN	Evening meal: $45

Guest rooms:
Ambience:
Setting/location:

Dinner, B&B rates $395-$595.

LOW   HIGH

186

Property features
- Central heating and log fire
- Friendly NZ born hosts
- Rural and mountain views
- Relaxed atmosphere
- Warm timber theme

Local features
- Guided Glacier walks/heli hikes
- Scenic flights
- Bush/lakes and coastal walks
- Horse trekking and kayaking
- White Heron sanctuary tour

Holly Homestead

Gerard and Bernie Oudemans
State Highway 6, Franz Josef Glacier
Tel: (03) 752 0299
Fax: (03) 752 0298
stay@hollyhomestead.co.nz
www.lodgings.co.nz/hollyhomestead.html

Franz Josef - 2 mins
Hokitika - 90 mins

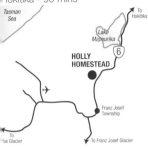

On SH6, 1.5km north of Franz Josef Glacier township.

This historic 1920's house is one of Franz Josef Glacier's oldest wooden homesteads and is built from the native timbers in the Arts and Crafts style. The hosts, Gerard and Bernie, have spent the last few years restoring the homestead and making it the warm and inviting place it is today. When I arrived, a comforting fire was burning in the fireplace in the main living room. I was invited to join Gerard and Bernie for a cup of tea and homemade muffins and they took the time to find out what I had planned for my stay and to provide me with tips of what I must see while I was there. The homestead has four ensuite guestrooms, all superbly appointed with old-world charm. The homestead is perfectly positioned for the outdoor activity the area is known for – hiking, guided glacier walks, scenic flights and kayaking, to name a few. I took time out in the afternoon for a scenic flight over the glaciers, which was a fantastic adventure. Breakfast is served at the large dining table just off the kitchen which overlooks the alpine views. Guests are seated with each other providing a great chance to meet other travellers and exchange travel tips while enjoying Gerard's cooking.

Accommodation available (NZ$)	♦	♦♦	+♦	🛏	🛁
2 Rooms	$160-200	$190-230		Q	EN
1 Room	$190-230	$220-250		SK or 2S	EN
1 Room	$190-230	$220-250	$70	SK or 2S	EN

Breakfast: Cooked

Guest rooms:
Ambience:
Setting/location:

LOW   HIGH

187

Wilderness Lodge Lake Moeraki

Dorothy Piper   Malcolm Edwards
SH 6, Lake Moeraki, South Westland
Tel: (03) 750 0881
Fax: (03) 750 0882
lakemoeraki@wildernesslodge.co.nz
www.lodgings.co.nz/wildernesslm.html

Property features
Incl. 4-course evening meal
Incl. shorter guided nature options
Trout fishing gear for hire
Canoe safaris/kayaks
Lunch available/laundry facilities
Knowledgeable nature guides
DOC concessions
Local features
Trout fishing/rainforest
Fiordland Crested Penguin
Seals

Wanaka - 3 hours
Hokitika - 3 hrs 30 mins

The Lodge is located 30km north of Haast and 90km south of Fox Glacier on SH 6.

Wilderness Lodge is set in the midst of the South West New Zealand World Heritage Area that protects lowland rainforest and wildlife. The lodge is the only human settlement within the 300 square-kilometre Moeraki valley. This is a unique area, one of the least affected by human population in New Zealand, with abundant bird life and a nearby coastline of wild beaches and wildlife such as penguins and seals depending on season. Included in the tariff are daily guided nature activities, such as rainforest discovery walks or easy canoeing trips. Many other activities can be arranged at an extra charge. The comfortable accommodation includes standard Lodge Rooms and superior Garden Rooms. Meals are served in the Riverside Restaurant and the Red Dog Saloon and include mains, such as slow-cooked star anise and orange duckling, cheesy baked potatoes, field and porcini mushrooms with red wine jus or grilled fillet of Akaroa salmon, risotto of king prawns and spinach with lemon cream sauce. This is one of the few successful ecotourism ventures in New Zealand—not only in what it provides, but how it is provided. The lodge generates its own power and recycles most rubbish. May more follow their lead. Warm and friendly atmosphere.

Accommodation available (NZ$)	![person]	![two people]	+![person]	![bed]	![bath]	
12 Rooms	$300-350	$400-500	Q+S	EN		Breakfast: Special cooked
6 Rooms	$300-350	$400-500	Q	EN		Evening meal: Included
5 Rooms	$350-450	$500-700	K	EN		Guest rooms:
5 Rooms	$350-450	$500-700	Q+S	EN		Ambience:
						Setting/location:

Changes will occur at the lodge fom Oct 1, 2006. Contact the lodge for information.

LOW   HIGH

Collyer House
Neroli Nolan
Jackson Bay Rd, Haast, South Westland
Tel: (03) 750 0022
Fax: (03) 750 0023
collyerhouse@xtra.co.nz
www.lodgings.co.nz/collyerhouse.html

Property features
Coastal views
Peace and quiet
Local history
Relaxed atmosphere
Spacious living areas
Local features
Bush walks
Hunting and fishing
Penguins in season
Scenic flights
Jet boating

Wanaka - 1 hour 45 minutes
Fox Glacier - 1 hour 45 minutes

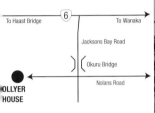

From State Highway 6 drive
approx. 12kms down Jackson Bay
Road. Drive over the Okuru River
bridge and turn right into Cuttance
Road North. Collyer House is 1km
down road.

I arrived at Collyer House on a winter's evening and was greeted by a roaring fire and a mixture of culinary aromas which whetted my appetite. This brand new home is warm and inviting and decorated with tasteful elegance. The rooms are beautiful and spacious, each with it's own ensuite and large comfortable beds. Host Neroli Nolan is an interesting and vivacious character, whose hospitality will delight and whose cooking skills will tempt the most jaded appetite. Request a dinner of whitebait fritters, venison and Neroli's decadent sticky date pudding. Expect to while the evening away with a bottle of wine and great conversation in front of the spectacular fireplace, which is cleverly constructed from local river rock. When I woke up in this cosy home, I was delighted by the stunning river and sea views from my bedroom window. While I indulged in an enormous country-style breakfast, Neroli was happy to give me guidance on the local sights. Her family has lived in the area for generations and she knows it well. I was reluctant to leave this charming accommodation and I am keen to make this a regular holiday retreat.

Guest pets by arrangement

Breakfast: Cooked
Evening Meal: $50pp
Guest rooms:
Ambience:
Setting/location:

Accommodation available (NZ$)	👤	👤👤	+👤	🛏	🛁
1 Room	$200	$250		SK or 2S	EN
1 Room	$200	$250		Q	EN
1 Room	$200	$250	$50	D+S	EN
1 Room	$200	$250		K	EN

Sumptuous food in top class restaurants.

Hanmer Springs
Malabar Restaurant and Cocktail Bar Alpine Pacific Centre, 5 Conical Hill Rd, Hanmer Springs. Tel: (03) 315-7745.

The Old Post Office
2 Jacks Pass Rd Hanmer Springs. Tel: (03) 315-7461. Award winning food served in historic surroundings.

Amberley
Nor' Wester Café
95 Main North Rd,
Tel: (03) 314-9411. Enjoy the courtyard, verandah, or open fire while sipping an espresso or tasting Canterbury cuisine.

Pukeko Junction Café SH 1, Leithfield Amberley
Tel: (03) 314-8834. A café and deli set in a sunny corner spot.

Christchurch
Annie's Wine Bar Art Centre, Tel: (03) 365-0566. Great wine list & ambience, delicious meals and picturesque setting in the cloisters of the Arts Center.

Café Metro
Cnr Kilmore & Colombo Street, Tel: (03) 366-4067. Trendy café – great service and coffee

Ciao Bella Restaurant & Bar
131 Victoria St, Tel: (03) 371-7288. The restaurant boasts a superb menu and fine local wines. The small bar is a very smart and stylish hangout for the cocktail set.

Indochine 209 Cambridge Tce, Christchurch Tel: (03) 365-7323. Food and cocktails to celebrate the very best of East meets West.

Le Café 78 Worcester Boulevard Christchurch, Tel: (03) 366-7722. Fish and chips come highly recommended.

Megawatt - Urban Food Kitchen
218 Manchester St,
Tel: (03) 363-9680.

Minx Dining Room and Bar
96 Lichfield Street,
Tel: (03) 374-9944. Top chefs, multi changing menu, choice of open or intimate seating.

Pedros Restaurant
143 Worcester St,
Tel: (03) 379-7668.
Authentic Basque/Castellano Spanish restaurant.

Pescatore Seafood Restaurant
The George Hotel, 50 Park Tce, Tel: (03) 371-0254. Dine on the best locally caught seafood in an atmosphere of chic sophistication.

Rotherhams of Riccarton
42 Rotherham Street Riccarton Tel: (03) 341-5142. Classic European and New Zealand cuisine.

Saggio di Vino 185 Victoria St, Tel: (03) 379-4006. Brilliant wine list and dining. Award winner in the eating out guide.

Simo's Moroccan Restaurant
114 City Mall, Cashel St,
Tel: (03) 377-5001. Exotic fresh North African flavours.
Bookings essential.

Strawberry Fare
114 Peterborough St, Christchurch Tel: (03) 365-4897. Famous for its mouth watering dessert menu.

The Daily Grind 149 Victoria St, Tel: (03) 377-0111. Contemporary café serving excellent coffee, great service.

Tiffanys 95 Oxford Terrace, Tel: (03) 379-1350. Known for its fine cuisine and superb wine list. Bookings essential.

T Teahouse 25 Marriner St, Sumner, Tel: (03) 326-7111 Offering over 30 different teas.

Akaroa
C'est La Vie 33 Rue Lavaud, Tel: (03) 304-7314. BYO restaurant serving French cuisine.
Bookings recommended.

Harbour 71 Restaurant & Bar
71 Beach Rd, Tel: (03) 304-7656.

Ma Maison
6 Rue Balguerie, Akaroa
Tel: (03) 304-7658. Waterfront location with panoramic views of Akaroa harbour

Church of the Good Shepard - Lake Tekapo.

Geraldine
The Easy Way Café & Bar Berry Barn Complex, Talbot St,
Tel: (03) 693-8090. Nachos, wild venison hamburgers and ostrich.

Fairlie
The Old Library Café
7 Allandale Rd, Tel: (03) 685-8999

Twizel
Hunters Café Bar 2 Market Pl, Tel: (03) 435-0303. Tasty food, big portions.

Rakaia River & Canterbury Plains

Cheltenham House

Len and Maree Earl
13 Cheltenham Street, Hanmer Springs
Tel: (03) 315 7545
Fax: (03) 315 7645
enquiries@cheltenham.co.nz
www.lodgings.co.nz/cheltenham.html

Property features
Spacious sunny rooms and suites
Breakfast at leisure in own suite
Quiet peaceful park like setting
Complimentary evening wine
Billiard table in guest lounge
Centrally heated throughout

Local features
200m to thermal pools & restaurants
Forest walks/tramps
Mountain biking
Golf course

Hanmer Springs - 2 mins walk
Christchurch - 1 hr 40 mins

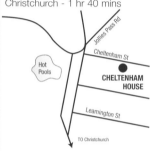

When entering Hanmer Springs village pass the Thermal Pools and turn right into Cheltenham Street. Cheltenham House is a short way u on your right.

Cheltenham House is set on large private grounds at the end of a peaceful side street, and yet is just a short stroll to the hot pools and cafes of Hanmer Springs. Cheltenham House has character and is equipped with modern facilities. Four rooms are available, two of which have their own private sunrooms. One has an intriguing sliding window over a half-door leading to the garden – the set up was conducive to lying out in the sun. The rooms have their own tea/coffee facilities, televisions, electric fans for summer and central heating for winter. If the weather isn't up to much, guests can always retire to the billiard room and have a turn on the full size table, serenade your partner at the upright grand piano, or sip a good Canterbury pinot noir in front of the open fire. In addition to the main house, there are two units, with adjacent parking, set back on the extensive grounds. The décor is fresh and modern, with comfortable seating and table and chairs – ideal for a long stay. Breakfast was served in my room – such decadence deserves at least a two-night stay so you can make the most of very slow mornings.

Accommodation available (NZ$)	🧍	🧍🧍	+🧍	🛏	🛁	Family pets on site Guest pets by arrangement
1 Room	$170	$200	$40	2Q	EN	Breakfast: Cooked
1 Room	$145	$168	$40	Q+S	PR	
2 Rooms	$187	$210		SK	EN	Guest rooms:
2 Studios	$157	$180		Q	EN	Ambience:
						Setting/location:

LOW   HIGH

Property features
All day sun, peaceful, private
Flexitime 3-course breakfast
Large ensuites/spa - guest wing
S/C villa with outdoor hot tub
Aircon in all suites/double glazing
In-room cinema/DVD
3 guest lounges & internet
Local features
Hot pools/cafés/shops/restaurants
18 hole golf course
Massage & pamper packages

Albergo Hanmer Lodge and Alpine Villas
Bascha and Beat Blattner
88 Rippingale Road, Hanmer Springs
Tel: (03) 315 7428
Fax: (03) 315 7428   Free: 0800 342313
albergo@paradise.net.nz
www.lodgings.co.nz/albergohanmer.html

Hanmer Springs - 2 mins drive
Christchurch - 1hr 40 mins drive

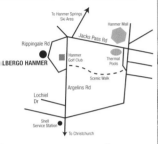

At junction before main village,
300m past Shell Garage, take
Argelins Rd (Centre branch), take
2nd road on left Rippingale Rd.
Albergo Hanmer is 700m down
on left.

Beat from Switzerland and Bascha, a New Zealander, have created this accommodation experience to follow their dream of providing a special place, similar to a small private hotel in Italy, which translated is 'Albergo'. On arrival I was warmly welcomed by Beat and immediately felt, I would be well looked after. The interior styling is contemporary, fresh and eclectic with a sense of fun. Main Lodge guestrooms and ensuite bathrooms are spacious and feature comforts for all seasons; under floor heating, and air conditioning to name just two. There are great views to the mountains from every window. The new self-contained Alpine Villa is adjacent to the main lodge, featuring a split level courtyard with private jacuzzi. Other decadent luxuries include in-room cinema with DVD library, full kitchen, and marble ensuite. The hosts are both chefs who love to create and a delicious breakfast which could be described as designer, was exquisitely presented and prepared from an expansive menu. Tailor made two-to-seven course dinners and authentic Swiss Fondues are popular. Book ahead to partake in an Albergo pamper package. The Thermal Pools, shops & cafes are just two minutes away. Albergo is truly where magic happens.

Accommodation available (NZ$)	👤	👥	+👤	🛏	🛁
Breakfast: Special cooked	1 Room	$140	$160-180		SK or 2S EN
Evening meal: $55-$110pp	1 Room	$170	$180-220		SK or 2S EN/Spa
Guest rooms:	1 S/C cottage	$200	$200-280	$60	K or 2Q EN
Ambience:	1 S/C villa	$290	$280-525	$60	CK or 2S EN/Spa
Setting/location:					

Hosts speak 6 languages. Children welcome by prior arrangement.

Frantoio Cottage

Barbara Smith
94 Isaac Road, Eyrewell
Tel: (03) 310 6144   Mob: 027 2511959
Fax: (03) 310 6133
bvtaylor@xtra.co.nz
www.lodgings.co.nz/frantoio.html

Property features
Log fire/TV/DVD/CD
Full kitchen for self-catering
Italian and basic Japanese spoken
75 acres of olives, nuts & grapes
Luxurious bathroom with bath
Local features
Swimming beaches nearby
Wine trails/vineyard restaurant
Close to golf course
Trout and salmon fishing
Christchurch Airport 30 mins drive

Rangiora - 12 mins
Christchurch - 30 mins

Take SH 1 to Waimakariri Bridge.
Take Tram Rd exit turn left into Tram
Rd. Travel 1.5 km turn left into South
Eyre Rd. Travel 14 mins and turn left
into Isaac Rd.

Tucked away on 75 acres planted with olives, nuts and grapes is Frantoio Cottage, named after one of the variety of Tuscan olives that grow on the land. Every detail has been thought of in this purpose-built cottage which has a fully-equipped kitchen, a lounge area, one large bedroom with a king-size bed, a bathroom almost the size of the bedroom and a deck with a barbecue. The host of this delightful property is Barbara who lives next door to the cottage and is around for guests if they need her. She had even thought to leave out a few snacks and a bottle of wine for me because she knew I had been travelling most of the day. The cottage, which is ideal in both summer and winter, has a large fireplace and I sat and enjoyed my wine in front of a roaring fire. Looking out the window I could have been anywhere in the world and then thoughts of Italy filtered through. Frantoio is a thirty-minute drive from Christchurch and the area around it offers fishing, vineyards visiting and horseback riding. Frantoio Cottage can be an easy escape from Christchurch or a perfect place to stop while travelling.

Accommodation available (NZ$)	👤	👤👤	+👤	🛏	🛁	Family pets on site
1 Room	$225	$225		SK or 2S	EN	Breakfast: Provisions provided

Guest rooms:
Ambience:
Setting/location:

Property features
Complimentary sherry & port
1 min to Merivale shops/cafes
Separate guest lounge
Historic Places Trust classification
Period furnishings/DVD in rooms
Native timbers & leadlight windows

Local features
Hagley Park and gardens
Antique shops/casino
Punting on Avon River
Golf courses nearby

City centre - 10 minutes
Dunedin - 4 hrs 30 mins

Elm Tree House
Karen and Allan Scott
236 Papanui Road, Merivale, Christchurch
Tel: (03) 355 9731
Fax: (03) 355 9753
stay@elmtreehouse.co.nz
www.lodgings.co.nz/elmtree.html

From north, continue on Main North Rd rather than turning into Cranford St (SH 74). Becomes Papanui Rd as it veers left. From south turn left at Hagley Park. Continue on to Harper Ave and left into Papanui Rd.

For those of you not familiar with Christchurch, Merivale is a haven for cafes, restaurants, antique shops as well as conventional retail outlets. Elm Tree House is just a short stroll to them all and, despite the busy nature of this location, the property has a relaxed feel to it, as it is set back from the road in a large garden. This character home has a civilised 'club' atmosphere in the communal areas. The rooms vary in style. My favourite is the Honeymoon Suite with its heavy timber-panelling, writing desk and separate lounge area. The Cromwell and Milford Rooms are downstairs. They have polished floors and French doors that lead to their own small courtyards and gardens. Although the interesting 1920's architecture is a real feature here, the thing that sticks in my mind is the thought Karen and Allan have put into ensuring their guests' comfort. They are continually thinking of ways to improve it, such as installing double-glazing in all of the bedrooms to eliminate road noise. Happy hour, where complimentary wine and cheese are served in the new conservatory or the garden, lives up to its name and many guests say that a stay here feels like coming home.

Family dog on site

Breakfast: Special cooked

Guest rooms:
Ambience:
Setting/location:

Accommodation available (NZ$)	👤	👤👤	+👤	🛏	🛁
1 Room	$235	$265		K/T	EN
2 Rooms	$265	$295		Q	EN
2 Rooms	$295	$325	$80	K/T	EN
1 Room	$295	$325		K	EN

Enquire about low season rates May - September.

Springfield Cottage

Noeleen and Michael Clarke
137 Springfield Road, St. Albans, Christchurch
Tel: (03) 377 1368
relax@springfieldcottage.co.nz
www.lodgings.co.nz/springfield.html

Property features
S/C heritage cottage
All modern comforts
Quality bed linen & fresh flowers
Private garden with BBQ
Single party bookings only
Self catering or breakfast provision
Local features
Botanic gardens
Garden City attractions
Merivale mall
Art centre 2km from city centre

Merivale Mall - 1.5km
Christchurch Centre - 2km

From airport take Memorial Ave to
Hagley Park. Turn left into Harper
Ave, continue into Bealey Ave turni
left into Springfield Rd. No. 137 is (
the left.

This was described as a self-contained heritage cottage built in the 1870's, recently refurbished, and offering a delightful combination of classic and colonial charm and modern comforts. I felt that was pretty accurate. When I entered through the classical front door, I immediately felt I had escaped to a peaceful hideaway in the city. I was aware of the city but relaxed and wandered through the open plan dining kitchen area into the sunny courtyard garden. Springfield Cottage is ideal for a romantic getaway in the center of an exciting and busy city. Restaurants and cafes are in abundance a short drive away, or you can gather delicious fare from the deli in Merivale and relax under the umbrella in the privacy of the courtyard. Provisions can be provided for cooked and continental breakfasts with a bottle of local wine and a fruit-and-cheese platter. How I wanted to stay for a day or two but I had work to do. I will be very happy to return and felt that if I could have spent a few days here, it would soon feel like home.

Accommodation available (NZ$)	👤	👤👤	+👤	🛏	🛁
S/C cottage	$150-250	$150-250		Q	PR

Breakfast: Provisions provided

Minimum stay 2 nights. Bookings essential.

Guest rooms:
Ambience:
Setting/location:

LOW   HI(

Hadleigh Heritage Home

Jon and Shirley Warring
6 Eversleigh St, Christchurch
Tel: (03) 355 7174   Mob: 027 4972871
Fax: (03) 355 7174
info@hadleigh.co.nz
www.lodgings.co.nz/hadleigh.html

Property features
- Category 2 historic listed home
- Classic performance cars (Porsche)
- Billiard & motorsport trophy room
- Separate guest lounge
- Small guest kitchenette
- Arts & crafts style architecture

Local features
- Botanical Gardens/Hagley Park
- Arts Centre/Casino
- Punting on the Avon River
- Antarctic Centre/Cathedral square

City centre - 17 mins walk
Airport - 15 mins drive

Bealey Ave borders central Christchurch to the north. From the airport or north Hagley Park continue along Bealey Ave and turn left into Springfield Rd. Hadleigh is on the corner of Eversleigh St on the right.

I love places that are full of character and history. This home, which is one of this country's best examples of the Arts and Crafts architectural style has been restored to the standard it deserves and is sympathetically furnished with a great deal of care. The four guest suites (two have two bedrooms) all have private bathrooms, comfortable seating, televisions, complimentary port and fresh flowers. They are spacious and well appointed. There is a small guest kitchen on the same level, where we could have made a light meal. The refrigerator was stocked with complimentary beverages and snacks. Jon and Shirley asked me to join them in the gracious sitting room, with its lattice bay windows overlooking the garden, for a drink before I went out for dinner. Jon has a specialised interest in Porsche racing and in order to house his three-car collection a facility of 150 square metres has been added to the house. I was welcome to explore the extensive gardens, to hone my skills in the billiard room, play the piano and peruse the small library. In the morning a full English-style breakfast was served with strawberries and peaches fresh from the potage garden.

Family dog on site

Breakfast: Cooked

Guest rooms:
Ambience:
Setting/location:

Accommodation available (NZ$)	🧍	🧍🧍	+🧍	🛏	🛁
1 Suite	$225	$265-275	$50	Q+S	PR
1 Suite	$275-290	$340-360		K/T	EN
1 Suite	$245-260	$310-325		Q	EN
1 S/C Suite	$290-310	$290-310	$50	K/T+Q	EN

Writing desk available in suite. Rates negotiable on 3-day plus stays.

Hambledon

Jo and Calvin Floyd
103 Bealey Avenue, Christchurch
Tel: (03) 379 0723
Fax: (03) 379 0758
hambledon@clear.net.nz
www.lodgings.co.nz/hambledon.html

Property features
Tranquil cottage gardens
Complimentary sherry & port
Guest lounge & library
Conservatory & verandahs
Antiques, oriental rugs & NZ art
Laundry service
Email kiosk
Local features
Hagley Park - 5 mins walk
Many restaurants close by
Cathedral & Arts Centre

City centre - 15 mins walk
Airport - 15 mins drive

From the city centre, take Colombo
Street north to Bealey Avenue. Turn
left and travel to Springfield Rd on
the right. Hambledon is on the corner
of Bealey Ave and Springfield Rd.

It doesn't matter what you are looking for in the way of bedroom or bathroom facilities, you will probably find something you like in this lovely old building built by George Gould in 1856. Hambledon has retained a high level of serenity and comfort. Modernising has improved amenities without sacrificing the depth and character of the building. The suites are so spacious that, Jo says, guests at breakfast are often surprised that there are other guests in the house. All suites have televisions, tea and coffee making facilities, comfortable seating areas, fridges and heaters, and are furnished with antiques, such as wonderful four-poster and Victorian halftester beds. With separate guest lounges and private, leafy corners throughout the pleasant garden, there are plenty of places to socialise or find solitude. The hosts greet their guests individually and help them with bookings for activities and restaurants. Some of the city's best restaurants are within a few minutes' walk from the house and if you have over-indulged and need to exercise, Hagley Park is just down the road. You are right in the heart of Christchurch here.

Accommodation available (NZ$)	👤	👤👤	+👤	🛏	🛁	
1 Suite		$330		K	EN	Breakfast: Special cooked
1 Suite		$295	$50	K+S	EN	
2 Suites		$285	$50	K+S	EN	Guest rooms:
1 Suite		$275	$50	Q+2S	EN	Ambience:

Setting/location:

LOW   HIGH

Property features
Separate guest entrance
Off-street parking
Courtesy transfers available
Opposite Hagley Park
Antique furnishings
Local features
Arts Centre - 5 min walk
Botanical Garden - 5 min walk
Golf course in Hagley Park
Restaurants/cafes - 5 min walk
Art gallery/museum - 5 min walk

City centre - 15 mins walk
Airport - 15 mins drive

The Weston House

Len and Stephanie May
62 Park Terrace, Christchurch
Tel: (03) 366 0234   Mob: 027 2839546
Fax: (03) 366 5254
enquiries@westonhouse.co.nz
www.lodgings.co.nz/westonhouse.html

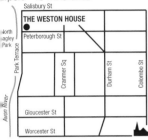

THE WESTON HOUSE

Salisbury St
Peterborough St
Park Terrace
Cranmer Sq
Durham St
Colombo St
Gloucester St
Worcester St
North Hagley Park
Avon River

Park Tce borders Hagley Park to the east. It can be accessed from Harper Ave (from Airport), Bealey Ave or the central city/Arts Centre area. The Weston House is on the corner of Park Tce & Peterborough St.

Len and Stephanie are only the third owners of this landmark Georgian-style mansion, and they have spent nearly two years working to return it to its intended grandeur within the confines of a category one, historic grading. It was once one of Christchurch's most prestigious homes - and so it is today. Where the cooks, nannies and housekeepers once lived is now an opulent, two-suited wing for guests. Both rooms have tiled ensuites, dressing and lounging areas and every conceivable convenience and extra, adding up to luxurious accommodation of the highest standard. At seven o'clock in the evening, I was invited to have a glass of wine with Len and Stephanie and other guests. This was served in the showpiece of the house - the very elegant drawing room, featuring lavish russet curtaining, butter-yellow walls and a glorious blend of antiques. In fine weather drinks are served on the sunny porch overlooking the formal garden, bordered by roses and native and exotic trees. Stephanie has decorated this grand old house with great flair and sympathy for the era it was designed for. The couple says they enjoy pampering guests and seeing other people appreciate the house as much as they do.

Family cat on site

Breakfast: Special cooked

Guest rooms:
Ambience:
Setting/location:

LOW   HIGH

Accommodation available (NZ$)	👤	👥	+👤	🛏	🛁
1 Room			$360-390	SK/T	EN
1 Room			$360-390	Q	EN

The Worcester Of Christchurch

Maree Ritchie   Tony Taylor
15 Worcester Boulevard, Christchurch
Tel: (03) 365 0936   Mob: 025 2203163
Fax: (03) 364 6299   Free: 0800 365015
info@worcester.co.nz
www.lodgings.co.nz/worcester.html

Property features
Separate guest lounge
Complimentary pre-dinner drinks
Art gallery - NZ art
Opposite tram stop
Quiet garden with sculpture
Antique furniture/Pure cotton linen
Wireless internet in house
Apartment has laundry and gym
Local features
Arts centre/cafes/restaurants
Botanical gardens/Hagley Park

City centre - 5 mins walk
Airport - 15 mins drive

Follow main route into city. Turn right
into Park Tce following onto Rollest
Ave. Turn left into Worcester
Boulevard opposite Canterbury
museum. No 15 opposite Arts Cent

Maree is a long-time art dealer. It should therefore come as no surprise that her taste is impeccable. All guestrooms have been furnished with flair and individually decorated. Both suites have their own lounge and feature original art, direct dial phones, television, desks and extra touches such as hand-made chocolates and speciality bathroom products. The Worcester Suite has a handsome, French-polished, walnut bedhead which dominates the super-king bed. In the Godley Suite a third guest can be accommodated on a rolled arm sofa-bed in the lounge. This property has, for me, all the features of a top hotel and at the same time, the individuality and character you expect of a boutique lodging. The house was built in 1893, for the Chief Constable of Lyttelton and retains some very distinctive architectural features of that time. Even with all this, one of the things I most appreciated was the location which is on the tramline, opposite the Arts Centre and a short stroll to the middle of town. The apartments are a few minutes walk away in the award winning West Fitzroy building. Apartments each have their own kitchen & laundry, and there is also a gymnasium on site.

Accommodation available (NZ$)	👤	👤👤	+👤	🛏	🛁	Family dog on site
1 Suite	$380	$380	$150	SK/T	EN	Breakfast: Cooked
1 Suite	$380	$380		SK	EN	
1 Apartment	$275	$275	$50	K+2S	PR	Guest rooms:
2 Apartments	$275	$275	$25	SK/T	PR	Ambience:

One suite also has sofa bed. Apartment is two blocks from The Worcester.

Setting/location:

LOW   HIG

Property features
Laundry and kitchen facilities
DVD's available
Elegant, minimalist décor
Local features
Museum - 5 mins walk
Botanical gardens - 5 mins walk
Art centre - 5 mins walk
Next door to convention centre
Avon river - 100 mtrs
Close to restaurant district

Metro Suites
Liz Barry
Cnr Colombo & Kilmore Street, Christchurch
Tel: (03) 366 4067   Mob: 021 365489
Fax:(03) 377 4665
inquiries@metrosuites.co.nz
www.lodgings.co.nz/metro.html

Christchurch city - 5 minute walk

From motorway, turn left at Papanui
into Cranford Street, turn right into
Bealey Avenue, left into Colombo
Street and it is the corner of the 3rd
block on the right.

Situated in the heart of Christchurch, on the second storey of the city's well-known Metro Cafe, are two luxurious and contemporary suites. The keys for the suites are collected from the café, where the staff made me feel welcome and took the time to show me to my suite which was through a separate entrance beside the cafe. Both suites have queen beds and are generous in size. One is decorated in a minimal, but still charming, style. The other has more design content, and both are furnished with quality furnishings. I chose the larger of the suites as I was unable to resist the opulent clawfoot bath, from which I still had a view over the city. There are many restaurants in close proximity to choose from. Two of them are owned and operated by Liz who also hosts the suites. I decided my suite was too comfortable to leave and instead ordered dinner-to-go so I could enjoy it in privacy. The next morning I had a very good breakfast, chosen from the café's menu downstairs. I thoroughly recommend the coffee which was one of the best I had on my travels.

Accommodation available (NZ$)	👤	👤👤	+👤	🛏	🛁
1 Room	$175	$175		Q	PR
1 Room	$195	$195		Q	PR

Breakfast: Continental
Evening meal: Enquire
Guest rooms:
Ambience:
Setting/location:

LOW   HIGH

Chatterley Manor

Isabella Hockey and Family
433 Old Tai Tapu Road, RD 2, Christchurch
Tel: (03) 329 6658   Mob: 027 4310773
Fax: (03) 329 6827
enquiries@ladychatterley.co.nz
www.lodgings.co.nz/ladychatterley.html

Property features
Swimming pool/billiard room
Tennis court/sauna/large spa
Fernery/summer house/farm animal
Old English-style gardens
Themed guest rooms
Lake with island & small chapel
Private guest lounge with bar
Local features
Horse riding/skiing
9 hole golf course - 3km drive
Vineyard/ restaurant/café nearby

Christchurch - 15 minute drive
Akaroa - 45 minute drive

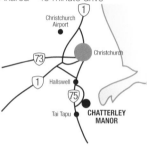

From Christchurch take SH75 south.
After Halswell turn left into Old Tai
Tapu Road. Chatterly Manor is
3.5kms on left.

Only 15 minutes from the centre of Christchurch, Chatterley Manor is a country retreat which provides space and peace to guest groupings of various sizes, and a base from which they can explore the Canterbury region. Children are welcome. Set on seven-and-a-half acres of farmland, native bush and established gardens, Chatterley Manor allows guests to spread out and be comfortable. I was encouraged to swim in the pool, play tennis or head up the road to go horse trekking. Chatterley Manor can accommodate up to 20 guests in the four large garden suites and five smaller suites in the main house. The suites are all individually themed and interestingly decorated to become the African Room, the Egyptian Room, Lady Chatterley's Room, the Mediterranean Room, the Lavender Room, the New Zealand Room and the Austrian Room. The garden suites all have mezzanine floors with a queen-size bed and two singles, downstairs the guest lounges have doors that open out to private patios, manicured lawns and gardens. What I liked best about Chatterley Manor was the easy going nature of Isabella and her family, the beautiful gardens and the relaxed family atmosphere. The Manor is fully licensed so guests are welcomed into the main house and lounge to enjoy a drink at the bar or relax in front of the large television.

Accommodation available (NZ$)	👤	👤👤	+👤	🛏	🛁	Guest pets by arrangement
4 Suites	$180	$280	$60	1Q + 2S	EN	Breakfast: Special continental
3 Rooms	$160	$220-280		2S	PR	Evening meal: $40pp
1 Room	$160	$250-320		1D + 1S	EN	Guest rooms:
1 Room	$160			1S	PR	Ambience:

TV available on request. Enquire about children's rates.

Setting/location:

LOW   HIGH

Property features
Rambling gardens
Tranquil rural setting
Mountain, city and ocean views
Guest sitting/dining room
Outdoor hot spa
Log fire
Local features
Scenic hill walks
Walk to Lyttleton or Sumner
Gondola
Beach/Sumner seaside village

City centre - 20 minutes
Akaroa - 1 hr 30 mins

Hornbrook

Darryn and Jo Shepherd
Summit Road, Mt Pleasant, Christchurch
Tel: (03) 384 0020
Fax:(03) 384 0320
hornbrook@xtra.co.nz
www.lodgings.co.nz/hornbrook.html

From city centre, follow signs to
Sumner. Shortly after the road joins
waterfront take Mt. Pleasant Rd on
your right. Drive approx. 5.5km to
Summit Rd T intersection. Hornbrook
is immediately on left.

Staying here is like being on top of the world in a quiet country location, and yet it is just a short drive to the city, Sumner Village and Lyttelton. The view from here is huge and takes in much of the city and South Shore, the estuary, and as far as the eye can see up the coast to the Seaward Kaikoura Mountains. This is a great area for walking the tracks and quiet roads of the Port Hills. I am told the walk to Sumner is not difficult but the walk back up is not for the faint hearted. The house has character and is laid out in such a way that you can either be sociable in the lounge, or sit quietly in the large dining room with its own sound system. A wall of glass doors opens to the front courtyard and garden where, under a vine-covered pergola, there is a spa pool and barbecue area. Jo and Darryn are happy to let guests take charge in this spacious and comfortable place, which was built in 1911 and named after the pioneer owner of the original Mt Pleasant sheep run. It was difficult to tear myself away from the view which took on different moods as the day advanced. Breakfast was a leisurely help-yourself affair with fresh fruit, cereals, yoghurt, toasts and juices.

Family pets on site	Accommodation available (NZ$)	♦	♦♦	+♦	🛏	🛁
Breakfast: Continental	1 Room	$150	$180		K	EN
	1 Room	$160	$190		K	EN
Guest rooms:						
Ambience:						
Setting/location:						

Meychelle Manor
Luxury Bed and Breakfast

Brian and Michelle Walker
SH73, Main West Coast Road, Darfield
Tel: (03) 318 1144   Mob: 027 2260118
Fax:(03) 318 1965
stay@meychellemanor.co.nz
www.lodgings.co.nz/meychelle.html

Property features
Lake/bar/heated pool/gym
2 guest lounges/DVD/CD/telescope
Massage & beauty- must pre book
Laundry/BBQ/use of kitchen
Garden-farm park and tour
5th generation friendly Kiwi family
Local features
Cafes/restaurants/shops/gallery
Trans alpine scenic train/skifields
Jetboat/horsetrekking/golfing
Walks/hunting/fishing

Darfield - 4 mins drive
Christchurch - 25 mins drive

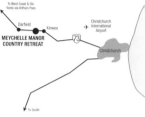

Take Highway 73 from Christchurch
Travel 25 mins and just after Kirwee
on left stands Meychelle Manor.

Overlooking the main road, this spacious modern home is definitely for those who would like the experience of a genuine New Zealand family. Set in rural Canterbury on a deer farmlet, I was greeted by a menagerie of animals and birds when I drove up the driveway. Brian and Michelle and their family are keenly interested in helping their guests enjoy their stay at Meychelle Manor and their visit to the region. Brian's family have owned this land for five generations so they know the area and history well. Treats for guests are the large heated swimming pool and home theatre and outside, the fountain and the lake with a row boat, fish and ducks. A telescope is available to view the galaxy from a southern perspective. The wide-open, night skies are wonderful here. Breakfast, with interesting variations such as venison sausages, is served in the sunny kitchen/family room. Courtesy driving is provided so that guests can dine in one of the excellent local restaurants. An international awareness is apparent, as the Walkers have hosted students from abroad from time to time. Guests can be met at the airport by arrangement. Meychelle Manor reflects true kiwi hospitality in a modern way.

Accomodation available (NZ$)	👤	👤👤	+👤	🛏	🛁	Family dog on site
1 Room	$130-150	$190-220	$20-80	SK or 2S+1S	EN	Breakfast: Special cooked
1 Room	$130-150	$190-220	$20-80	SK or 2S+1S	EN	Evening meal: Yes
1 Room	$130-150	$190-220	$20-80	SK or 3S+1S	PR	Guest rooms:

Ambience:
Setting/location:

LOW   HIG

Property features
Panoramic harbour views
Private, tranquil garden setting
Stone and timber cottages

Local features
Sea activities - harbour cruises
Variety of local craft shops
Restaurants/wineries/cafes
Local walkways/gardens to visit
Historic French village of Akaroa
Swim with the dolphins
Golf course - 15 mins

Loch Hill Country Cottages
Managers: Jill and Murray Gibb
SH 75, Akaroa
Tel: (03) 304 7195
Fax:(03) 304 7672   Free: 0800 456244
lochhill@xtra.co.nz
www.lodgings.co.nz/lochhill.html

Akaroa - 10 minutes walk
Christchurch - 1 hour drive

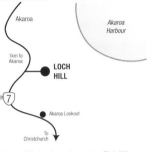

From Christchurch, take SH 75.
Loch Hill is situated on the right,
1km before Akaroa township.
Stone entranceway is well
signposted.

There is a little piece of paradise to suit everyone here. Not only are the cottages of varying sizes, styles and layouts, but they vary in location, and all but two (which are tucked into the trees) take advantage of the view across the harbour. A great deal of thought has gone into making each as private as possible. The property is large, with park-like grounds edged by forest. The driveways complete the picture with the hosts' home off to one side. While the focus here is privacy, Jill and Murray are friendly, knowledgeable hosts with an abundance of local knowledge. But these stone and timber cottages all have two common elements in that they are finished to a high standard and are well appointed. They range from studio style with kitchenettes to the spacious Ashcroft Cottage that could take three couples. This has kitchen, bath and shower, leather chairs, air-conditioning and French doors leading to a balcony. Depending on your cottage, you might luxuriate in a spa bath, snuggle up in front of a fire, enjoy a bed with a view down to the harbour and township, or relax on your balcony listening to the bell birds calling from the bush.

Family cat on site

Breakfast: Extra $12pp

Guest rooms:
Ambience:
Setting/location:

Accommodation available (NZ$)	👤	👥	+👤	🛏	🛁
3 S/C cottages	$185		$20	SK/T+2Q	EN, PR
2 S/C cottages	$175		$20	SK/T+Q	PR
4 S/C cottages	$170		$20	K	EN
2 S/C cottages	$145		$20	K or Q	EN
2 Studios	$140		$20	Q	EN

Maison de la Mer

Carol and Bruce Hyland
1 Rue Benoit, Akaroa
Tel: (03) 304 8907   Mob: 021 986221
Fax: (03) 304 8917
maisondelamer@xtra.co.nz
www.lodgings.co.nz/maison.html

Property features
Historic villa
Extensive views across harbour
Fifty metres to beach
Local features
Restaurants - 5 min walk
Dolphin watching/swimming
Historic homes/village
Museum
Vineyards/wineries short drive

Akaroa - 3 minutes walk
Christchurch - 1 hr

Maison de la Mer is situated in the heart of the village opposite the main swimming beach on the corner of Rue Lavaud (main road) and Rue Benoit.

This graceful house, which was built in 1910 with the fortunes of an entrepreneurial businessman called Thomas Taylor, has recently been restored to the same dignified and elegant standard it originally must have presented. One of its strengths as an accommodation place is its marvellous locality in the middle of Akaroa Township, close to and overlooking the harbour. Bruce and Carol have used a combination of soothing natural colours, furniture collected from their travels around the world and a delicious breakfast menu to make a stay at this bed and breakfast a special treat. Each bedroom faces out to the serene Akaroa harbour. I sat and wrote my diary in the sun room, off my room, and watched yachts and fishing boats coming in and out of the harbour. Rolling green hills surround the harbour and isolate it from the rest of the peninsula. Guests at Maison de la Mer have their own lounge with thick leather couches placed in front of a large, gas fireplace and with a small library in the corner. There are two luxurious guestrooms in the main house and a separate, self-contained apartment with its own entrance outside. Keen yachties, Bruce and Carol have decorated the apartment in a nautical theme. I liked the flagpole in the front yard.

Accommodation available (NZ$)	👤	👤👤	+👤	🛏	🛁	Family dog on site
1 Room	$295			Q	EN	Breakfast: Cooked
1 Room	$295		$50	Q+S	EN	
1 S/C unit	$295			Q	EN	Guest rooms:
						Ambience:
One room has spa bath.						Setting/location:

Property features
Restored historic cottage
2.5 acre garden
Tranquil rural setting
Local features
Historic township
Harbour trips
Walking tracks
Swimming with dolphins
Vineyards/wineries
Scenic drives

Mill Cottage

Cliff and Louisa Hobson-Corry
81 Rue Grehan, Akaroa
Tel: (03) 304 8007   Mob: 027 4949062
Fax: (03) 304 8007
millcottage@xtra.co.nz
www.lodgings.co.nz/millcottage.html

Akaroa - 10 minutes walk
Christchurch - 1 hr 15 mins

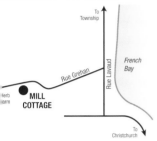

When driving into Akaroa, turn first left into Rue Grehan. Drive 800 metres and Mill Cottage is on your left.

The character and charm of this cottage, which has historic place classification is hard to beat. For those interested in history, this is an opportunity to live in it, while not going without modern-day comforts. The cottage has a lounge, master bedroom, bathroom and dining area downstairs. Climb the old timber stairs (not recommended for the infirm) to the attic with two authentic, single bedrooms with dormer windows. As the cottage only has microwave facilities I decided to try one of Akaroa's quality restaurants for dinner. French doors open out to the sunny verandah which is a good place to relax with tea, or perhaps a gin and tonic. This tranquil setting was once the site of Canterbury's first water-driven flour mill. Rarely have I seen such a good restoration, with such sympathetic decoration and furniture. The hosts, Louisa and Cliff, care for the enchanting, park-like grounds and continue to enhance the surroundings with shrubs and gardens that blend in well with a number of well-established trees. Their house is a short distance away and faces away from the cottage to preserve a feeling of privacy. Here you will find the spacious Akaroa suite which takes up the entire top floor.

Accommodation available (NZ$)	👤	👤👤	+👤	🛏	🛁
1 S/C cottage	$225	$250	$50	Q+2S	PR
1 Suite	$225	$250	$50	Q+2S	PR

Breakfast: Special continental

Guest rooms:
Ambience:
Setting/location:

Cooked breakfast $20pp extra. Suite is top floor of main building.

Maison des Fleurs

Margy and Dai Morris
6 Church Street, Akaroa, Banks Peninsula
Tel: (03) 304 7804   Mob: 021 1370500
Fax: (03) 304 7804
luxury@maisondesfleurs.co.nz
www.lodgings.co.nz/maisondesfleurs.html

Property features
Kingsize spa bath
Port/chocolates/organic juices
Open fire/CDs/magazines/guitar
Tranquil courtyard with swing seat
Sunny private balcony
Local features
Historic village walks/tramping
Restaurants/shopping 100 metres
Harbour cruise/swim with dolphins
Local winery/cheese factory
French history museum/golf

Akaroa - 1 minute walk
Christchurch - 1.5 hours

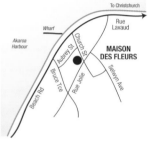

On reaching Akaroa township, drive along Rue Lavaud, past the beach into Rue Jolie. Then turn right into Church St. Maison des Fleurs is 10mtrs on left.

By the time I'd reached Maison des Fleurs, Christchurch city seemed a million miles away although it is not a long drive. This handcrafted timber house, located in the pretty harbourside town of Akaroa, is constructed of macrocarpa and native rimu timber. It is a 'green' house, built of non-toxic materials without the use of paints or polyurethane. The interior is set up for love-in-luxury; the guest book is full of comments from happy honeymooners and couples celebrating anniversaries and birthdays. After the drive from Christchurch Airport in the cool night air, the warmth from the gas fire was welcoming. I had picked up dinner provisions on the way and was able to heat them in the small stylish kitchen. But I made plans to dine out the following evening at one of Akaroa's renowned restaurants which are only a few minutes walk away. The living area is upstairs and guests relax in front of the open fire and listen to the sound of ambient jazz. After a soak in the spa bath, I slept in a bed also made entirely of natural products. A stay at Maison des Fleurs seems to inspire creativity. Margy and Dai have provided an acoustic guitar and an art book for any guests who are taken by the muse.

Accommodation available (NZ$)	👤	👥	+👤	🛏	🛁
1 S/C cottage		$250-325		Q	EN

Guest rooms:
Ambience:
Setting/location:

LOW   HIGH

Property features
Award winning restaurant on site
Luxurious accommodation
Open fires/spa/claw baths
Private balconies
Glass of champagne
Fruit & chocolate platter
Local features
Wineries/trout fishing/hunting
Art galleries/museums
Skiing/tramping/golf
White water rafting

Kavanagh House

Juilearna and Killian Kavanagh
State Highway One, Winchester, South Canterbury
Tel: (03) 615 6150   Mob: 021 701301
Fax: (03) 615 9694
info@kavanaghhouse.co.nz
www.lodgings.co.nz/kavanagh.html

Geraldine - 5 mins drive
Temuka - 5 mins drive

On State highway 1 at Winchester,
1.5 hours South of Christchurch.

Kavanagh House, which is located in rural South Canterbury, has the sophistication and luxury that you might find in boutique lodging in New York, London or perhaps Dublin. On the other hand, from the verandah, I was able to gaze across fertile pasturelands. The dramatic flaming torches at the entrance are in keeping with the experience to be found within. Attention has been given to detail, with luxurious linen, towels and décor. Each room is named and themed; the Rococo room, the Van Cleef room and the New York room. All of the guestrooms have immaculately restored hand-painted ceilings and either a claw-foot or spa bath - perfect for soaking in while sipping a complimentary glass of champagne. A welcoming open fire is always burning in the elegant sitting room downstairs, alongside which is an award winning in-house restaurant, serving café-style food during the day and innovative cuisine in the evening. The food is a highlight of any stay and a gourmet breakfast is included in the rate. The owner, Juliearna, commutes between Ireland and New Zealand, bringing refreshed ideas for her managers to execute and her energy is reflected in the lively and vibrant atmosphere of the lodge.

Family cat on site Guest pets by arrangement	Accommodation available (NZ$)	♦	♦♦	+♦	🛏	🛁
Breakfast: Special cooked	1 Room	$250	$320		K	EN
Evening meal: $30-40pp	1 Room	$220	$295		Q	EN
Guest rooms:	1 Room	$180	$210		K	EN
Ambience:						
Setting/location:						

LOW   HIGH

Lake Tekapo Luxury Lodge

Lynda and John van Beek
24 Aorangi Crescent, Lake Tekapo
Tel: (03) 680 6566   Mob: 021 1299439
Fax: (03) 680 6599   Free: 0800 525383
lake.tekapo.lodge@xtra.co.nz
www.lodgings.co.nz/laketekapo.html

Property features
Views to Lake Tekapo & Mountains
Separate guest entrance & lounge
Walkway to shops
Handmade furniture by local artists

Local features
Clearest skies for star gazing in NZ
Scenic flights over Glaciers/Mt Cook
Scenic walks to lakes & mountains
Historic church and monument
Fishing/golf/horse trekking
Shops/restaurants/post office

Lake Tekapo - 2 minute walk
Timaru - 1 hour drive

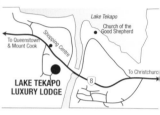

When arriving from Christchurch or Queenstown you will arrive on SH8. Opposite Lake Tekapo Tavern is Aorangi Cres and the sign to the Lodge. Drive to end of Cres, the Lodge is #24.

Set at Lake Tekapo, in the heart of the breathtaking MacKenzie country, this luxury lodge overlooks the brilliant turquoise-blue of Lake Tekapo. Welcomed at the door by Lynda and John, I entered through antique, arched, church doors and was led into the dining room to admire the exposed beams and handmade furniture. The views to the lake and the surrounding Southern Alps were continuous and in the evening, at sunset, the colours of the mountains were magnificent. I enjoyed the views while sipping coffee on the deck in front of my room. The separate guest lounge provided a host of things to do in-house, and has tea and coffee making facilities, comfortable leather lounge suites, and a gas fire. On a clear night take the time to look skyward out of the star-gazing window. Lake Tekapo offers some of the clearest skies in the country. The lodge is located next to a walkway, perfect for visiting the shops, restaurants and the historic Church of the Good Shepherd at the lake's edge. This is a very picturesque location and a good base from which to enjoy all there is nearby.

Accommodation available (NZ$)	🧍	🧍🧍	+🧍	🛏	🛁	
1 Room		$295-335	$40	SK	EN+Spa	Breakfast: Special cooked
1 Room		$295-335	$40	SK	EN	
1 Room		$295-335	$40	Q+S	EN	Guest rooms:
1 Room		$200-250	$40	Q+S	EN	Ambience:

Three of the rooms have their own decks.

Setting/location:

LOW   HIGH

Property features
Lake & mountain views
Separate guest lounge & entry
Spacious guest rms/native garden
Fishing guide on site
Local features
The Church of the Good Shepherd
Restaurants nearby
Mt Cook - 75 mins
Skiing/ice skating/fly fishing
Scenic flights and drives
Glacier fed lake

Creel House Bed and Breakfast

Grant and Rosemary Brown
36 Murray Place, Lake Tekapo
Tel: (03) 680 6516
Fax: (03) 680 6659
creelhouse.l.tek@xtra.co.nz
www.lodgings.co.nz/creel.html

Lake Tekapo - 3 minutes
Fairlie - 35 minutes

From SH 8, 100 metres east of dam bridge, turn onto Greig St. Follow road round onto Jeune St & proceed up to the top of the hill, turn right onto Murray Pl. Creel House is signposted on the left hand side of the street.

Family cat on site

Grant and Rosemary have dedicated a lot of time and energy into creating a bed and breakfast that has all the comforts of home and better views than most. The guestrooms are of generous proportions with plenty of light, fresh flowers and fluffy towels. The upstairs front room, with its own balcony and views over Lake Tekapo, was my choice, although all rooms are of the same standard and have comfortable seating and tea and coffee facilities. The room on the lower level would be good for a longer stay with its large bathroom and separate bath. Creel House is a perfect place to stop if you are travelling between Christchurch and Queenstown. If you intend driving to Mt Cook, this is the most logical place to stay for the night. The lake, Church of the Good Shepherd and shops are within walking distance. Grant and Rosemary have a family, and the guest accommodation is quite separate from theirs. They are happy to host guests in the large guest lounge, which overlooks the lake. A bonus of staying at Creel House is that Grant is a professional fly-fishing guide (NZPFGA), so if you are interested in fishing for trout or salmon, here is a good opportunity for you to try your luck.

	Accommodation available (NZ$)	♦	♦♦	+♦	🛏	🛁
Breakfast: Special continental	2 Rooms			$150-160	Q	PR
	1 Room	$70-80		$150-160	2S	EN

Guest rooms:
Ambience:
Setting/location:

LOW　HIGH

Off-season rates apply May to September.

Lake Tekapo Grandview

Leon and Rosemary O'Sullivan
32 Hamilton Drive, Lake Tekapo
Tel: (03) 680 6910   Mob: 021 1113393
Fax: (03) 680 6912
info@laketekapograndview.co.nz
www.lodgings.co.nz/laketekapograndview.html

Property features
Local photographs
Stunning lake/alpine views
Garden
Hand embroidered bed linen
Rimu furniture throughout
Local features
Star watching
Scenic walks
Horse riding/fishing/hunting
Scenic flights
Skiing in Winter

Lake Tekapo -10 minute walk
Timaru - 1 hour drive

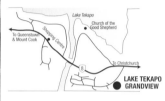

From the south take 2nd right into Hamilton Dr. From north turn left into Hamilton Dr 600 metres before the village.

Any room that I was in at Lake Tekapo Grandview afforded a wonderful view of the mountains that meet the lake. The property certainly has views worthy of its name. The accommodation was purpose built in 2002 and has four good-sized rooms with king-size beds and ensuites. Three rooms have decks and, after the long drive to get here, I enjoyed relaxing al fresco with a cup of tea. Drinks and hors d'oeuvres were served in the early evening, which gave me the chance to meet other guests and to get to know my hosts. Leon and Rosemary both come from New Zealand farming backgrounds and were pleased to share their knowledge of the land with me. They take a big interest in their guests, even tracking where they come from on a world map that hangs in the entrance to the house. It was an easy walk from the property into town where there were several restaurants to choose from. On the walk home I took a moment to enjoy the night sky. It was a very still, clear night, and because of the lack of city lights, a myriad of stars were visible in all their glory.

Accommodation available (NZ$)	👤	👥	+👤	🛏	🛁	
1 Room	$270			SK	EN	Breakfast: Special cooked
1 Room	$250			K	EN	
1 Room	$250			K	EN	Guest rooms:
1 Room	$220		$60	SK+S	EN	Ambience:

Setting/location:

LOW   HIGH

Property features
Spectacular mountain views
Exclusive accommodation
Private pond with trout
Peace and tranquility
Excellent dining
Local features
Fly fishing
45 min to Aoraki/Mt Cook
Heli Flight seeing/gliding
Hunting/bushwalking
Endangered Black Stilt programme

Matuka Lodge

Rosalie and Russell Smith
Old Station Road, Twizel
Tel: (03) 435 0144
Fax: (03) 435 0149
info@matukalodge.co.nz
www.lodgings.co.nz/matukalodge.html

Twizel - 5 minutes
Queenstown - 150 minutes

Approaching Twizel from the North, on Inland Scenic Route 8, cross the Twizel River, turn right into Glen Lyon Road, travel 3km then left into Old Station Road.

Set among spectacular scenery deep in the heart of the South Island's Mackenzie Country, Matuka Lodge is luxury accommodation and has some of the best fly-fishing in New Zealand close by. Anyone who stays here is fortunate. The lodge is elegant and intimate with an ambience created by original artworks and antiques blending with contemporary furniture. My suite had a king-size bed, individual climate control, mountain views and a verandah that overlooked a large ornamental pond. In the ensuite bathroom was under-floor heating, a heated, towel rail and cosy bathrobes. I was woken in the morning by the sun streaming in my window and had breakfast on the main deck that leads off the lounge and extends out over the pond. Trout swam lazily by. I didn't want to leave this peaceful haven but Rosalie and Russell had recommended a tour to the natural wonderland of nearby Aoraki/Mt Cook National Park. After an action-packed day, I came back to a pre-dinner drink on the deck. On the menu that night were fresh salmon and venison accompanied by delicious wine. Matuka opens all summer but is sometimes closed in the winter. It's an ideal place to stop on the way from Christchurch to Queenstown.

Accommodation available (NZ$)	👤	👤👤	+👤	🛏	🛁
1 Room	$390	$590		K	EN
2 Rooms	$450	$680		SK or 2S	EN

Breakfast: Cooked
Evening Meal: Included
Guest rooms:
Ambience:
Setting/location:

All inclusive rate: Breakfast, pre-dinner drink, dinner & accompanying wine.

Outdoor eating under clear blue skies, Queenstown.

Alexandra

Shaky Bridge Vineyard Café
Graveyard Gully Rd, Alexandra,
Tel: (03) 448-5111. Enjoy a relaxed
lunch at the Otago gold miner's
cottage. Picturesque setting.

Clyde

Post Office Cafe & Bar
Blyth St, Clyde, Tel: (03) 449-2488.
Olivers Restaurant
34 Sunderland St, Clyde,
Tel: (03) 449-2860.

Cromwell

Fusée Rouge 64b The Mall,
Tel: (03) 445-4014.

Wanaka

Cardrona Hotel & Restaurant
Cardrona Valley Rd,
Tel: (03) 443-8153. Est. in 1863,
one of NZ's oldest establishments.
Outstanding views, al fresco and
fireside dining. Worth a stop.
Relishes Café 1/99 Ardmore St,
Tel: (03) 443-9018. Alfresco dining
in summer, fireside dining in winter.
Licenced & BYO café.

Arrowtown

Blue Door Bar 18 Buckingham
St, Tel: (03) 442-0885. Cosy
fireplace, comfy
couches, dim lighting.
Good place to have a
drink before/after
dinner.
**The Postmaster's
House Restaurant**
54 Buckingham St,
Tel: (03) 442-0991. An
upmarket intimate

restaurant that focuses on regional
fare.
Saffron 18 Buckingham St,
Tel: (03) 442-0131. Delicious,
innovative food, good selection of
local wines.

Queenstown

Amisfield Winery Bistro
10 Lake Hayes Rd,
Tel: (03) 442-0556. Enjoy organic
and locally sourced produce in
architecturally award winning
surroundings. Play petanque in the
courtyard. Great wine.
Eichardt's
Marine Parade, Tel: (03) 441-0450.
Superb food for lunch and
designer cocktails and bar snacks
from late afternoon.
Fergburger Ltd Cow Lane,
Tel: (03) 441-1232. Great takeaway
burgers, vegetarian and meat.
Joe's Garage Camp St,
Tel: (03) 442-5282. Excellent
coffee, fast service, tasty food –
very popular.
Prime Upstairs, No 2 Rees St, Tel:
(03) 442-5288. Indoor/outdoor
dining, largest open fire in town. A
steakhouse with great views.
Solera Vino
25 Beach St, Tel: (03) 442-6082.
Spanish-style wine and tapas bar.
The Bathhouse
28 Marine Parade,
Tel: (03) 442-5625. Waterfront at
Lake Wakitipu. Café by day and
fine dining at night.
The Bunker Restaurant & Bar
Cow Lane, Tel: (03) 441-8030.
Expect leather armchairs, log fires,
ambient music, excellent menu.
The Cow Cow Lane,
Tel: (03) 442-8588.
Busy atmosphere, great pizzas.
Do not take bookings.
Vudu Café 23 Beach St,
Tel: (03) 442-5357, BYO café
serving café style cuisine.
Internet access.
Wai 23 Beach St, Steamer Wharf.
Tel: (03) 442-5969. Delicious menu
with focus on seafood and oysters.
On the waterfront.

Sea Kayaking, Fiordland.

Events
Craft Market Saturdays.
Queenstown Winter Festival
June/July Runs for about 10 days.
Wine & Food Festival
First weekend of February.

Te Anau

La Toscana 108 Town Centre,
Tel: (03) 249-7756. Relaxed casual
dining at this pizzeria spaghetteria.
Olive Tree Garden 52 Town
Centre, Tel: (03) 249-8496.
Good coffee, courtyard dining.
Redcliff Café 12 Mokonui St,
Tel: (03) 249-7431. A bar and
restaurant with atmosphere and
character.
Events
Gore Boat Club "Poker Run" –
Easter Saturday, Manapouri.

Dunedin

Bean Scene Café & Restaurant
18 Octagon, Tel: (03) 471-7372.
Bell Pepper Blues 474 Princes St,
Tel: (03) 474-0973. Still considered
one of the best in town. Creative
menu. Bookings recommended.
Conservatory Restaurant
Corstorphine House, Milburn St,
Tel: (03) 487-1000. Exceptional
food, magnificent views and old-
world charm.
**Etrusco at The Savoy Pizzeria &
Spaghetteria** 8a Moray Place,
Tel: (03) 477-3737. Overlooking
the ocean, superb pizzas.
Mazagram Espresso Bar
36 Moray Place,
Tel: (03) 477-9959. Small café,
coffee roasted on-site.
Nova 29 The Octagon,
Tel: (03) 479-0808. Popular
city-style café with tons of
ambience and great food.
Adjacent to Public Art Gallery.
Plato 2 Birch St, Tel: (03) 477-4235.
Restaurant and bar in Dunedin's
upper harbour area. Serving
contemporary food surrounded
in 1960's décor.
Table Seven 44 Hanover St,
Tel: (03) 477-6877. Modern, trendy,
Pacific Rim cuisine.
Two Chefs 428 George St,
Tel: (03) 477-9117. Fine dining,
delicious food, open fire, nice
atmoshphere.
Events
ID Fashion Week March.
Otago Farmers Market
Every Saturday, 8am-1:30pm.
Railway Station, north carpark,
Anzac Avenue.

Takitimu Mountains, Southland.

Milford Sound/
Fiordland

Wanaka page 217

St Bathans page 216

Queenstown page 224

Te Anau page 238

Athol page 237

Manapouri page 241

Dunedin
page 243

Riverton page 251

Invercargill page 252

Stewart Island
page 253

Constable Cottage and Gaol

The Vulcan Hotel
St Bathans township
Tel: 0800 555016
info@stbathansnz.co.nz
www.lodgings.co.nz/stbathans.html

Property features
Laundry & kitchen in S/C cottage
TV/video/stereo in S/C cottage
Phone S/C cottage
BBQ
Lake views
Local features
Gold mining history
Swimming
Cycling
Walking
Boating

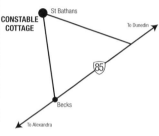

Alexandra - 40 minutes
Queenstown - 1 hr 30 mins

From SH 85, turn towards St Bathans from Becks. The cottage is on your right just before you reach the centre of town.

There are few places in Central Otago that retain their historical character as much as St Bathans does, with its restored stone and earth-brick buildings, the silent lake and strange columns of clay left by the sluicings. There are about 20 buildings in the town but only seven residents. The accommodation is in the original police cottage and the small gaol behind it, on an elevated site overlooking the lake. My stay here was memorable. The days were warm and bright, the nights cool and quiet. I lit the fire in the lounge, cooked up an easy meal in the well-equipped kitchen, soaked in the deep bath and slept soundly in a comfortable bed that smelt of lavender. Although the characteristics of a 19th-century dwelling have been kept in the cottage, it is not at the expense of modern amenities such as television, video and CD player. Continental breakfast ingredients were left for me to prepare myself, or I could have visited the Vulcan Hotel, a short walk away, for cooked breakfasts and dinners. Guests can also spend a romantic night in the small, one-room gaol and experience the novelty of an outdoor bath. The Rail Trail is nearby for biking enthusiasts.

Accommodation available (NZ$)	🧍	🧍🧍	+🧍	🛏	🛁	Guest pets by arrangement
1 S/C cottage	$220	$220	$40	2Q+2S	PR	Breakfast: Provisions provided
1 Cottage	$100	$100		Q	PR	Evening meal: Enquire

Phone available in S/C cottage. S/C Cottage weekly rate is $1000.
Gaol weekly rate is $500.

Guest rooms:
Ambience:
Setting/location:

LOW · HIGH

Property features
Croquet and petanque
Lunch hampers - by arrangement
Complimentary pre-dinner drinks
Guest pick-up available
Mountain bikes available
Feature garden
Local features
Skifields
Golf course
Fishing/lakeside walks
Jet boating/kayaking

The Stone Cottage
Belinda Wilson
Dublin Bay, Wanaka
Tel: (03) 443 1878
Fax:(03) 443 1276
stonecottage@xtra.co.nz
www.lodgings.co.nz/stonecottage.html

Wanaka - 10 minutes
Queenstown - 1 hour

From Wanaka, drive 4km towards Lake Hawea / West Coast on SH 6, then turn left into Dublin Bay Rd. The Stone Cottage is near the end of the road on your left.

Although the Stone Cottage is just a short drive from Wanaka, I could easily have imaged I was marooned on an island. The proximity to the lake and the magnificent view are important features of staying here. The view extends across the lake to Treble Cone ski field and, if the timing is right, you might be able to lie in bed at night and see the lights of the snow groomers on the mountains in the distance. The two suites occupy the upper level of Belinda's home and are accessed independently by staircases at each end of the building. The larger suite has more substantial facilities, such as a full stove, and French doors leading to a balcony taking full advantage of the view. The smaller suite is newer; it also takes in the views and has an outdoor table and chairs on the landing - great for an alfresco breakfast. If you're are travelling on your own opt for the smaller suite; with others in tow, an adjoining door can be opened to create a 'super-suite', with loads of living space. Belinda loves to 'play' in the kitchen so you would be well advised to eat in. A visitor from Hong Kong wrote: 'So there is a heaven on earth! The silence and solitude are unbelievable. Thanks a million.'

Family dog on site

Accommodation available (NZ$)	♠	♠♠	+♠	⬆	🛁
1 S/C unit	$220	$240-270		SK	EN
1 S/C unit	$220	$260-300	$50	D+2S	EN

Breakfast: Cooked
Evening meal: $65pp
Guest rooms:
Ambience:
Setting/location:

LOW   HIGH

Aoturoa

Jon and Lesley Davies
Rapid #3396, Highway 6, Cromwell Rd, Wanaka
Tel: (03) 443 5000   Mob: 021 2986484
Fax:(03) 443 5001
stay@aoturoa.co.nz
www.lodgings.co.nz/aoturoa.html

Property features
Two minutes stroll to the river
Trout fishing when in season
Swimming
Walk along the river terraces
Mountain views
Four luxurious suites
Super-king beds
Local features
15 minute drive to Wanaka
15 minutes to restaurants/vineyards

Wanaka - 15 minute drive
Queenstown - 1 hour drive

Aoturoa is 17 kilometres from
Wanaka and 3 kilometres from
Luggate on your left hand side on
Highway 6.

Aoturoa is located just a few minutes drive away from Wanaka. Although I had no expectations, I was still surprised by the impressive modern house that stood at the end of the long, private driveway. Aoturoa, meaning "world of light", was aptly named. The light and colour that surrounds this amazing property are ever changing. Jon and Lesley, who had searched long and hard for a place to build, fell in love with this perfect spot. Well, who wouldn't? Their land, surrounded by mountains and next to the Clutha River, comprises two miles of river flat, which is perfect for fishing, swimming, walks and leisurely picnics. As for the accommodation, there are four lavish guestrooms to choose from, two of which have French tubs large enough to fit two people. The décor is minimal so as not to overwhelm the fantastic alpine and river views. Dinners are arranged on request and I recommend dining in for at least one night of any stay. The menu, the local wine and the company made for a great experience. After dinner we gathered with other guests in one of the lounges and sat talking around a log fire until late into the evening.

Accommodation available (NZ$)	🧍	🧍🧍	+🧍	🛏	🛁	
3 Rooms	$490	$490		SK	EN	Breakfast: Cooked
1 Room	$490	$490		2 KS	EN	Evening meal: $70pp

Guest rooms:
Ambience:
Setting/location:

LOW   HIGH

Property features
Ten acres of landscaped grounds
Uninterrupted mountain views
Swimming pool/spa pool
Pitch and putt golf course (5 holes)
Helipad
Stylish guest lounge with open fire

Local features
Mt Aspiring National Park/hiking
Treble Cone/Cardrona ski resorts
Lake activities/trout fishing/kayaking
Scenic flights/vineyards/golf

Lime Tree Lodge

Sally Carwardine   Rebecca Butts
672 Ballantyne Road, Wanaka
Tel: (03) 443 7305   Mob: 021 529118
Fax:(03) 443 7345
revive@limetreelodge.co.nz
www.lodgings.co.nz/limetree.html

Wanaka - 6 minutes drive
Queenstown - 1 hour drive

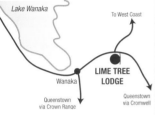

From Wanaka town centre travel approximately 6km towards Cromwell on SH6. Lime Tree Lodge is on the corner of Ballantyne Road just past the West Coast turn-off.

Lime Tree Lodge has recently undergone an extensive, interior makeover and I was enchanted with the results which far exceeded any expectations I'd had from the outside of this purpose-built building. Sally and Rebecca have put their hearts and souls into this property and the result is a lodge that manages to be both sophisticated and unpretentious - very easy to relax in, but still with all modern conveniences and luxuries. Four of the guestrooms open to a patio, an expansive lawn and a large pool area. Beyond are the mountains, and their changing moods became a big part of the experience of staying here. Among the six rooms, two new, ultra-modern suites, called Black Peak and Linden, are extravagant in detail. Sally and Rebecca have thought of everything. I favoured Black Peak suite because it has a log fire, a private terrace and great views of the mountains. There are other excellent facilities for guest use, such as a swimming pool, spa pool, a five-hole pitch-and-putt golf course and a helipad. The lodge is only six kilometres from Wanaka but because it is set on ten acres of land, it feels well away from the busy world.

	Accomodation available (NZ$)	🧍	🧍🧍	+🧍	🛏	🛁
Breakfast: Cooked	1 Room	$330	$350		Q	EN
Evening meal: $95pp	3 Rooms	$330	$350		K, SK or 2S	EN
Guest rooms:	1 Suite	$430	$450		SK or 2S	EN
Ambience:	1 Suite	$530	$550		SK+2S	EN
Setting/location:						

Minaret Lodge

Gary and Fran Tate
34 Eely Point Road, Wanaka
Tel: (03) 443 1856
Fax: (03) 443 1846
relax@minaretlodge.co.nz
www.lodgings.co.nz/minaret.html

Property features
Tennis
Petanque
Sauna
Spa pool
Drying room
Ski storage facilities
Spacious grounds
Local features
Short walk to lake
10 minute walk to Wanaka

Wanaka - 10 mins walk
Queenstown - 1 hr drive

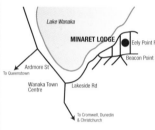

From Wanaka township, drive North along Lakeside Road. Continue on Lakeside Road for 2km, turn right into Eely Point Road.

Gary and Fran have restored and re-created this inviting lodge, which is set in rambling rustic grounds and aptly named after the Minaret Peaks across Lake Wanaka. The house is hung with interesting local art and is perfectly set for pursuing the various activities in the adventure playground around Wanaka. Gary and Fran's architect used natural and non-toxic building materials for the lodge and natural oil has been used on the woodwork. For LOTR fans there is "Barlimans Room" - themed Lord of the Rings kingsize room with special hobbit menu! All rooms have four-channel Sky television and a mini-bar. Every detail has been thought of in these very attractively decorated rooms which all have easy access to the outdoors, where you can take a spa or use the outdoor games room. A tennis court is set among trees. Should your stay be in winter there is good ski storage and a drying area, and on-site ski maintenance. Gary and Fran invite guests to have a glass of Central Otago wine with hors d'oevres before dinner. Transfers to local restaurants are also provided. Minaret Lodge is quiet and peaceful set in very spacious grounds, a short walk to the lake and close to town.

Accommodation available (NZ$)	👤	👤👤	+👤	🛏	🛁	Family pets on site
4 rooms	$375	$395	$60	SK or 2S EN		
1 Suite	$495	$495	$60	K or 2S EN		

Breakfast: Special cooked
Evening meal: $85pp
Guest rooms:
Ambience:
Setting/location:

LOW   HIGH

Property features
Large gardens with natural springs
Private hot tub in garden setting
Lake and mountain views
Business facilities/office
Tourism Award finalist 2001/2002
Local features
Lake Wanaka - short walk
Fishing/hunting guides available
Scenic flights/ski fields
Vineyards/golf course/jet boat rides
Walk to town centre/cafes

Wanaka Springs Lodge

Murray and Lyn Finn
21 Warren Street, Wanaka
Tel: (03) 443 8421   Mob: 025 2414113
Fax:(03) 443 8429
relax@wanakasprings.com
www.lodgings.co.nz/wanakasprings.html

Wanaka - 3 mins walk
Queenstown - 1 hour

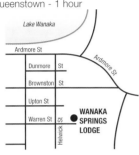

From the lakefront, travel up Helwick Street. Turn left into Warren Street, Wanaka Springs is on your left.

Purpose-built in the centre of Wanaka, this boutique hotel is proving a quiet and popular choice for travellers. Murray and Lyn welcomed me and explained that they had their own accommodation, so that I could see as little or as much of them as I wanted. I was shown the inviting guest lounge where there is a television, cosy couches, small library and a fireplace that made me wish it was winter. Drinks are offered here in the evening. All the bedrooms are comfortably appointed and immaculate, with brocade duvets on the beds. Many have outlooks to the garden or the lake and mountains. Our view also incorporated the stream that wells up from a natural spring and winds through the garden where, in one corner, there is a luxurious spa house. Breakfast in a sunny room, or on the deck, was a lavish affair and pleasantly social with plenty of variety to cater for different tastes. I had a very early start and Murray and Lyn could not have been more warm and accommodating. Afternoon tea with scones was also served everyday in the breakfast room, as part of the tariff. The lodge has a separate well-appointed small office where guests are able to access a good information system.

Accommodation available (NZ$)	🧍	🧍🧍	+🧍	🛏	🛁
5 Rooms	$275	$295		Q	EN
1 Room	$275	$295		2S	EN
2 Rooms	$310	$330		K	EN

Breakfast: Special cooked

Guest rooms:
Ambience:
Setting/location:

Rollaway beds available (extra charge). TV on request.

Wanaka Stonehouse Boutique Lodge

Jaime and Anna Kate Hutter
21 Sargood Drive, Wanaka
Tel: (03) 443 1933
Fax: (03) 443 1929
indulge@wanakastonehouse.co.nz
www.lodgings.co.nz/wanakastone.html

Property features
Lodge exclusively for guests
Large lounge with open fire
Separate mezzanine reading room
Tranquil private garden
Spa and sauna
Local features
Golf course with lake views
Ski fields within 30 mins drive
Kayaking/jet boating/paragliding
Walks/trout fishing/scenic flights
Easy walk to lake and vineyard

Cromwell - 30 mins drive
Queenstown - 50 mins drive

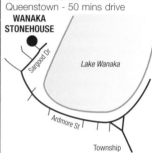

From Wanaka lake front (Ardmore St) take the third right into Sargood Drive. We are approximately 300 metres along on your left – 21 Sargood Drive.

Jaime and Anna Kate, new owners of the lodge, have thought of everything in this character, hunting-style lodge. This young and enthusiastic couple live in a separate house across the garden and although they were there for anything I needed, they take a non-intrusive approach to this boutique lodging. I arrived to be greeted by the temptation of home baking straight from the oven, and I enjoyed sitting in the garden under the umbrella quietly chatting over a cool drink. In this region, where there are so many outdoor adventures, guests enjoy coming back here and reviving their weary bodies in the beautiful sauna and spa sanctuary. The breakfast menu changes daily and I was treated to snacks and drinks throughout the day. I was also welcome to help myself to cookies and fruit from the kitchen. Wanaka township is only a short stroll away, so evening meals can be enjoyed in town or picked up and taken back to the lodge. Beds are turned back in the evening and the linen and towels in the rooms are a luxurious quality. Situated midway between two ski fields, this lodge is a good choice for a winter stay.

Accommodation available (NZ$)	👤	👥	+👤	🛏	🛁	
						Guest pets by arrangement
1 Room	$395		$50	K or 2S	EN	Breakfast: Special cooked
1 Room	$395			K or 2S	EN	
2 Rooms	$345			Q	EN	Guest rooms:
						Ambience:
						Setting/location:

LOW   HIGH

Property features
3-seater cedar hot tub
Cosy guest lounge with open fire
DVD/Sky TV
Breath taking mountain views
Drying room and ski storage
Local features
Mt Aspiring National Park
Golf course/horse trekking
20 mins to ski fields
Heli-skiing/mountain biking
Fishing/boating

Mountain Range
Melanie Laaper   Stuart Pinfold
Heritage Park, Cardrona Valley Road, Wanaka
Tel: (03) 443 7400
Fax:(03) 443 7450
stay@mountainrange.co.nz
www.lodgings.co.nz/mountainrange.html

Wanaka - 5 mins drive
Queenstown - 45 mins drive

From West Coast or ChCh, take SH
84 towards Wanaka. Follow lake
front and turn left into Macdougall
Street. Heritage Park is approx 2 km
on the left. Once in the park
Mountain Range is on the left.

Stuart and Melanie recently took over this ranch-style lodge set on ten acres of parkland at the foot of the ranges from which it takes its name. Even though it's only a three-minute drive from the township, the property is surrounded by open space and is overlooked by the dramatic peaks of the rugged mountains. I was made very welcome and in the afternoon, I relaxed in front of a roaring, open fire before the thought of a soak in the Canadian cedar hot tub, which is set in the native garden, got the better of me. In the evening I took a 'trip' around the Southern Hemisphere's night sky through a telescope that is made available to guests. The rooms are presented with an understated elegance. All have spacious ensuites, and luxurious beds and they open onto private verandahs with spectacular views. Stuart and Melanie are young, outdoor enthusiasts who are well travelled and they are generous with their hospitality. I don't play golf but for those who do there is a course right next door and Stuart joins his guests for a round when he has time. Mountain Range is a stylish and comfortable retreat and a great base from which to explore the Wanaka region.

Accommodation available (NZ$)	🛈	🛈🛈	+🛈	🛏	🛁
1 Room	$165-235	$210-280		SK	EN
6 Rooms	$165-235	$195-265		SK or 2S	EN

Breakfast: Special cooked

Guest rooms:
Ambience:
Setting/location:

Skyview Magic

Jef Desbecker   Robina Bodle
44 Jeffery Road, Crown Terrace R.D. 1, Queenstown
Tel: (03) 442 9405   Mob: 027 4337232
Fax:(03) 442 9405
info@skyview.co.nz
www.lodgings.co.nz/skyview.html

Property features
25 m solar heated non-chem pool
3 km walking/running track
Set on 168 acre property
Privacy/silence/seclusion
Incredible mountain views
Climbing wall/sunny verandahs

Local features
Mountain/road cycling/fishing
Skiing/boarding/heli-skiing
Whitewater rivers/50km lake
Wineries/cafes/shopping/golf

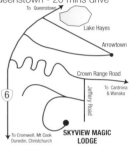

Arrowtown - 12 mins drive
Queenstown - 20 mins drive

To Queenstown
Lake Hayes
Arrowtown
Crown Range Road
To Cardrona & Wanaka
Jeffery Road
6
To Cromwell, Mt Cook
Dunedin, Christchurch
SKYVIEW MAGIC LODGE

Travel 19 km from Queenstown on Hwy 6 towards Cromwell, turn up Crown Range Road. Travel 5km, tu right onto Jeffery Road. Travel 1/2 km, turn right at "Skyview" sign. Take left at driveway fork.

Only a short 20-minute drive from Queenstown, you can find yourself in this alpine oasis. Located on Crown Terrace above the Wakitipu Basin the views are magic – 360 degrees of mountain and lake, fields of tall wild grasses, young forests and, in season, colourful flowers. This rustic lodge is located on a 168-acre property, with three kilometres of walking tracks, an on-site climbing wall, and a 25-metre solar-heated, indoor chlorine-free swimming pool. It is central to five local ski areas. The location alone is enough to make you gasp, but when I entered the lodge, my attention was drawn to the sawn timber and log slabs, the 100-year old bridge beams, a floor of recycled kauri, puzzle walls of timber pieces, and driftwood banisters on the stairway. This lodge is truly unique. The guestrooms are all spacious with comfortable beds and all have funky, bright, ensuite bathrooms with modern fittings. Downstairs there is a fully equipped kitchen, comfortable furniture and beautiful Indian carpets. The high stud ceilings give a great sense of space. The lodge is fully insulated with underfloor heating on all tiled areas, double-glazed windows and a wood burner, so even in the middle of winter it is cosy. Skyview Magic could cast a spell that will make you never want to leave.

Accomodation available (NZ$)	👤	👥	+👤	🛏	🛁	Family cat on site
1 S/C lodge	$500	$500	$40-85	2SK/T,2Q,4S	4 EN	

Breakfast: Not available
Dinner: Enquire
Guest rooms:
Ambience:
Setting/location:

Lodge has 4 bedrooms + mezzanine.
Sleeps up to 12 people. Min 2 night stay.

RECOMMENDED
BOUTIQUE LODGINGS
LOW   HIG

Property features
Suites open to 2 acres of gardens
Lounge with stone fireplace/library
Mountain views
Peaceful rural retreat
Private patios
Local features
Swimming/fishing in Lake Hayes
4 golf courses within 15 min drive
Coronet Peak skiing 15 min drive
Vineyards/wineries 15 min drive
Arrowtown is a historic mining town

Bellini's of Queenstown

Melinda Hayton   John Lapsley
578 Speargrass Flat Rd, Queenstown
Tel: (03) 442 0771   Mob: 021 341245
Fax:(03) 442 0715
holiday@bellinis.co.nz
www.lodgings.co.nz/bellinis.html

Arrowtown - 4 minutes
Queenstown - 15 minutes

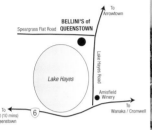

From Queenstown Airport turn right
down Highway 6 towards Cromwell.
Drive approx 8 mins, turn left
towards Arrowtown at Amisfield
Winery. Drive 3 mins then turn left
into Speargrass Flat Rd.

Set on two acres of secluded grounds and gardens and surrounded by spectacular Queenstown countryside, Bellini's is a retreat that is sure to impress. Inside, stone schist, massive timber beams, lavish Persian carpets, artworks, and carefully chosen furnishings, are combined to superb effect. All three spacious guest suites are well appointed, with Egyptian cotton linen, Sky television, stereo and DVDs, and have private patios opening directly out to the expansive property. I stayed in the Mountain Suite which had alpine vistas stretching out to The Remarkables mountains. Guests have the option of breakfast in the dining room, with its stone wall, pyramid arched ceiling, and striking dining table. But I was there on a sunny day and breakfast was served under a willow tree in the garden. John and Melinda were happy to help me with plans to see the area, suggesting scenic drives, walks, golfing and fishing venues, as well as restaurants for that evening. Their fishing guide guarantees that both experienced anglers and beginners might catch a wild trout for the guest barbecue. In the evening we swapped traveller's tales over cocktails served beside the large open fire that warmed the lounge and library, before enjoying dinner at one of the fine restaurants in nearby Arrowtown.

Accommodation available (NZ$)	🚹	🚹🚹	+🚹	🛏	🛁
1 Studio	$350	$400	$100	K or 2S	EN
2 Suites	$400-450	$450-500	$100	Q	EN

Breakfast: Cooked

Guest rooms:
Ambience:
Setting/location:

LOW   HIGH

225

The Turret

Mark and Martha Arrowsmith
Lake Hayes, Queenstown
Tel: (03) 442 1107   Mob: 021 2987085
Fax: (03) 442 1160
theturret@xtra.co.nz
www.lodgings.co.nz/turret.html

Property features
Lake and mountain views
Separate guest dining & lounge
Award winning garden
Overlooking wildlife reserve
Local features
Skifields - 20 minutes
Several golf courses nearby
Restaurants/cafes - 5 minutes
Day tours Milford/Doubtful Sound
Vineyards/wineries - 2 minutes

Arrowtown - 5 minutes
Queenstown - 15 minutes

Cardrona Ski Area
Arrowtown
Coronet Peak Ski Area
Lake Hayes
Queenstown 6
THE TURRET
Remarkables Ski Field

From Queenstown, take SH 6 towards Cromwell approx. 12km, Tɪ Turret is on your right. From Cromw / Wanaka continue past the second Arrowtown turnoff. The Turret is on your left.

Mark and Martha are the hosts of this charming lodge and, when I met them, the first thing I noticed was the depth of their life experience. I was warmly welcomed to share a glass of wine in the sunny living room overlooking the lovely front garden and Lake Hayes. This is a house of strong character with a lively and inviting ambience, which is impossible not to enjoy. If you are looking for time by yourself, there are some wonderful enclaves on the patio, in the beautifully landscaped garden, or on the nearby Lake Hayes walking track. The front door of the house opens to the guest dining area and adjacent is a quiet and cosy guest-dedicated living room dominated by a large open fireplace. Downstairs two attractive bedrooms open to the patio and a tranquil outlook over Lake Hayes and up to Coronet Peak. But the piece de resistance is the large turret suite upstairs, which, with its exotic décor, walk-in change room and spacious bathroom with shower and a claw foot bath, is like a room in a Moroccan palace. In the attached turret is a intriguingly decorated, private sitting room with a stunning view. This house is different and very interesting and a great base from which to explore the district.

Accommodation available (NZ$)	👤	👤👤	+👤	🛏	🛁
1 Room	$135	$165	1S+1D	PR	
1 Room	$165-195	$165-195	Q	EN	
1 Suite	$200	$295	Q	EN	

Breakfast: Special continental

Guest rooms:
Ambience:
Setting/location:

LOW   HIɪ

Property features
Private trout fishing
Sheep and cattle farm
Peaceful rural location
Midway Queenstown/Arrowtown
Mountain views
Local features
Skifields - 20 minutes
Adventure activities
Vineyards/wineries - 15 minutes
Lake Hayes - 5 minutes
Golf course - 5 minutes

Arrowtown - 10 minutes
Queenstown - 10 minutes

From Queenstown, drive approx.
?km on SH 6 towards Cromwell.
Alec Robins Rd is on the right,
Bridesdale is at end. From Cromwell/
Wanaka drive past Arrowtown
turnoffs & Lake Hayes. Alec Robins
Rd is on the left.

Bridesdale

Fran and King Allen
Alec Robins Road, Lake Hayes, Queenstown
Tel: (03) 442 0864   Mob: 027 4360403
Fax: (03) 442 0860
bridesdale@xtra.co.nz
www.lodgings.co.nz/bridesdale.html

Bridesdale is a striking country home set at the foot of the Remarkable Mountains with a view across the valley to Coronet Peak. It is the hub of a 140-acre farm, which runs sheep and beef cattle. Through a stone archway next to the house is an attractive, well-appointed cottage with two bedrooms, a lounge, kitchen and a warm ambience. But first, Fran and King welcomed me into their own ample lounge, which opens to a broad terrace and garden. Over tea I heard about the farm and how King enjoys taking his guests around it, and down to the trout-rich Kawarau River which runs though the property where there is good fishing. I returned from the tour and enjoyed a complimentary drink with the couple before leaving for an evening meal. Bridesdale is halfway between Arrowtown and Queenstown and therefore handy to a wide range of restaurants, cafes and activities, it also takes on all the peace and quiet of the countryside. Nearby are several very well known vineyards which are well worth a visit. A full continental breakfast will be served in the cottage if you want morning privacy. However, if you are happier to bring your own provisions you, will have all you need to prepare them. The cottage is a good choice for a longer stay.

Family pets on site Guest pets by arrangement	Accommodation available (NZ$)			+		
Breakfast: Breakfast: Extra $12pp	1 S/C cottage	$200	$225-275	$60	SK+Q or 2S+Q	PR

Guest rooms:
Ambience:
Setting/location:

LOW   HIGH

Pear Tree Cottage

Terry and Erina McLean
Rapid no. 51 Mountain View Rd, Queenstown
Tel: (03) 442 9340   Mob: 027 4370935
Fax: (03) 442 9349
info@peartree.co.nz
www.lodgings.co.nz/peartree.html

Property features
Set in 7.5 acres incl. mature garden
Historic S/C cottage (circa 1870s)
Full kitchen/stocked pantry
TV/video/stereo
Spa pool/BBQ/petanque
Guest laundry
Local features
Skifields - 15 mins
Three golf courses - 15 mins
Fishing/jet boating/rafting
Arrowtown - history/museum

Queenstown - 12 minutes
Arrowtown - 12 minutes

From SH 6, take Lower Shotover R
Turn left into Domain Rd. Name
changes to Dalefield Rd, continue
and take Mountain View Rd on you
left. Cottage is on your left.

Neither photographs nor words can do Pear Tree Cottage justice. Inside the cottage, guests are surrounded by antiques and pieces of kiwi memorabilia; collections of irons, chamber pots, and New Zealand Rail oil cans among them. I would be here all day if I listed everything! I'm pleased I don't have to dust this place - the hosts must spend hours ensuring cleanliness is not compromised by the rustic ambience. The original part of the cottage dates back to the 1870's, with recent renovations making room for a separate lounge, two bedrooms, bathroom and large country kitchen/dining. A winter stay would be a real treat here - a radiator system throughout the house and a huge open fire in the lounge make a winter holiday in Queenstown a delight. All modern conveniences such as dishwasher, washing machine, television, VCR, CD collection are here and so are many other special touches. Terry and Erina are passionate gardeners and guests at Pear Tree Cottage can enjoy lounging in the outdoor furniture, the shade of large established trees and the perfume of the extensive flower gardens. The cottage is private but the hosts are so welcoming and the cottage so delightful it is very hard to leave.

Accommodation available (NZ$)			+		
1 S/C cottage	$335	$240-350	$50-60	Q+D+S	PR

Breakfast: Special continental
Evening meal: $75pp
Guest rooms:
Ambience:
Setting/location:

LOW   HIG

Four guests $340-470 per night, other tariffs on request.

Property features
Cliff-top hydrotherapy jacuzzi
Panoramic river/mountain views
Bedrooms with private balconies
Day spa/massage therapies
Breakfast menu changes daily
Pre-dinner drinks & hors d'oeuvres
Hosts NZ Tourism Award Winners
Local features
Walk to Shotover jet/rafting
Stables/hiking trails - 2 mins
Quiet & secluded - town 5 mins

Queenstown - 5 minutes
Wanaka - 1 hour

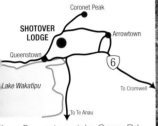

From Queenstown take Gorge Rd
towards Coronet Peak / Arrowtown.
Drive several minutes and cross
bridge (Shotover Jet operation to
your left). Turn right into Atley Rd
500m past bridge. Lodge is
signposted.

Shotover Lodge

Steve and Jeanette Brough
61 Atley Road, Arthurs Point, Queenstown
Tel: (03) 441 8037
Fax:(03) 441 8058
luxury@shotoverlodge.com
www.lodgings.co.nz/shotoverlodge.html

Perched high above the Shotover River this private paradise contains all guests need for a blissful stay. Quality appointments and conveniences go without saying but what makes this lodge stand apart is the extras, the location and attention to detail. You can soak up the views from the jacuzzi or request any of a huge range of day spa services. Play snooker and take advantage of the wine cellar or just relax in front of the fire with an espresso coffee. Indulge in breakfasts that could include items such as compote of spiced apricot and red berries with baked honeyed ricotta, or leg ham and jarlsberg cheese croissants. Of course you don't come to Queenstown just to relax. The convenient location is a bonus. Queenstown's most popular activities - Shotover Jet, horse riding, the white water rafting base & four restaurants are within walking distance. Hiking & mountain biking trails lead directly from the lodge. Shotover Lodge can arrange a day's fly fishing for anglers of all abilities. The entrance to Coronet Peak, Queenstown's premier ski resort, is only five minutes away. Steve and Jeanette are the Winners of a Travel & Leisure magazine 'World's Best Award' and a New Zealand Tourism Award - assurance of a special experience.

Accommodation available (NZ$)	👤	👤👤	+👤	🛏	🛁
3 Rooms	$405	$450		Q+S	EN

Breakfast: Special cooked

Guest rooms:
Ambience:
Setting/location:

LOW   HIGH

Enquire about tariff for additional guests in room.

229

Trelawn Place

Michael Clark   Nery Howard
off Gorge Road, Arthurs Point, Queenstown
Tel: (03) 442 9160
Fax: (03) 442 9167   Free: 0871 7311014 (UK only)
trelawn@ihug.co.nz
www.lodgings.co.nz/trelawn.html

Property features
Absolute river front
Panoramic views from rural setting
Guest laundry/internet facilities
All rooms have balcony/patio views
Riverside jacuzzi
In-room tea/coffee/fridge/TV
Local features
Ski field 15 mins away
Local tours pickup guest here
River access/walks from Trelawn

Queenstown - 4 mins
Arrowtown - 15 mins

SH6a into Queenstown turn right a
the 2nd roundabout into Gorge Rd
towards Coronet Peak, travel 4kms
the blue B&B sign on the right.
Trelawn is at the end of the drive.

It was hard to believe when I arrived at the delightful rural setting of Trelawn Place, that I had only driven four minutes from central Queenstown. Set on two acres at the edge of the Shotover River the property is surrounded by dramatic mountains. The main house, built in 1978, and the two cottages are made of schist and dark timber with low-slung, corrugated-iron roofs. The creeping wisteria, gardens of roses and manicured lawns reflect Nery and Michael's passion for gardens. Private places have been created throughout the property – terraces and verandahs off guestrooms, a cliff-side gazebo with hot-tub and dining table, and walking trails that lead guests through the garden or down to the river's edge. I chose to eat our generous, cooked breakfast at the large table in the main house. The cosy room was warmed by the morning sun and an old coal range. It was a wonderful way to start the day. Cottage guests have the option of breakfasting in their cottage. After 25-years of hosting bed and breakfast accommodation, Nery and Michael have developed a small library with an extensive range of travel guides and information. The hospitality and tranquility of Trelawn makes it a place people visit again and again.

Accommodation available (NZ$)	🧍	🧍🧍	+🧍	🛏	🛁	
						Family pets on site
						Guest pets by arrangement
1 Cottage		$295	$50	Q+2S	PR	Breakfast: Cooked
1 Cottage		$350		K	PR	
1 Room	$250	$295	$50	K+S	EN	Guest rooms:
2 Rooms	$250	$350		K	EN	Ambience:
						Setting/location:

LOW   HIG

Property features
Spectacular views
Central Queenstown - 4 min walk
15 guestrooms including suites

Local features
Walking tracks
Golf courses
Skifields
Vineyards/wineries
Rose gardens

Queenstown House

Louise Kiely
69 Hallenstein St, Queenstown
Tel: (03) 442 9043
Fax: (03) 442 8755
queenstown.house@xtra.co.nz
www.lodgings.co.nz/queenstownhouse.html

Queenstown central - 4 min walk
Dunedin - 3 hours

From Hwy 6, drive down hill to roundabout in central Queenstown, turn right into Ballarat St, left into Hallenstein St. The house is 50 metres on right on the corner of Malaghan St.

The main house of this small boutique hotel was established over 20 years ago. More recently Louise has built The Villas which join onto the existing 14 bed and breakfast rooms. The rooms range in size and are comfortable with ensuites and views or private patios. Stone steps and several joining patios connect the two buildings. Yucca trees, native grasses, lavender and roses line the way and create numerous private areas and spaces for guests. The Villas include two stylishly appointed, self-contained suites and two lake-view suites. Our party of four booked the upstairs two-bedroom suite. The spacious living area and open-plan kitchen was ideal. We could dine inside or out on the private patio looking over Queenstown's city centre, Lake Wakatipu and Walter Peak. It was only a four-minute walk down to Queenstown's numerous restaurants and cafes. The large blue leather couches in front of the schist-stone, gas fireplace were comfortable for lounging on after a day of Queenstown adventures. Breakfast is served daily in the stylish dining room in the main house where, in the evening, the popular pre-dinner hour is held where there are complimentary drinks, a chance to meet other guests and to sample New Zealand cheeses.

Accommodation available (NZ$)	👤	👥	+👤	🛏	🛁
3 Rooms	$250	$295		Q	EN
8 Rooms	$250	$295		K or 2S	EN
2 Suites	$350	$395		K	EN
1 S/C unit	$425	$495		K	EN

Breakfast: Special cooked
Evening meal: Enquire
Guest rooms:
Ambience:
Setting/location:

Evening meals by prior arrangement

The Stone House

Jo and Steve Weir
47 Hallenstein St, Queenstown
Tel: (03) 442 9812   Mob: 027 4573903
Fax: (03) 441 8293
stone.house@xtra.co.nz
www.lodgings.co.nz/stonehouse.html

Property features
500m from central Queenstown
Garden spa
Fireside wine & cheese
Tour booking/laundry service
All rooms have: hairdryers/elec blkts
alarm clocks/bathrobes/telephones
Local features
Golfing/fishing
Jetboating/Milford Sound flights
Shopping/winetasting
Skiing/boarding

Queenstown - 5 mins walk
Dunedin - 3 hours

From the town centre, cross Stanley
St and head up the hill on Ballarat S
Turn right onto Hallenstein St, The
Stone House is on the left.

The Stone House is well known to Queenstown visitors and, in the high season, it's important to book ahead. Like the rest of this beautifully restored 1874 home, the bedrooms are authentic and well appointed. The guest lounge contains complimentary sherry, orange juice, hot chocolate, tea & coffee, a television, a CD player and a selection of books and games. This is where guests congregate in the evening for complimentary wine and cheese by the fire. Breakfast is delicious and can include croissants, fluffy omelettes, pancakes, waffles and eggs Benedict. Served in the dining room overlooking Cecil and Walter Peaks, this could be the highlight of the day. The building is listed by the Historic Places Trust and it is a treat to experience the charm of New Zealand's past in such comfortable modern style and only 500 metres from central Queenstown. The hosts, Jo and Steve, are well-informed and happy to offer suggestions about what to do in the Queenstown area. Guests from the United States recently wrote, 'beautiful spot, warm hospitality and gourmet breakfasts!'

Accommodation available (NZ$)						Family cat on site
3 Rooms	$250		K	EN		Breakfast: Special cooked
1 Room	$250		K	PR		

Guest rooms:
Ambience:
Setting/location:

LOW   HIGH

Rms can accommodate a couple only - no facilities for extra guests in rms.

The Dairy, Private Luxury Hotel

Elspeth Zemla
Corner Isle and Brecon Streets, Queenstown
Tel: (03) 442 5164
Fax: (03) 442 5166 Free: 0800 333393
info@thedairy.co.nz
www.lodgings.co.nz/thedairy.html

Property features
Lake and mountain views
Large lounge and private library
Close proximity to town/gondola
Open fireplace/central heating
Ski storage/hydrotherapy spa
Internet access

Local features
Skifields - 30 min drive
Tramping/nature walks
Scenic flights/fishing/jetboating
Vineyards/wineries - 30 min

Queenstown - 1 min walk
Arrowtown - 15 minutes

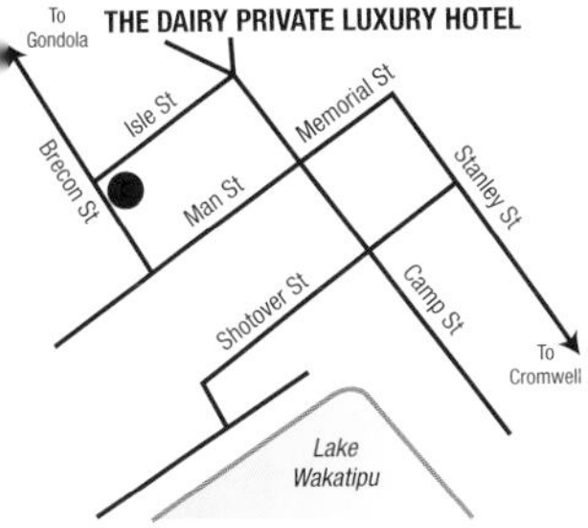

Entering Queenstown on SH 6A, continue along Stanley St to roundabout. Turn left into Shotover St, right into Camp St and left into Isle St. The Dairy is on the corner of Isle and Brecon Sts.

10

If you want to stay in the heart of Queenstown but out of the way of the noise, this private luxury hotel suits perfectly. There are thirteen rooms, some of which have views over the lake and Remarkables mountains and the others that overlook the town. The hotel was recently refurbished and offers contemporary comfort with items such as silk cushions, mohair rugs and superb linen. The Dairy takes its name from the original 1920's corner store, and exudes a timeless elegance. The large guest lounge is comfortable and is decorated with style. It boasts generous leather couches and is warmed by the roaring open fire. It was a perfect place to unwind and one that I could imagine guests sitting and sharing travelling tales. Throughout The Dairy, old New Zealand product, packaging and dairy items hint at its past. A highlight for me was afternoon tea where delicious home baked goods, which The Dairy has become renowned for, were available. This is an ideal place from which to experience all the activities in the area. The hosts make recommendations for restaurants, services and tourist operators, and will book them if guests wish.

Breakfast: Cooked

Accommodation available (NZ$)					
9 Rooms	$355-390	$385-420		SK/T, 1Q	EN
4 Rooms	$325-360	$355-390		SK/T, 1Q	EN

Guest rooms:
Ambience:
Setting/location:
LOW HIGH

Cooked breakfasts/afternoon teas.

Browns Boutique Hotel

Nigel and Bridget Brown
26 Isle Street, Queenstown
Tel: (03) 441 2050
Fax: (03) 441 2060
stay@brownshotel.co.nz
www.lodgings.co.nz/browns.html

Property features
Views over lake to Remarkables
Quiet location close to town centre
Central heating
Guest lounge with open fire
Courtyard/outdoor seating
Ski room

Local features
Skifields/outdoor pursuits
Restaurants/cafes - 5 min walk
Lake/water sports/jet boating
Gondola - 5 min walk

Queenstown - 3 mins walk
Wanaka - 1 hour

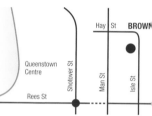

Entering Queenstown on SH 6A,
continue on Stanley St to
roundabout. Turn left into Shotover
St, first right into Camp St and
second left into Isle St. Lodge is near
the top of the hill on the left.

Browns Boutique Hotel is, as its name suggests, a ten-bedroom purpose-built accommodation, which is situated right in the heart of Queenstown. A three-minute walk down a lane brought me to the action part of town - the cafes, restaurant bars and boutique shops. The hotel building hints at a Mediterranean style in the white, rough-plastered walls of the spacious rooms and the glass doors that open to Juliet balconies, where guests get the full advantage of views of the Remarkable Mountains, Queenstown Hill and Lake Wakatipu. Each room is similar and thoughtfully equipped with everything you might need (the two downstairs ones don't have such a good view and have showers but no baths). The bathrooms in all rooms are fully tiled and the fittings and furnishings throughout are of a very high quality. Downstairs an attractively tiled and walled courtyard with outdoor furniture and a good view of the mountains is a great place to catch the sun. For colder weather there is a large lounge/library with an open fire and leather chairs with the ambience of an exclusive club. Breakfast which is either cooked or continental is served in the well-appointed dining room.

Accommodation available (NZ$)	♦	♦♦	+♦	⬦	⬦	Family dog on site
10 Rooms	$240-260	$260-280		K/T	EN	Breakfast: Cooked

Guest rooms:
Ambience:
Setting/location:

LOW   HIGH

234

property features
- Lake and mountain views
- All rooms are large suites
- Enormous ensuite bathrooms
- Outdoor spa/garden/fireplace
- Double vanity/spa baths
- Sky TV/mini bar/internet
- 4 course breakfast/4 acres

Local features
- Vineries/jetboating/skiing
- Day tours Milford/Doubtful Sound
- Hike/golf/fishing/rafting

Queenstown - 5 minute drive
Arrowtown - 15 minute drive

Take 6A (Frankton Rd) towards
Queenstown. After the Shell Petrol
Station travel 1.2km and turn right
into Greenstone Terrace Apartments.
Take private drive straight ahead up
hill to Pencarrow.

Pencarrow

Bill and Kari Moers
678 Frankton Rd, Queenstown
Tel: (03) 442 8938   Mob: 027 4131567
Fax: (03) 442 8974
info@pencarrow.net
www.lodgings.co.nz/pencarrow.html

   Located just on the outskirts of town this modern lodge is not far from Queenstown centre. Pencarrow, named after New Zealand's first lighthouse, is perched on a hillside overlooking Lake Wakatipu and the Remarkables Mountains. Bill and Kari were warmly welcoming. The couple has been in the hospitality industry for some time and both are well versed in the small details that add to guests' comfort. At one side of the entrance to the lodge is a spa pool and outdoor fire. I made a mental note to spend time there later in the evening. My suite was the complete package with plenty of space, a king-size bed, a huge bathroom with a spa bath, and a selection of products to enjoy. Before I went into town to find dinner I had a game of snooker in the 'games room', as Bill and Kari call it. Here there are also darts, books and photos and other entertainment. Pencarrow, with its four large suites, is well proportioned and warmed by colours that have been carefully chosen to enhance the interiors. A country breakfast is served in the dining room, on an outdoor terrace or deck, or in your own suite. You'll be spoiled by the hosts at this five star property.

Accommodation available (NZ$)	👤	👤👤	+👤	🛏	🛁
1 Suite			$450-500	$60	K	EN
3 Suites			$450-500	$60	SK	EN

Breakfast: Special cooked

Guest rooms:
Ambience:
Setting/location:

Remarkables Lodge

Colleen Ryan   Brian Savage
595 Kingston Road, SH6, Queenstown
Tel: (03) 442 2720   Mob: 021 619539
Fax: (03) 442 2730
contact@remarkables.co.nz
www.lodgings.co.nz/remarkables.html

Property features
Cosy bar with snooker table
Spacious lounge with log fire
Swimming pool/sauna/spa pool
Tennis court/croquet
Helipad for heliskiing/fishing
Outside seating areas/fireplaces

Local features
Remarkables ski field - 2 mins
3 golf courses - within 10 mins
Walking trails from Lodge
En route to Milford Sound

Queenstown - 10 mins drive
Arrowtown - 10 mins drive

Follow SH6 (to Milford Sound/
Invercargill) at Frankton, passed the
airport and over the one-way bridge.
Continue passed the Remarkables
Ski resort and the lodge is on the left

Nestled at the foothills of the Remarkables mountain range, this newly refurbished historic lodge is set on two acres of peaceful, landscaped gardens. It wasn't difficult to see why the original station owners chose this location for their home. This picturesque playground showcased gardens of fruit trees, deer in surrounding fields and a walk to a waterfall. Inside the lodge, a bar and games room, formal dinning area and a roaring log fire in the lounge in the winter are the height of luxury. I was invited to mingle around the pool table for pre-dinner drinks, although there was a temptation to sneak away to enjoy Colleen and Brian's impressive library of books. All seven bedrooms were ensuite with clawfoot baths and each suite had a balcony. I was greeted in the morning by the the sight of the stunning Remarkables towering into the sky virtually out of the back garden. Breakfast was a delight prepared by the resident chef, with homemade breads and pastries, bottled fruit from the garden and a choice from the cooked breakfast menu. A six-course dinner is also included in the tariff. Only a ten-minute drive from Queenstown's centre, Remarkables Lodge is an ideal place to stay in any season.

Accommodation available (NZ$)	👤	👥	+👤	🛏	🛁	Guest pets by arrangement
4 Suites	$750	$990-1080		SK or 2S	EN	Breakfast: Special cooked
3 Rooms	$650	$850		SK/Q	EN	Evening meal: Included

Guest rooms:
Ambience:
Setting/location:

Ski gear drying room available.

Nokomai Valley Accommodation

Ann and Brian Hore
Nokomai Station, RD 3, Lumsden, Southland
Tel: (03) 248 8850   Mob: 027 2429480
Fax: (03) 248 8841
nokomai@xtra.co.nz
www.lodgings.co.nz/nokomai.html

Property features
- Personalised tours/activities
- Historic stone homestead for dining
- On-site Brown trout fly fishing
- On-site helicopter flights
- Hiking/farm tours/mountain bikes
- Part of Northn Sthland Heritage Trail
- Hunting/horse trekking

Local features
- Kingston Flyer Steam Train
- Queenstown/Milford Sound Tours
- Skifields/shopping/vineyards

Queenstown - 60 minute drive
Invercargill - 90 minute drive

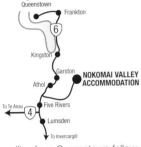

Travelling from Queenstown follow SH6 south past Lake Wakatipu until you reach the township of Athol. The turn-off to Nokomai Station is sign-posted 7km past Athol on the left hand side.

These three, purpose-built, country cottages near the Queenstown/Milford Sound highway, are set on a 100,000 acre, high-country sheep and cattle station, one of the biggest in New Zealand. They stand among pastures that extend the length of the valley that is surrounded by mountains. The only sounds were the wind rustling the trees, dogs barking in the distance, and the whistling of sheep musterers. The station has operated since 1950, but Ann has only recently built the cottages. Guests have dinner in the restored schist cottage nearby. The aromas emanating from the country kitchen and the warm fire crackling in the grate made me think that a cowboy might saunter in at any moment. Ann serves real country fare – cooked breakfasts to order, picnic lunches, and for dinner a heart-warming selection of dishes, such as roast lamb, venison steaks or beef hotpot. The cottages are simple with super king-size or king-single beds, kitchenettes, lounge and dining areas, and private terraces with views that stretch down the valley. With the Mataura River weaving its way through their property and a helicopter on site there is much to do - fly-fishing, horse trekking, walking one of the numerous farm tracks, watching farm activities or just relaxing with a book.

Family pets on site Guest pets by arrangement	Accomodation available (NZ$)	👤	👥	+👤	🛏	🛁
Breakfast: Special cooked	1 S/C cottage	$310			2SK or 4S	GS
Evening meal: $65pp	2 S/C cottages	$250			SK or 2S	EN
Guest rooms:						
Ambience:						
Setting/location:		Sofa bed in lounge. Packed lunches avail. $20pp.				

Mt Prospect High Country Station

Joan and Ross Cockburn
1338 Kakapo Road, Te Anau
Tel: (03) 249 7082   Mob: 025 6589643
Fax:(03) 249 7085
prospect@fiordland.net.nz
www.lodgings.co.nz/prospect.html

Property features
Working high country station
Guided mountain drive
Garden setting/mountain views
Family property since 1913
Complimentary NZ wines
Local features
Te Anau gateway to Fiordland
Fiordland World Heritage Park
Milford and Doubtful Sounds
Kayaking/fishing/walking/golf
Scenic flights (heli & plane)

Te Anau - 15 minutes
Queenstown - 2 hrs

Kakapo Rd runs north off SH 94
approx. 5km east of Te Anau
(between Te Anau and Mossburn).
Drive approx. 16km up Kakapo Rd.
Mt Prospect Station is well
signposted.

If you stay on this high-country station you will probably leave, as I did, feeling like part of the family. Joan and Ross are relaxed and attentive hosts, who have genuine interest in the people who visit them and enjoy sharing aspects of life on a 8,400 acre merino sheep and cattle farm. The homestead has been extensively altered and upgraded to provide guests with comfortable, ensuite bedrooms, each of which opens to its own tiled courtyard and small garden. It's a treat to have pre-dinner drinks in the guest lounge with the hosts and other guests. The room is fronted by a tiled, glassed-in porch, so that the beautiful country garden, the pastures of the White Stone River valley and the Murchison Mountains are all in view. Dinner was a platter of roast lamb with vegetables from the kitchen garden, followed by creme brulee with ginger and fresh fruit - well-presented, country fare. Another way to get a taste of this country environment is to go out on the farm with Ross. He takes guests on a farm tour, the highlight of which is the lofty peak of Mt Prospect. It affords a panoramic, 360-degree view of the regions dramatic mountains, lakes and valleys. The air is especially crisp and clear here.

Accommodation available (NZ$)	👤	👥	+👤	🛏	🛁	
2 Room	$410	$510		K	EN	Breakfast: Cooked
2 Rooms	$410	$510		K/T	EN	Evening Meal: Included
						Guest rooms:
						Ambience:
						Setting/location:

Reduced tariff for two nights or longer. TVs avail. in all bedrooms.

Fiordland Lodge

Ron and Robynne Peacock
472 Te Anau - Milford Highway, Te Anau
Tel: (03) 249 7832
Fax: (03) 249 7449
info@fiordlandlodge.co.nz
www.lodgings.co.nz/fiordland.html

Property features
Log construction/lake views
Large open fireplace
Rural setting/farm animals
Laundry facilities
Cot and highchair
Local features
Guided fishing/hunting/golf course
Milford and Doubtful Sound
Milford/Routeburn Tracks
Hollyford/Kepler Tracks
Nature walks/birdwatching/kayaking

Te Anau - 5 minutes
Queenstown - 2 hrs

From Te Anau, drive north
approximately 5km on SH 94
towards Milford Sound. Just past
Sinclair Rd turn right into driveway
signposted Fiordland Lodge.
Continue to end of driveway.

Suiting the grandeur of the surrounding landscape, Fiordland Lodge's site is elevated and looks out over rolling pastureland to the expanse of Lake Te Anau and the mountains of Fiordland National Park. I was very warmly welcomed in the main foyer, where the log structure and stone fireplace are enormous. A trophy Wapiti deer head, shot by a local hunter in 1966, hangs on one wall, and the light fittings are uniquely modeled to represent fishing flies or game fish. Bedroom suites are both up and down stairs and are appointed to the highest standard. There are beechwood cabinets, Oregan pine ceilings, swamp kauri bathroom counters and views from every room. A purpose built conference facility is available for smaller groups. Meals are top New Zealand cuisine and both dinner and breakfast are gastronomic treats. The two original, loft-style log cabins have recently been stylishly revamped and now having comtemporary furnishings with natural tones and fibres. Each has comfortable seating, a spa bath, a queen-size and two twin beds. Robynne and Ron (he is a fishing guide) are passionately involved in the open-air activities in this spectacular country. After enjoying the clear starlit evening, I retired to bed to the sounds of deer roaring in the distance.

	Accommodation available (NZ$)	👤	👤👤	+👤	🛏	🛁
Family pets on site						
Breakfast: Special cooked	Lodge Room	$580	$760		SK or 2S	EN
Evening meal: $95	Exec Suite	$780	$980		SK or 2S	EN
Guest rooms:	1 S/C log cab	$260	$360	$100	Q+3S	PR
Ambience:	1 S/C log cab	$260	$360	$100	Q+2S	PR
Setting/location:	Log cabin incl B&B, children $75.					

Blue Ridge

Julia and Phillip Robertson
15 Melland Place, Te Anau
Tel: (03) 249 7740   Mob: 027 2589877
Fax: (03) 249 7340
info@blueridge.net.nz
www.lodgings.co.nz/blueridge.html

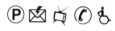

Property features
Views of Keppler/Murchison moun▮
Beautiful gardens
Outdoor spa pool
Guest BBQ
Local features
Numerous cafes/restaurants
Glow worm caves
Milford Sounds - 2 hours
Doubtful Sounds cruises
Guided and independent walks
Trout fishing/kayaking/horse riding

Te Anau - 5 minutes walk
Manapouri - 15 minutes drive

From Te Anau, follow Luxmore Drive
right at Caltex station into Bowden
Street, right onto Pop Andrew Drive
right on Jackson Street then right in
Melland Place. Down long driveway.

As I woke early I was greeted by pink-tinged, snow-capped mountains at Blue Ridge bed and breakfast. They rise majestically from the clear, sparkling waters of Lake Te Anau, which is reached by a short walk through quiet residential streets. For guests who prefer a more leisurely start to the day, the mountains can also be viewed from the comfort of their room or while they're enjoying a relaxed breakfast in the home of the friendly hosts, Julia and Phillip Robertson, a couple well suited to the hospitality industry. As well as a double room provided within their own home (which comes with a private bathroom), there are three modern, purpose-built studio units adjacent to the main house. Each comes with a spotlessly clean kitchenette, an ensuite bathroom with underfloor heating, quality robes and towels, luxurious linens and richly textured curtains and spreads. Breakfast is a veritable feast with a delicious range of favourites on offer including traditional bacon and eggs, French toast, scrambled eggs with smoked salmon or an omelette stuffed with a choice of fillings, and cooked to perfection. Alternatively, for those who wish to breakfast in the privacy of their room, a continental breakfast basket hamper is provided.

Accommodation available (NZ$)	🧍	🧍🧍	+🧍	🛏	🛁	Family cat on site
1 Room	$125-145	$135-155		Q	PR	Breakfast: Special cooked
1 S/C unit	$175-195	$195-225		Q	EN	
1 S/C unit	$175-195	$195-225		K or 2S	EN	Guest rooms:
1 S/C unit	$175-195	$195-225		K or 2S	EN	Ambience:

Setting/location:

LOW   HIGH

Property features
100 metres to lake/river
Sep guest lounge/dining room
Coffee/tea/robes in rooms
Pet deer/lake views
Helicopter landing area
Historic lodge (circa 1889)
Local features
Doubtful Sound/Milford Sound
Kayak/canoeing/scenic flights
Walking tracks - Kepler/Milford
Trout fishing - guide available

Murrell's Grand View House

Jack and Klaske Murrell
7 Murrell Ave, Manapouri, Fiordland
Tel: (03) 249 6642
Fax:(03) 249 6966
murrell@xtra.co.nz
www.lodgings.co.nz/murrells.html

Te Anau - 20 minutes
Queenstown - 2 hrs 30 mins

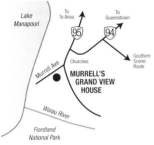

At the Churches in Manapouri, turn right into Murrell Ave. Murrell's is the first house on the left behind the hedge. Reservations are essential.

Murrell's is a good place to stay if you are considering exploration of the Milford Sound and Te Anau areas. Jack and Klaske's oasis in Manapouri is not only strategically located but the couple have an extensive knowledge of the area. I was welcomed with the offer of tea and was ushered into the comfortable guest lounge, which was warmed by a large log fire. If it had been summer, we would have moved to the verandah, from where the view of the lake and the sharp peaks of the Kepler and Hunter Mountains is breathtaking. No matter - all three bedrooms have windows that take in the view. There were once more bedrooms, but today's hosts have incorporated ensuite bathrooms. The history here is extraordinary. The house was built in 1889, by Jack's great grandparents as tourist accommodation and since then, has been continually operated by Jack's family. On the walls are some intriguing historic photographs of the area. We had an excellent breakfast, with homemade jams and muffins, in the Victorian dining room which is hung with early 19th-century prints, lace curtains and light shades and furnished with antique cabinets and a small organ. All in all, a fascinating stay.

Family cat on site	Accommodation available (NZ$)	👤	👥	+👤	🛏	🛁
Breakfast: Special cooked	2 Rooms	$240-260	$260-280		Q	EN
	1 Room	$260	$260-280		K/T	EN

Guest rooms:
Ambience:
Setting/location:

Cont breakfast in room for guests leaving early. Reservations essential.

Cathedral Peaks B&B

Janice and Neal Duncan
44 Cathedral Drive, Manapouri
Tel: (03) 249 6640
Fax: (03) 249 6648
cathedralpeaks@ihug.co.nz
www.lodgings.co.nz/cathedralpeaks.html

Property features
Panoramic lake and mountain views
Separate guest lounge/dining room
TV in rooms
150 metres from lake
Writing desk in rooms
Local features
Doubtful Sounds boat departure
Restaurants - 3 mins walk
Milford Sounds - 2-2.5 hrs drive
Walking tracks/fishing/kayaking
Scenic flights/golf course - 20 mins

Te Anau - 20 mins drive
Queenstown - 2 hrs drive

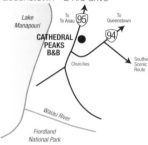

From highway 94 turn right onto
95/Cathedral Drive. Travel approx
1/2km, Cathedral Peaks is the large
2 storey cream house. If you get to
the Hotel, you have gone too far.

You need to see the magnificence of Lake Manapouri and the majestic peaks of Fiordland National Park to understand how beautiful they are. Aptly named, Cathedral Peaks faces directly out to this scene. Easy to find on the main road into Manapouri, this two guestroom bed and breakfast has been purpose-built by Neal and Janice so that they can share their slice of heaven. The furniture in the downstairs guestrooms are made of recycled rimu. I stayed in the room with a queen-size bed; the other has a super-king-size bed, which can be divided into twins. Both rooms have ensuite bathrooms and are complete with televisions, tea and coffee-making facilities and small fridges. Large glass doors lead out to private terraces. The bedrooms are separated by an open-plan, guest dining room and lounge, which is ideal for two couples travelling together as there is privacy as well as a place to socialise. All rooms take full advantage of the views. It is only a short walk to local restaurants, the lakeside and the wharf where the boat leaves from to travel to Doubtful Sound. There is much to do in this area; golf courses, fishing, kayaking and the scenic-flight airstrip are a short drive away.

Accommodation available (NZ$)	♦	♦♦	+♦	🛏	🛁	
1 Room	$120-200	$150-250		Q	EN	Breakfast: Cooked
1 Room	$120-200	$150-250		SK or 2S	EN	

Guest rooms:
Ambience:
Setting/location:

Property features
Panoramic mountain/sea views
21 acres of private country grounds
Hand feed friendly animals
Sundeck/BBQ/helipad
Eco-friendly design/energy efficiency
Local features
Royal Albatross colony/rare penguins
Beaches/wildlife/wild flowers
Fine dining/cafes/museums
Art galleries/botanic gardens
Hiking/mountain biking/kayaking

Dunedin Airport - 15 min drive
Dunedin Central - 15 min drive

Highland Peaks

Di and Peter Espie
333 Chain Hills Road, RD 1, Dunedin
Tel: (03) 489 6936   Mob: 021 1629489
Fax: (03) 489 6924
info@highlandpeaks.com
www.lodgings.co.nz/highlandpeaks.html

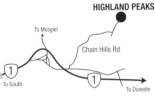

From SH1 take Mosgiel exit, turn towards Kinmont. Continue along Quarry Rd and Morris Rds over motorway. Turn left into Chain Hills Rd, take left fork to road end.

Centrally positioned between Dunedin city and the airport, Highland Peaks felt as if it were its own world. The site of this new purpose-built bed and breakfast is on a hill and looks as if it might mark the gateway to Central Otago. The views of the ranges of Lammerlaw and Silver Peaks to the east are spectacular. The Silver Peaks room has a private bathroom with a spa bath; the Lammerlaw room is ensuite with views to Ocean View Beach and Green Island. Both rooms are furnished with New Zealand kauri timber furniture. Food is a focus at Highland Peaks; both Di and Peter enjoy cooking and are happy to organise dinner by prior arrangement. Homemade Bircher muesli with seasonal fruit and cream, followed by scrambled eggs with smoked salmon, was on the breakfast menu for my first morning. Guests enjoy this in the sunroom, which has a large bay window and extensive valley views. This room is also a nice place to relax in during the day. The lounge has comfortable, blue leather couches and a wood-burning fireplace. Peter is a grassland ecologist and qualified to organise tailor-made tours to the Otago Peninsula, The Catlins, Central Otago or Moeraki.

Family pets on site	Accommodation available (NZ$)	♀	♀♀	+♀	🛏	🛁
Breakfast: Special cooked	1 Suite	$175-275	$195-295		K	EN
Evening meal: Enquire	1 Suite	$175-275	$195-295		SK or 2S	PR
Guest rooms:						
Ambience:						
Setting/location:		Evening meals by prior arrangement.				

Glenfield House

Lyndsey and Guy Farland
3 Peel Street, Mornington, Dunedin
Tel: (03) 453 5923   Mob: 021 564615
Fax:(03) 453 5984
glenfieldhouse@xtra.co.nz
www.lodgings.co.nz/glenfieldhouse.html

Property features
Antique billiard room & table
Private dining on request
Adjacent to park
Sunny private garden
Guest kitchen
Local features
Art gallery/museum
Carisbrook rugby stadium
Railway station
Speights brewery tour
Dunedin wildlife

Dunedin Central - 3 mins drive
Queenstown - 3 hour drive

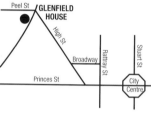

From the Octagon drive south toward Princes St. At Casino right into Rattray St. First left onto Broadway. At lights right into High St. Peel St at very top on the left.

Built in 1884, Glenfield House is surrounded by established gardens and it is only two kilometres away from the centre of Dunedin (The Octagon). After a warm welcome from the hosts, Lyndsey and Guy, I was shown to the delightful Garden Room. This sunny, spacious, ensuite guestroom is on the ground floor and has French doors opening out to a private terrace to look over a beautiful, lush country garden. The four other guestrooms are positioned for privacy throughout this large house, each tastefully decorated to reflect the warmth and elegance of a past era. The Deluxe Suite is a spacious and romantic room with extra features that include a clawfoot bath on a raised platform overlooking the harbour, a solid-wood, king-size bed and a sun room for private breakfasts and special dinners. Guests are invited to use the entire house, which includes a billiard room, a guest lounge, dining rooms and a large self-contained kitchen. The hosts live a phone call way across the street. Lyndsey is a trained chef and, by prior arrangement, is happy to cook dinners for small groups. Guy and Lyndsey are delightful hosts, who ensure their guests are welcomed and looked after, and they and have restored this house with the distinction it deserves.

Accommodation available (NZ$)						
1 Suite	$275	$275	$15	K or 1S	EN	Breakfast: Special cooked
1 Room	$200	$200		Q	EN	Evening meal: Enquire
1 Room	$185	$185		Q	EN	Guest rooms:
1 Room	$185	$185		Q	PR	Ambience:

Please enquire about the twin double option.

Setting/location:

Property features
Separate guest lounge
Complimentary port and shortbread
Unique architecture (circa 1865)
Open fireplaces/four poster beds
Local features
Larnach Castle
Albatross colony
Yellow-eyed penguins
Taieri Gorge train
Botanical Garden
Historic Olverston House

Lisburn House

Olivia Richmond-Johnston   Alan Johnston
15 Lisburn Avenue, Caversham, Dunedin
Tel: (03) 455 8888
Fax: (03) 455 6788
stay@lisburnhouse.co.nz
www.lodgings.co.nz/lisburn.html

City centre - 5 minutes
Queenstown - 3 hours

Just south of the city centre, turn off SH 1 (motorway) at Caversham (first set of traffic lights on motorway south). Continue on South Rd and turn left into Lisburn Ave on your left.

Dunedin's first brick-built house (circa 1865) has a distinctive profile. Its steeply pitched rooflines, pointed gable ends and bold geometric patterns, formed by cream bricks against the red, make it instantly recognisable. The front door, inset with colourful motifs in glass, is opened to me and I entered into the marble-tiled foyer and a circle of warmth that remains for the rest of my stay. Seated in deep leather chairs around logs burning in a raised oval fireplace, Alan and Olivia tell me how they spent three years trying to purchase this Victorian/Gothic-style house and how they have set up an intimate and exclusive restaurant in the front drawing room. As was expected this has been a huge success and Olivia stresses how important it is to book so as not to be disappointed. The foyer is a fitting introduction to the style of the rest of the house - its panelled dining room with a heavily carved fireplace inset with copper, the elegant Victorian parlour and the hanging staircase leading to the three guest bedrooms. These are light and spacious with whimsical canopies over the beds. This house is a charming place in which to experience some of the history and character of Dunedin.

Accommodation available (NZ$)	♦	♦♦	+♦	🛏	🛁
Breakfast: Cooked	1 Room	$220	$265		Q	EN
Evening meal: Menu	1 Room	$175	$195		Q	PR
Guest rooms:	1 Room	$200	$235	$70	Q+S	PR
Ambience:						
Setting/location:						

LOW   HIGH

Corstorphine House

Irina and Nico Francken
23A Milburn St, Corstorphine, Dunedin
Tel: (03) 487 1000
Fax: (03) 487 6672
info@corstorphine.co.nz
www.lodgings.co.nz/corstorphine.html

Property features
Historic mansion (1863)
Extensive gardens (12 acres)
City & harbour views
Licensed restaurant
Organic produce grown on site
Laundry facilities included
Fr, Ger, Spa, Dutch & Rus spoken

Local features
Historic buildings/museums
Albatross colony/penguins
Taieri Gorge Railway/golf courses

City centre - 10 minutes
Oamaru - 1 hour

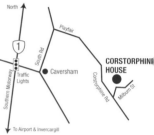

Take Caversham turnoff from SH 1, just south of city centre. Turn into South Rd (crossing over railway line). Turn right into Playfair St. Continue to Corstorphine Rd then left into Milbur St. Lodge is on your left.

It is difficult to do justice in a few words to this grand old Dunedin mansion. It was once one of the city's grandest homes - Edwardian in style with huge rooms, ornate ceilings, panelled walls and intricately carved fireplaces. It is set in 12 acres of private garden. Nico and Irina have restored the historically classified building with thoroughness, sensitivity and great deal of flair so that they can offer their guests a taste of the gracious lifestyle that the home was designed for. Seven enormous bedrooms have been decorated with country themes - The French, Scandinavian and Scottish Rooms are delicately designed with marvellous bathrooms, the Indian room with rich colours, the Egyptian Room with walls the colour of sand and so on; and these themes have been carried through to every element of the décor. All the ensuite bathrooms are large and modern with underfloor heating, de-mister mirrors, heated towel rails and bidets. There is also a room available for accompanying drivers, pilots or nannies. There are five guest areas including drawing rooms, a music room and a formal dining room on a grand scale. But many guests choose to dine in the historically rated Conservatory, in a restaurant that must be among the best in the country for its food and atmosphere.

Accommodation available (NZ$)						
6 Rooms	$545	$595	$45	K	EN	Breakfast: Special cooked
1 Room	$545	$595	$45	2Q	EN	Evening meal: Menu

Guest rooms:
Ambience:
Setting/location:

Off season rates available.

LOW   HIGH

Property features
Panoramic views over city
Separate guest lounge
Proximity to peninsula/wildlife
Host is wildlife tour guide
Nature pkgs for max. 4-6 people
Local features
Numerous cafes/restaurants
Larnach Castle/Otago University
Glenfalloch Gardens
Golf courses/beach walks
Historic homes/museums

City centre - 7 minutes

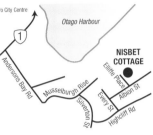

From SH 1, take Andersons Bay turn off. Follow the main traffic route for approx. 3 km. Turn left into Highcliff Rd and left into Every St. Take first right into Albion St. and first left into Elliffe Place.

Nisbet Cottage / Nature Guides Otago

Hildegard and Ralf Lubcke
6a Elliffe Place, Shiel Hill, Dunedin
Tel: (03) 454 5169
Fax: (03) 454 5369
info@natureguidesotago.co.nz
www.lodgings.co.nz/nisbet.html

The Otago Peninsula is a wildlife area and Hildegard, hostess of Nisbet Cottage, is a licensed and experienced wildlife guide. This pleasant accommodation is exclusive to guests on the nature-based packages Hildegard offers. The packages combine two or more nights bed and breakfast with guided wildlife tours of Dunedin, the Otago Peninsula, and the Catlins. All packages include the Sunrise Penguin Walk and Albatross viewing and can be tailored to suit special interests. The groups are led by a professional guide and have a maximum number of six people, so that flexibility to suit individual requirements is no problem. Nisbet Cottage is located on the way out to the Peninsula and just seven minutes from the heart of Dunedin. My room had a stunning night view out over the city lights of Dunedin. Guestrooms have been pleasantly decorated each with their own tea/coffee making facilities, television, and ensuites. There is a cosy guest lounge and a dining room, which opens through French doors to a large deck overlooking Dunedin and the hills beyond. Don't get confused with the name 'cottage' - this is a large character home with a history spanning back to 1930, when the Presbyterian Church built it as part of the original orphanage.

Accommodation available (NZ$)

Breakfast: Cooked	2 Rooms		K+1S or SK	EN

Guest rooms:
Ambience:
Setting/location:

LOW   HIGH

Rooms exclusive to nature-based packages - priced from $525pp for 2 night B&B + full day tour. May-Sept: B&B guests welcome

247

The Cottage

Julz Asher   Lutz Ritter
Broad Bay, Dunedin
Tel: (03) 476 1877   Mob: 027 2283380
Fax: (03) 476 1873
thecottage@xtra.co.nz
www.lodgings.co.nz/thecottage.html

Property features
Birdlife and wildlife
Located over the road from the sea
Local features
Penguin colony
Albatross colony
Larnach Castle
Natural history tours
Harbour wildlife cruise
Fishing trips
Coastal walks

Dunedin - 25 minutes
Portobello - 5 minutes

From Dunedin, follow Peninsula signs. Broad Bay is approx. 18km from the city along Portobello Rd. The Cottage is 1km beyond Broad Bay Boat Club on the corner of Bacon St. Please telephone first.

Don't be put off by the twenty five-minute drive to Dunedin city. The benefits of the attractions on the peninsula, the natural surroundings, and the harbour across the road more than make up for it. This early 1900s cottage has been lovingly restored to reflect a bygone era. The Cottage is tucked in amongst bush and trees and has plenty of atmosphere. The décor is quite simple and features the odd piece of original New Zealand art and numerous curiosities from yesteryear - cake tins, old scales, interesting old bottles among them. Over the road from the secluded cottage is Broad Bay where there is plenty of birdlife, beach walks and swimming (when the weather permits). The hosts live nearby on the peninsula. They were responsible for the scrumptious basket of ingredients for breakfast which was delivered to my cottage during the afternoon for me to have the next morning. Further sustenance is available a short drive away in Portobello. The Peninsula on which The Cottage is located, is a wildlife treasure with its penguin, albatross and seal colonies which are unique and can be visited any time of the year. Larnach castle is well worth a visit and is just a five-minute drive away.

Accommodation available (NZ$)	👤	👤👤	+👤	🛏	🛁	
1 S/C cottage	$140	$140		D	EN	Breakfast: Extra charge

$175 per night with special breakfast hamper.

Guest rooms:
Ambience:
Setting/location:

LOW   HIGH

Property features
Fully S/C historic cottage
Two double and one single bedroom
Separate guest lounge with TV/DVD
Centrally heated
Old world bathroom
Charmingly furnished
Fully equipped kitchen
Complimentary wine and chocolates
Local features
Close to city and local restaurants
Cafes/bars/hospital/casino nearby

Dunedin - 5 mins drive
Dunedin Airport - 25 mins drive

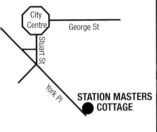

From Octagon up Stuart St, left onto York Place. Up hill until traffic lights, right and hard left into top of York Place. Signposted on corner to both B&B and historic cottage.

Stationmasters Cottage
Brendon & Amanda Colmore-Williams
300 York Place, Dunedin, Dunedin
Tel: 0800 327333
Fax: (03) 473 1160   Free: 0800 327333
info@stationmasters.co.nz
www.lodgings.co.nz/stationmasters.html

This beautiful cottage is as pretty as a picture. The sign identifying The Stationmaster's Cottage blows gently in the wind and beyond it is the cottage, set in a garden lined by rose bushes and a white, picket fence. This three-bedroom, classical, Georgian-style cottage is centrally heated and quite spacious with a guest lounge, one twin and two queen rooms, a bathroom and a self-contained kitchen. The large bathroom has a clawfoot bath and separate shower, which tastefully combine with the period furnishings and pictures. At the rear of the cottage is a small paved courtyard set among established native trees and ferns. This comfortable cottage is well furnished with kauri floors in the hall and carpeted bedrooms. Throughout is the fragrant scent of roses. It is a perfect set up for families and there is the option of a single booking. A cot and high chair are available on request. Located at the upper end of York Place, only a short distance from central Dunedin, this self-contained cottage is a popular option for parties of up to six guests wanting to self-cater while staying in Dunedin to enjoy the city's sights. For those seeking bed and breakfast accommodation, Peacocks Bed and Breakfast is next door.

Accommodation available (NZ$)	👤	👤👤	+👤	🛏	🛁
1 S/C house	$225	$250	$35	2S+2Q	PR

Breakfast: Special continental

Guest rooms:
Ambience:
Setting/location:

LOW   HIGH

Peacocks

Brendon and Amanda Colmore-Williams
304 York Place, City Rise, Dunedin
Tel: 0800 327333
Fax:(03) 473 1160
info@stationmasters.co.nz
www.lodgings.co.nz/peacocks.html

Property features
Ensuite bedrooms/honeymoon suite
Antique furnishings
Luxurious linen and towels
Quality fittings and fixtures
Children accepted
Local features
Near city/local restaurants/cafes/
bars/casino
Near Otago University/
Dunedin Hospital/Aquatic Centre/
Olveston Historic House

City Centre - 3 minutes
Airport - 20 minutes

From Octagon up Stuart St, left ont
York Place. Up hill till traffic lights,
right and hard left into top of York
Place. Signposted on corner to bot
B&B and historic cottage.

Located at the top end of York Place in residential Dunedin, Peacocks is a convenient distance from the city's downtown cafes, shops and restaurants but also offering peace and quiet. The first thing I noticed at Peacocks was the stunning antique furniture. The owner is an antique dealer, so the five ensuite guestrooms are furnished with striking antique pieces, which are very apt for this house, built in the 1800's. My favourite room was coloured with deep blues and golds. The décor is luxurious with no expense spared on furnishings and linen. The Honeymoon Suite had an in-room bath, a mahogany gas fireplace and a queen-size antique bed, as well as stunning drapes and chandeliers. Every room at Peacocks has something novel: upstairs two of the rooms have queen-size beds and views out to Dunedin Harbour from the balcony; another has an authentic clawfoot bath. All bedrooms have modern ensuite bathrooms with underfloor heating and designer fittings. Downstairs there is a guest lounge with a television, stereo and DVD player and a designated dining room where breakfast is served. Peacocks bed and breakfast offers old-world charm with modern conveniences for both corporate and leisure travellers. For those seeking self-contained accommodation The Stationmasters Cottage is next door.

Accommodation available (NZ$)					
3 Rooms	$250-350	Q	EN		Breakfast: Special cooked
1 Room	$250-350	D	EN		
1 Room	$250-350	2S	EN		Guest rooms:

Twin room available on request.

Ambience:
Setting/location:

LOW   HIG

Property features
Large spa bath/open fire/BBQ
Large decks/panoramic ocean views
Nautical theme
1 hour historic tour in Mercedes
Local features
Restaurants/cafes nearby
Fishing trips/jet boating/beaches
9-hole golf course
Heated swimming pool/massage
Art centre/Maori art centre
Heritage trail/museum

Nautical Haven
Tommy and Gail White
9 Ivy Street, Riverton
Tel: (03) 234 8755   Mob: 021 1592758
Fax:(03) 234 8755
info@harbourviewhouse.co.nz
www.lodgings.co.nz/nauticalhaven.html

Riverton - 5 minute drive
Invercargill - 35 minute drive

From Riverton Centre take Richard St towards the Riverton Rocks. Turn right into Roy St then left into Ivy St. Nautical Haven is on your left.

    This bright, spacious, three-bedroom home sits at the southern-most end of the seaside town of Riverton at the bottom of the South Island. Separated by a large front deck, two of the guestrooms have queen-size beds and spectacular views out to the ocean. I lay in bed and listened to the tranquil sounds of birds calling and waves breaking on the beach – absolute peace. The lounge and two front bedrooms have French doors opening out to the deck. Suited to all seasons, guests can barbecue on the front deck, soak in the large spa bath or get cosy by the open fire. Throughout the house, Gail has displayed many interesting treasures and pieces that fit the nautical theme. Although self-catered, Gail leaves breakfasts for guests – fruit, yoghurt, cereals and gourmet-filled croissants - which I enjoyed while I sat on the deck overlooking the panoramic view.   A highlight for me was the one-hour, driving tour of historic Riverton in Tommy's '86 Mercedes. Gail packed us a lunch and I grabbed a bottle of wine and sat back to listen to stories about the oldest town in the South Island. Nautical Haven is a perfect place to stop for a few days if you are exploring the Deep South of New Zealand.

Breakfast: Special continental

Accommodation available (NZ$)	👤	👥	+👤	🛏	🛁
2 Rooms	$180	$240-265	$100	2Q	PR
1 Room		$240-265		2S	PR

Guest rooms:
Ambience:
Setting/location:

251

Tudor Park Country Stay & Garden

Joyce and John Robins
21 Lawerence Road, Ryal Bush, RD6, Invercargill
Tel: (03) 221 7150   Mob: 025 310031
Fax: (03) 221 7150
tudorparksouth@hotmail.com
www.lodgings.co.nz/tudorpark.html

Property features
20 acre semi-retirement property
Prize winning gardens
Large pergolas/ponds/canal
Peonies grown commercially
Cattle, horses and sheep grazing
Local features
Fly fishing
Parks/gardens/bush walks
Connections to Stewart Island
Anderson Park Art Gallery
Southland Museum

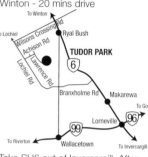

Invercargill - 15 mins drive
Winton - 20 mins drive

Take SH6 out of Invercargill. After
100km speed sign, take 2nd road o
left Branxholme/Makarewa Rd. Trave
approx 7km to Achison Rd (Tudor
Park sign here) turn right, 1km right
into Lawrence, 1st on left.

Located 20 minutes north of Invercargill, Tudor Park Country
Stay and Garden is a neo-Tudor-style house set on 20-acres of
farmland with three-acres of established country gardens.
Hosts, John and Joyce, are passionate about gardens and
have spent the last nine years designing and developing their
own, which is now earned the accolade of being an assessed
garden by the RNZ Institute of Horticulture NZ. At the right
times of the year, guests come across the lovely fragrance and
colours of roses, paeonies and hellebores. Other features of the
garden are two large, nine-pillar pergolas and a sundial. Small
weddings and functions are popular here. On a delightful walk
around the property, I saw grazing Simmental stud cattle,
racehorses and sheep. John and Joyce welcome guests into
their home to share genuine country living in the Deep South of
New Zealand. Tudor Park is near the Southern Scenic Driving
Route and it's a peaceful place for an overnight stop on the
way. There are three guestrooms; two have queen-size beds
with pretty outlooks onto the garden and the third has two king-
single-size beds. One of the queen rooms and the twin room
are ensuite and the other queen room has a private bathroom.

Accommodation available (NZ$)	👤	👤👤	+👤	🛏	🛁	Family dog on site
1 Room	$140	$180		Q	EN	Breakfast: Continental
1 Room	$140	$160		Q	PR	Evening meal: $45pp
1 Room	$100	$130		2S	EN	Guest rooms:
						Ambience:

Cooked breakfast available by arrangement.

Setting/location:

LOW   HIGH

Property features
Native bird watching/fodder trees
Quiet/central location/views
Itinerary packages avail.
On-site chef/gourmet meals
Local features
Kiwi spotting/rain forest/bush walks
Ulva Island bird sanctuary
Scuba diving/fishing/sea kayaking
6-hole golf course/clay bird shooting
Living botanical fossils & orchids
Boat trips/scenic flights

Stewart Island Lodge

Doug and Margaret Wright
14 Nichol Road, Halfmoon Bay, Stewart Island
Tel: (03) 219 1085
Fax:(03) 219 1085
silodge@xtra.co.nz
www.lodgings.co.nz/stewartisland.html

Oban - 1 minute walk
Invercargill - 20 minute flight

Oban Township

STEWART ISLAND LODGE

Stewart Island 23km from the port
of Bluff, accessible by 60 minutes
sailing time or 20 minutes flying
time from Invercargill airport.
Courtesy transfers provided.

As I flew over Stewart Island, the raw beauty of the island's white sandy beaches, clear water and untouched native forests lay enticingly below. Within ten minutes of arriving at Stewart Island Lodge, I saw native tui and kaka birds four metres from where I was standing – the birdlife is obviously abundant. The lodge's five purpose-built suites face out to views of Halfmoon Bay. They have recently been upgraded and have ensuites and dressing rooms. Earth-toned walls are interrupted by bi-folding doors that lead to a deck and allow good views of the sea. All suites have super-king-size or twin beds, a desk, two lounge chairs and comfortable outdoor furniture. From the deck, I watched a flock of albatross gliding and diving out in the bay. Fishing trawlers and private yachts lined the inner harbour. Doug helped me plan my time on the island. His extensive knowledge was invaluable and I was able to do many of the things I had hoped to achieve on the island. I went kiwi spotting and fishing for blue cod. I watched albatross, visited Ulva Island and went on bush walks. Every morning I was sent off with a packed lunch to have during the day's activity. With an on-site chef, every meal was a treat at this sophisticated lodge.

Accommodation available (NZ$)					
Breakfast: Special continental	5 Rooms	$300	$600		SK or 2S EN

Evening Meal:
Guest rooms:
Ambience:
Setting/location:

LOW   HIGH

Tariff incl. dinner, B&B, airport transfers, cocktail hour. TV avail. on request.

Index

For your convenience we have alphabetically listed the place names of centres or areas where we have properties. Appropriate page numbers are then listed for property reference.